JAMES EARL JONES
VOICES AND SILENCES

JAMES EARL JONES
VOICES AND SILENCES

JAMES EARL JONES
and PENELOPE NIVEN

CHARLES SCRIBNER'S SONS
NEW YORK

Maxwell Macmillan Canada
Toronto
Maxwell Macmillan International
New York Oxford Singapore Sydney

Charles Scribner's Sons
Macmillan Publishing Company
866 Third Avenue
New York, NY 10022

Maxwell Macmillan Canada, Inc.
1200 Eglinton Avenue East
Suite 200
Don Mills, Ontario M3C 3N1

Macmillan Publishing Company is part of the Maxwell Communication Group of Companies.

Library of Congress Cataloging-in-Publication Data
Jones, James Earl,
James Earl Jones: voices and silences/by James Earl Jones and Penelope Niven.
p. cm.
Includes index.
ISBN 0-684-19513-5
1. Jones, James Earl. 2. Actors—United States—Biography.
I. Niven, Penelope. II. Title.
PN2287.J589A3 1993
792'.028'092—dc20   93–19021
[B]   CIP

Macmillan books are available at special discounts for bulk purchases for sales promotions, premiums, fund-raising, or educational use. For details, contact:

Special Sales Director
Macmillan Publishing Company
866 Third Avenue
New York, NY 10022

10   9   8   7   6   5   4   3   2   1

Printed in the United States of America

Permissions on page 394.

TO
Robert Earl Jones, my natural father,
and
Professor Donald Crouch,
father of my resurrected voice
—JEJ

To Jennifer and Flynn,
voices of tomorrow
—PEN

ACKNOWLEDGMENTS

We wish to thank the following people for their contributions to this book: our editor, Robert Stewart; Regan McLemore, our invaluable research and photographic assistant; Cecilia Hart Jones; Flynn Earl Jones; Robert Earl Jones; Matthew Earl Jones; Jennifer Niven McJunkin; Barbara Hogenson and Beth Gardiner of the Lucy Kroll Agency; all of the people who worked on the book at Scribners and Macmillan, especially Lisa Drew, Mark LaFlaur, Carol Cook, Angella Baker, and Estelle Laurence; Doris Barron, Lisa Von Sprecken, Penny Miner, Valerie Kindle, and Joseph Kraemer, who worked on transcriptions and research; Jane Aire; Butch Anderson; Sharyn Bamber; Richard Bauman; Pamela Printy Bohnert; Richard Brown; Gerald Friedman; Coddy Granum; Claribel Baird Halstead; Linda Dovi Hutchison; George Joseph; David Hume Kennerly; Aubrey Lewis; Jeffrey Lyon; David Lust; Ernie and Kay Mott; Dale Olson; Jo Kaiser Raksin; Tim Redman; Mitchell Ryan; Ed Setrakian; Madge Sinclair; Mel Winkler; Anne Wittig; Richard Wood, Len Clark and George Silver of Earlham College, Richmond, Indiana, who gave indispensable computer support; Bessie Jolly

Taylor, whose book of family history illuminated the Jones family story; and all the members of the Connolly family who contributed memories, time, letters and photographs, especially Terry and Eugene Connolly and Ozella Connolly Walker. Finally, we offer singular thanks and tribute to Lucy Kroll.

James Earl Jones and Penelope Niven
Los Angeles, April 1993

CONTENTS

PART THREE   VOICES DISCOVERED   97

PART FOUR   VOICES CHOSEN   181

This book tells two tales, the story of my origins and the story of my career. I have explored the history, the energies, and the urgings which led me to become an actor. That tale of my childhood and family life I have found fascinating to evoke, "a round unvarnish'd tale" worth telling.

It has been much more difficult to tell the story of my work as an actor. I have faced that task with overwhelming reluctance, finding it almost impossible to put into words who I am and what I do as an actor;

> *". . . the story of my life,*
> *From year to year,—the battles, sieges, fortunes,*
> *That I have pass'd."*

I have just told you what I remember, as it happened, of the art of the world I work in. The best I have been able to do is to tell the story of key roles and productions, the story my time as an actor has to tell.

—James Earl Jones

FOREWORD

Penelope Niven

Out of excavations of memory, James Earl Jones has resurrected his history. For nearly four years we have worked together on this book. Hundreds of hours of taped dialogue have yielded hundreds of pages of manuscript, clay to be molded. We have interviewed others and read widely. We have combed the papers of our agent, Lucy Kroll, a consummate archivist, who kept the records of James Earl's long career, and persuaded him at last that he should write a book. He resisted for a long time. This is a life and career in progress.

Because he is a stutterer, he shapes written and spoken language uniquely, and works with even more care than most writers do. His hands linger over every sentence. His eyes and ears are attuned to the resonance of words. And his years of silence have forged a sensitive listener and observer. His journey back into childhood memory eventually evoked scenes witnessed through a child's eyes, told in the child's voice. That voice grew in complexity as his life story unfolded.

James Earl Jones travels constantly—Colorado, Louisiana, California, New York, Thailand, Kenya, Alaska, in the space of only a few weeks—migrating from one world to another, from movies to television to theatre to commercials to narrations. Work propels him, keeps him airborne, but so does hunger for experience, variety, home. In one day, he flies from Texas to California to New York.

We have written this book in trailers on movie and television sets; on board ship; at his family home in rural upstate New York; in Los Angeles and Manhattan and Hahnville, Louisiana; in Chicago and Dallas and San Antonio, Texas; in Hamilton, Bermuda, and San Juan, Puerto Rico.

I have followed him on many of his rounds, to watch him at work. In Colorado in 1989, he was honored at the Ninth Annual Breckenridge Festival of Film, surrounded by fans. Patient and courtly, he is as genuinely interested in people as they are in him. He enjoyed the mountain altitude, remembering the exhilaration of his Army Ranger training, and his work with the Mountain Cold Weather Training program in Colorado in 1953. He canvassed the Breckenridge shops in brilliant September sunlight, looking for gifts to take home to his wife and son. Everywhere people stopped him, introducing themselves, producing cameras, asking to have pictures made at his side. Later, a guide took him up into the rugged mountains, altitude fourteen thousand feet, the air too pure and transparent to breathe. He seemed more at home in that remote solitude than in the crowded village.

In October of 1989, he went on location to Homeplace Plantation in Hahnville, Louisiana, to play a modest role in *Convicts*, a film written by Horton Foote and starring Robert Duvall. James Earl Jones is deeply attuned to the spirit of place: hemmed in by sugarcane fields, he was depressed by the strands of history and doom woven into the atmosphere. It was more than the sultry air, the cane fields with their ghosts of pain and time. He was reading a book about cane harvesting, as brutal today as in 1904, the movie's time, when black and white convicts worked the fields under duress, and almost as brutal as the time when slaves worked with lacerated hands in the endless, lucrative fields.

The somber history of this place is in his bones. It transformed him into an older man, broad shoulders sagging, eyes grieving. The resignation on his face had nothing to with makeup or script. His dejected metamorphosis into the character of Ben Jackson was complete.

He moved on to Chicago to shoot the pilot for his television series "Gabriel's Fire," his first since "Paris" in 1979–80. The reality is overwhelming on Chicago's South State Street where he was filming on a bitter, windy March day, moving from location to location, down through degrees of poverty into hopelessness, desperation, danger. Many buildings stand abandoned, battered as if by war. Security guards surrounded him as he walked the short blocks from his trailer to the set. The street overflowed with people who really live there. Their voices haunted him: "They think I can give them something. They don't know what."

People recognize him everywhere. From Africa to the Caribbean, for instance, people have seen him play Eddie Murphy's father in *Coming to America,* and call him the King.

In New York in June of 1990, he presented a Tony Award, which he himself has won twice: as best actor for the 1968–69 season in *The Great White Hope,* and for the 1986–87 season in *Fences.* Of all his professional worlds, the theatre is home. He is at home in Washington, too. On Memorial Day in 1990, he stood before the Capitol to narrate Aaron Copland's *Lincoln Portrait* in a performance with the National Symphony Orchestra. In July of 1992, he received from President George Bush the National Medal for the Arts. At a State Department dinner, he stood as tribute was paid him, his enigmatic green eyes full of tears. In 1993, he returned to Washington to speak at the Lincoln Memorial during inaugural festivities for President William Jefferson Clinton.

He has traveled a long road to reach Washington. The cadences of his voice were shaped in Mississippi and transformed in Michigan. As a child he lost the power of speech and retreated into silence. The reasons, like his roots, reach back to Arkabutla

Township near Coldwater in Tate County, Mississippi, fifty miles south of Memphis, Tennessee.

I wanted to see his homeplace. I, too, am a Southerner. ("Can a black Southern man and a white Southern woman really work together?" someone from elsewhere in the country wanted to know.) We grew out of the same time and place and history. Our grandmothers taught us the same hymns, cooked the same greens with fatback, the same fluffy biscuits, the same red-eye gravy. James Earl and I know the same landscapes, the music Southern voices can make, the heavy burden of our shared history.

As I traveled through Mississippi, Tennessee, and Texas to interview his relatives, I discovered that while he is the most famous member of his vibrant family, James Earl is by no means the only remarkable one. I sat in family living rooms, heard stories and memories, looked at picture albums and letters, everywhere warmed by hospitality, good food, and laughter. I met the oldest family member, James Earl's great-aunt Sidney, afflicted in her nineties with Alzheimer's disease. Her face was smooth as a child's, and when we showed her a picture of her family and of herself, at the age of eight or nine, memory rekindled for an instant. She told us about the day the picture was made by an itinerant photographer, and about the shoes she was wearing then, and the dress.

One day in this rich odyssey stands out in my memory: I fly to Memphis for my first meeting with James Earl's Connolly cousins, Yvonne Denton from Memphis and Terry and Eugene Connolly from Michigan. They pick me up at the airport, and we drive the fifty miles to Coldwater, Mississippi. We take pictures of each other on the town square in front of the "Welcome to Coldwater" sign before we go on to Arkabutla Township.

A country store stands in Arkabutla, near two other small buildings. That is all there is of a town. The old church pew on the front porch of the store holds four shrewd and genial elderly men, three black, one white. In two of the faces black and Indian genes meld into regal profiles. Yes, they remember Ruth Connolly Jones and Robert Earl Jones. Yes, they know the old Connolly place.

James Earl bought the place years ago, then sold it to his cousin Terry. It is hard to find. The route to James Earl's birthplace splays off a gravel road drifting away from the paved county road. You have to walk through a wilderness to reach the homestead now. Someone will guide us by foot, through the woods, past the ravine, to the house itself. We are warned of bees and snakes, for no one has lived there for years. All of us who grew up in the South know the voluptuous power of summer and kudzu to camouflage buildings and landscapes. By August, when the air is dense with humidity, the rampant vines and grass consume the land, swallowing fences, trees, even derelict houses.

In the late afternoon heat, we follow our young guide far into the woods, walking deeper into the tall grass, the warm fragrant air, the drone of insects. All of a sudden, we come upon the house. Fragile and broken, it barely stands. Bees swarm in and out. Behind are pear and plum trees, the vestiges of a well and cistern, the bones of a fence. Here is James Earl's beginning, the true beginning, the homestead. . . .

PROLOGUE

There is a warm golden light. It shines from a coal oil lamp sitting on a potbellied stove. The stove is used to heat a four-room house filled with family—eleven in all. It is the middle of the night. Most of the family is asleep.

The woman Maggie sends her husband John to fetch a midwife, who comes as dawn approaches. She has taught Maggie her birthing skills: she has lifted all the children from Maggie's womb, three sons, seven daughters.

Now Ruth, Maggie's oldest daughter, is lying swollen and still. The water has long since broken. There is only silence.

Ruth asks for castor oil.

"Castor oil!?" Maggie's impatience grows.

"Go ahead. Let her have anything she wants," the midwife says. "It can't hurt."

"It won't come," Ruth says. "It's dead already."

"No—it's *not* dead."

Maggie vents her fury. She quietly heaps abuse on Ruth, and then, louder and louder, modulates into uncharacteristic profanity.

Ruth lies pained and frightened.

"Bear down. Work harder," the midwife says, simply encouraging her. The midwife and Maggie work, each in her own way, the midwife urging, Maggie willing the child into life.

At 6:05 on the morning of January 17, 1931, the midwife lifts Maggie's first grandchild from Ruth's womb.

I remember the warmth of the light. My mother, Ruth, told me the other details of my birth as she remembered them, but the light of the coal oil lamp that night floats in my memory. I have no conscious recollection of anything else . . . except for the light.

James Earl Jones

PART ONE

VOICES
OVERHEARD

1.

MY MOTHERS
AND
MY FATHERS

Early in my awakening memory, two grown men lean on a rail fence talking about livestock. It is spring of 1935. Since I am only four, they seem very tall to me. One of the men is my maternal grandfather, John Henry Connolly, grandson of a slave and an Irish indentured servant. The other man in my memory is my paternal grandfather, Robert Jones, also a slave's grandson. I do not really know this grandfather, and I am not sure why he has come. I live with my grandfather John Henry, who owns forty acres of land in Arkabutla Township, Mississippi.

In the center of his land, he has built a four-room house, the house where I was born. Twelve people live in that house, and we work our own forty acres and sharecrop others. We grow vegetables and fruit, hunt game, butcher pigs and cows, gather milk and butter from the cows. It is the middle of the Depression, but we never want for food.

Why has my grandfather Jones come this day? To buy cattle? To talk about me? I have no way of knowing. My grandfather John Henry leans on that rail fence and talks about his livestock because he says he is going to sell everything and move his family north to Michigan. He believes he can start over there, and he knows there will be better schools for his children. He cares about education. My grandmother Maggie Anderson Connolly is all for the move. She, too, believes there will be better schools, and better husbands for her daughters. Besides, she has a big thirst for adventure. That is why she wants to move to Michigan—that, and her hatred of Mississippi.

My grandparents have three sons and six daughters. There are seven children at home now, and one grandchild, me. All of us work hard, even the youngest children. Our land has belonged to the Connolly family since Reconstruction. It is beautiful land, sold cheap after the Civil War on the theory that it was worthless. For sixty years my family has proved that theory wrong. We love the tough, poor earth, the stubborn gullies and rises, the deep ravines, the freedom to roam over land that belongs to us. I know as I watch my grandfathers standing there, and as I listen to their talk, that my life is about to change. What is going to happen to me? I am very young, and I am more curious than afraid.

There is fear in another early memory. It is dark and I am supposed to be sleeping, but I cannot sleep because Maggie and my mother, Ruth, are arguing, and the argument is about me. Me and Goofer Dust. My grandmother is very angry about Goofer Dust. In New Orleans even today, cocaine is still called Goofer Dust. In the thirties, the use of cocaine was sanctioned, made cheap for farm and plantation owners. As they passed through to pick up their tools each morning, migrant workers pulled out their shirt pockets and received a thimbleful of cocaine to help them work productively and get through the day.

I don't know how my grandmother knew this, but she is keeping me awake arguing about Goofer Dust. My father is long gone, and my mother is saying that she wants to leave and go off with another man to the Mississippi Delta. There is no work for her in Arkabutla Township. In the Delta, she will become a migrant worker, harvesting whatever is in season. The man is the preacher's stepson, but Maggie does not trust him, or Ruth, or all that Goofer Dust, or the Delta. She says it is no place for a child, and she will keep me on the farm with the rest of her children.

All through the night, I hear my mother and my grandmother arguing. There is no privacy in a four-room house with thin wood walls, and ten people sleeping where they can—on pallets, even on the porch.

I am sad, and afraid, and very quiet.

* * *

I remember that the next day I found myself alone in a room with my mother. She was bathing me in a large basin, and she was wooing me.

"Do you want to come with me to the Delta?" she asked me.

"Nooo," I said. I don't think she knew that I had listened in the dark to her argument with Maggie. As I heard their angry voices rise and fall, I made up my mind that I did not want to go to the Delta with anybody, not even with my mother. The Delta was damp, uncomfortable, dangerous. There was Goofer Dust there.

Ruth asked me once more. We were alone again that evening, and she asked me to go with her to the Delta. I am not even sure how old I was then—between two and four. I was already walking, talking, just beginning to think for myself—and suddenly I was required to make a decision. I had to make the first significant choice of my life, the choice between the mother I loved and craved, and the grandmother I loved and trusted.

Again, I said no to my mother.

My aunts tell me that Maggie and Ruth struggled fiercely over who would take better care of me. My mother finally gave in. Almost everyone gave in to Maggie. She had a strong will, especially when she thought she knew best, and most of the time, that is exactly what she thought. I do not remember the ongoing battle. I just remember their words that night. And my own choice to stay, and my mother leaving without me.

When I reach far back into my memory, I see dimly some days in a city which must have been Memphis. My mother stays in a small room, and I have come for a visit. We eat rice three times a day. Sometimes at breakfast, there is an egg scrambled in the rice. Sometimes there are peas in the rice at lunch. Sometimes at supper, there is a little ground meat cooked with the rice. Surely my mother worked, but I do not remember that she left me alone or with someone else.

At night, we sleep together. Her body is warm, and timidly, I reach inside the softness of her gown to touch her breasts. I am trying to call her mama. I shape the word on my lips, but she awakes before I can say it.

"What's wrong? What do you want?"

"Nothing."

She goes back to sleep, and soon I sleep, the word unspoken.

There is one more early memory, only a flickering instant, but one that haunts me. My mother and I are walking along a railroad track. I do not know where we are, or where we are headed, or when, or why. I don't remember. I just see us walking there, side by side. She is holding my hand, and telling me to hurry, but I am tired, and afraid, and sad, mostly sad.

I remember scooping up some rocks from the railroad grade that day, and stuffing them into my pocket to take back to Ruth's room. Later, she built a fire in the fireplace, and as it burned taller, I threw those stones into the fire.

Suddenly they exploded like bullets. The noise scared us both, and my mother began to weep. Even then, I knew she was crying about much more than stones. Out of her own unspoken sadness and disappointment, my mother wept most of the time.

When Ruth was seventy-five, her sister Ozella had asked her to write down something about her life. "I feel all used up," Ruth wrote, but she promised Ozella to try to put something of herself on paper. She began writing about her parents first:

> *How it started*
>
> *Maggie and Johnnie, a young courting couple started dating. She lived on one side of the Bottom and he lived on the other, she in Desoto County [Mississippi] and he in Tate County. Maggie and Johnnie got married, bought 40 acres of ground [and] built a four-room house with porches and raised ten kids [one died young]. . . . In toil they raised everything that would grow and more besides. Cotton was the money crop but they grew*

peanuts, etc., Sure good eating. . . . They first moved to Douglas Park, Tennessee . . . then to Arkansas . . . things was rotten . . . then moved to St. Louis . . . living quarters was not good but we was rolling then there was work at the steel mill so Johnnie gave up farming a while and went to work in a steel mill, but no suitable place to live. He worked in Detroit a while. On his way back to Missouri he stopped in Gary and got a job at the steel mill. . . . Would you believe he found a brand new house, six rooms and bath and basement he could rent with options to buy. The two rooms upstairs was an apartment so we rented it out to help with expenses. . . . We went to Gary on the train. . . . Papa had bought some used furniture. We lived there about eighteen months. Ruby [the oldest daughter] was ill. Papa was doing only about three days at the mill but in the meantime the Swaggart County [office] was selling land sight unseen in Michigan. With Ruby being sick, work scarce, back to Arkabutla we went. Things was sort of slim pickin'. We could still count on the garden, a cow and a few pigs to get us through. I was ten years old that summer. . . . Spring was good but . . . lots of work—fruit, berries, plums. . . . The saddest part of it all was the school system for black children. They had about four months to go. Pa made a couple of attempts to get the kids in a better school. Could [not] board that many out. One fall he rented a house in Memphis. We all moved in to go in the city which was good. But with no other livelihood than farming it was hard. Pa was back on the farm trying to get things going. One or two years the oldest stayed in Memphis some and went to school there with kin. . . .

That is as far as my mother got in putting her early life down on paper. Only fragments of my history can be discovered now by going back to the front rooms and to the porches of my relatives, to the circle of aunts and cousins under the trees at family reunions, and to various family Bibles, letters, and pictures. Each aunt holds pieces of the family puzzle; uncles and cousins furnish other pieces. Much is lost in time and memory.

In Ruth's handwritten memoir, almost empty of punctuation and full of misspellings, the reality burns. It fits that her handwriting fades at the memory of "the saddest part of it all," for education meant a great deal to her. The love of reading and book learning is in our bone memory.

Oral tradition gives us our scant knowledge of our family history. Because we know so little of my maternal great-great-grandparents, Brice and Parthenia Connolly, I often wonder about the reality of their lives. Who kidnapped Brice and his two small brothers from their home in Africa and forced them into slavery? What was Brice's real name? Was it day or night, I wonder, when this ten-year-old boy was stolen from his family? Was he playing in some familiar place, or sleeping in his bed? How did he spend that last day of freedom? We know nothing of the mother and father who gave him life, named him, and taught him to speak. How did they feel when they discovered that their three small sons were gone? Were they, too, subjugated? We have no record of the terror the three children must have felt, or the hardships they endured on the long agony of their journey to a North Carolina port.

I try to visualize the three of them facing powerful strangers, adults speaking words they could not decipher. Bound and fed and moved at the mercy of men they did not understand, these children were sold separately, to different masters in different places. How then did they cope with the final separation from each other, and with the lonely fears of new perils lying ahead?

The boy who was to be my great-great-grandfather was sold to someone in Mississippi. There he toiled as a slave on a cotton plantation. Thirty-five or forty years later, after the Civil War, he was "freed" into a life of ongoing economic hardship, with no access to education for himself or his children, and little hope of improving his fate.

Yet he had a wife who could read and write, and who taught him how. Parthenia Connolly, my great-great-grandmother—what drove her to this country from Ireland before the Civil War? What dreams led her to indenture herself and travel alone to the United States? How did she get to Mississippi, and how did she encounter Brice?

Their first child was born in 1844. There were 436,631 slaves in Mississippi in 1860, and only 773 free blacks. There were 353,899 white people. Laws aside, there were liaisons between blacks, Indians, and whites, and, not uncommonly, between indentured servants and slaves, for some indentured servants were treated like slaves, housed and fed with slaves.

What were the day-to-day obstacles in the face of this romance between Brice and Parthenia? What power drew them together? How did they manage, what did they suffer for it, what were the transcending glories that fortified their bond to each other?

When the Civil War ended, Brice had his freedom and the need for a last name. We have been told that his brothers took the names of their masters—becoming Tom Evans and Ben Butler. Brice did not want his master's name.

"We know mine," Parthenia told him. "Take mine."

Connolly thus became our family name. Parthenia had given her children a surname, and had taught her husband to read and write. Their children were thirsty for education: education was true liberation, true power.

Brice and Parthenia had nine children in all; I am descended from their third child, Wyatt. Sometime after slavery days, during Reconstruction, Wyatt began to buy cheap land, until he had assembled more than three hundred acres in Arkabutla, Mississippi. There, according to my aunts, he read every book and pamphlet he could find, scouring each one for anything that would help him to cultivate his land. In the center of the farm, he built a house with a wide front porch. He called it the Home House. He had married Sharlett Jeeter, part African, part Indian, and she bore him eleven children in the Home House. The birthright of each of their six sons was forty acres of land, which they had to earn and pay for. That is how their son, my grandfather John Henry, came by the land he loved and farmed, and then relinquished when he gave up Mississippi for Michigan.

Brice died in 1910 at the age of one hundred, long before I was born. Parthenia, the old great-great-grandmother, lived into her nineties. Their buried history is in my blood.

"The saddest part of it all . . ." for my mother Ruth's childhood was the deprivation of mind and spirit. Because she could only go to school about four months a year, the rest of the time she and her brothers and sisters worked, much as our ancestors had, in fields they planted with cotton, peanuts, or tobacco, now and then making a journey to the city or the steel mill, before turning again to the land.

Ruth was the darkest of John Henry and Maggie's daughters. She was pretty, but considered less eligible in those days than her fairer-skinned sisters, who were thought to be more desirable. My father Robert Earl Jones fell in love with Ruth Connolly almost on sight, finding her beautiful and very intelligent. Because he had only a third-grade education and Ruth had completed sixth grade, he was impressed by her. She in turn was impressed that his family owned a lot of land, and had built a nice house in Coldwater, the only real town near Arkabutla.

My aunts have told me that long before my parents met, Ruth taught school in the church my great-grandfather Wyatt built near the Home House. When he first put up the church and founded the school, he knew that the state of Mississippi would not pay to build a school for black children, but that once there was a building and pupils, the county would have to pay for a teacher. Wyatt wanted all his children and grandchildren to know how to read and write. Ruth was one of a procession of teachers, but a popular one, even with her own brothers and sisters. She also wrote and directed pageants for her students to perform, often designing and making the costumes, for she was even then a skilled seamstress. People came from all over that part of Tate County to see Ruth's pageants. Then, for some reason nobody from this side of history can remember, she stopped teaching and went to work in Memphis as a maid.

My father, Robert Earl, came from a family of preachers and dreamers. His father Robert Washington Jones, the grandson of slaves, bought some land in Arkansas and tried to start a Utopian settlement he designed and named Peace. For years he and his cousin and compatriot Isaac Jolly rode the train from Mississippi to Arkansas, struggling to get their ideal community underway. Their dreams never came to pass.

I hardly knew my grandfather Jones, but I remember him as tall and handsome, with a deep voice. He was a "jackleg" preacher, not an ordained minister. He just suddenly felt called to preach one day, and he probably figured it would be an adventure. I tend to paint him as a rogue. He was so good-looking he had to be a rogue. But he was really a vagabond, loving the open road, and, it is said, loving women. He and Elnora, Robert Earl's mother, divorced when Robert Earl was a boy.

Both my grandfathers stand in my memory at the same rail fence. My grandfather Jones held that passion for the open road. My grandfather Connolly stayed home, steadfast as the earth, working hard to provide for the twelve of us, taking pride that he could feed and clothe that many people, working us as hard as he worked himself. Like my aunts and uncles, I called him Papa, and Maggie, Mama.

Papa was not affectionate, but he was there, dependable, available, sure as the seasons. I followed him all over the farm, sewn to him like his shadow. After working outside all day in Mississippi and later in Michigan, he would come into the house in the winter and build a fire, and without shame, stand in front of the fire rubbing his groin. He was as sensuous as nature. There was a mad note of sexual passion between my grandparents, although they never expressed it openly in front of the rest of us. In our small house, there was no privacy, and I overheard interesting conversations between Mama and Papa. In Michigan, growing older, Maggie would bemoan the changes in her body, remembering how beautiful, black, and silken her pubic hair used to be. John Henry would reassure her that she was still beautiful. This was a man who made love to his wife until they were very old.

I don't know what Mama and Papa thought about the Joneses, but they were apparently not too fond of Robert Earl as a suitor for Ruth. As "Battling Bill Stovall," Robert Earl achieved some success as a Golden Gloves boxer in the late twenties in and around Memphis, about fifty miles from Arkabutla. How did he get there? Who was the boy who became my father?

Late one night in 1923, in a sharecropper's cabin near Coldwater, Mississippi, a thirteen-year-old boy listens in the dark to a quarrel in the next room. His father's voice is fierce, his mother's cold. She has caught his father once more with another woman. He is a preacher as well as a farmer, she reminds him. He should know about sin. The edict is clear. His father will have to leave, banished this time for good. The boy knows as he listens in the dark that his world is changing forever, and there is nothing he can do about it.

His name is Robert Earl Jones. He is called Earl. His father gives him a makeshift reason for the departure he is about to take. They are close. Earl looks like his father, and depends on his love and approval. He listens to the advice his father is giving him:

"Never mind that you only completed third grade. You are strong and smart. You know how to work hard. Take care of your mother. Make something of yourself."

There is an emotional leave-taking. Time passes. Earl works hard on the farm, trying to please his mother Elnora, cares for their cabin, tends the farm acres his parents have leased. He grows taller, stronger, more handsome—more like his father. His voice deepens to sound like his father's did when he preached at revivals and gospel meetings.

His mother seems to want less and less to do with Earl. He feels rejection where her love and warmth used to be. It is something he learns to fear and expect in women. Once, in frustration, he journeys to visit his father in Arkansas, to see if he can live with him. Sadly, he realizes that will not work. He goes back to Elnora's house. He seldom sees his father after that.

In 1929, Earl and his mother give up farming and move to Memphis. He works odd jobs as a gardener, a janitor, an errand boy. His mother works as a maid. He is cocky, jaunty, wearing a veneer to mask his insecurity. He is always aware of his lack of schooling. He likes to read, but many words elude him. He lives with his mother's silent disapproval, feeling inadequate to please her. Girls like him because he is handsome and strong, but he never lets anyone come close to him.

He is a good athlete, and tries prizefighting and Golden Gloves boxing in Memphis. He is good at it. His manager gives him the fighting name of "Battling Bill Stovall." He enjoys the applause and the money he can sometimes win, but he has no heart for the sport. And win or lose, work or not, he cannot satisfy his mother, who is retreating more and more into her religion.

In the summer of 1929, on the eve of the Depression, Earl and Elnora go back to Coldwater for a church picnic and reunion. There, he sees Ruth Connolly, a year younger than he. He knows her father John Henry, a hardworking landowner from nearby Arkabutla Township, and her mother Maggie, part black, part Indian. Some people fear Maggie, for she is mysterious, aggressive, unpredictable. Some people say she knows magic, and can make her husband and children do whatever she wants.

Earl is immediately attracted to Ruth. She is beautiful and smart. She has more schooling than he, and has been a teacher in her grandfather's school. He begins to court her, and by early spring of 1930, they are married.

In Memphis he has found them jobs, hard to come by now that the Depression has hit. She will be a maid, he a butler and chauffeur for a rich white family. They can live on the estate for free in a garage apartment. They can save money to buy their own house. He is proud of the way he has provided for his beautiful wife.

Earl and Ruth are happy together sometimes, but most of the time she is unpredictable—now cheerful, now morose and depressed. Her moods change in an instant. She will not talk to him. He begs her to tell him her troubles, but she will not, or cannot. Maybe that is just the way of women, he thinks—or maybe he is just a failure as a son and a husband.

Maggie comes to Memphis to visit them in the apartment over the garage. Earl has been proud of it and of their plans for the future—until Maggie comes. She does not approve of the life they have begun to stitch together. Ruth is listening to Maggie. Things are worse between him and Ruth after Maggie leaves. Her moods grow deeper, her silences longer. He must not be good enough, strong enough, smart enough. He loves Ruth as well as he will ever love anyone, but he believes this is not enough for her. Sometimes she is vivacious, even flirtatious, like the girl he met at the picnic. But most of the time she is sad, withdrawn—a stranger.

To this day, my mother's sisters are fond of my father, and he of them. Robert Earl tells me that there was something deeply wrong on a personal level between him and Ruth. Emotionally, she was never complete. Robert Earl speculated that she might have been assaulted or even sexually abused before they met. My mother once confided in me that when she told Robert Earl she was pregnant, he said in disbelief, "It can't be. We only did it once. You have no woman's nature." Ruth told me that my father in his panic even said, "It must be my brother Charles's child." Only once did Ruth ever tell me about a book that meant something to her—*The Well of Loneliness,* Radclyffe Hall's treatment of lesbian love, of some women's need to find comfort in each other. I do not think Ruth ever had a liaison with a woman, except, perhaps, for reaching out for some kind of warmth in friendship. She was married twice more, but she never seemed to find lasting understanding and affection with men.

That girl teaching and running her own little pageants near the Home House in Arkabutla became a migrant worker in the Delta, a domestic in Memphis, a tailor and a seamstress in the Midwest. Some wedge of history or experience or inhibition fractured her marriage to my father. They were separated before I was born. Ruth went back to John Henry and Maggie's house for my birth, and I stayed there while she went out to work where she could. There was little work to be had in Arkabutla in the best of times, and the Depression dried up any opportunity Ruth might have had for work she might have truly enjoyed. She was barely twenty, and black, and a single working mother.

Robert Earl stayed on in Memphis for a time after I was born, boxing, working at odd jobs, feeling his guilt about the marriage, and believing himself a failure as a man, a husband, and now, a father. He and my aunts have told me that some of the family persuaded Ruth and Maggie to allow Robert Earl to see me when I was an infant. He came, and pulled back the netting from my carriage—and I looked into his face. He lifted me up and I squalled. I was a baby. He was a stranger to me. He took it as a personal affront, and left, and we never saw each other again until I was twenty-one.

The father void was in some ways easier to bear than my mother's long absences from me. I never knew Robert Earl, or expected to know him or even to see him. Ruth came and went, reentering my life, only to leave again. I counted the days until she arrived to visit in the summer—and as soon as I saw her I would go to the calendar and mark the day of her leave-taking. Every moment of her visit, I dreaded that inevitable last day. I knew no matter how many presents she brought, no matter how much fun she had with me and her brothers and sisters, it was just a matter of time until she would go away somewhere and leave me once again.

I felt sometimes as a child that I had killed my mother. Sometimes I felt that she had killed me by leaving me behind, no matter how much I had protested that I wanted to stay. I rejoiced in her visits, yet her impending departure brought me to grief.

But Maggie and John Henry were always there, day by day, and they became for me, once and for all, my mama and my papa.

2.

BOYISH DAYS

Othello: Her father lov'd me; oft invited me;
Still question'd me the story of my life,
From year to year, the battles, sieges, fortunes,
That I have pass'd.
I ran it through, even from my boyish days. . . .

OTHELLO, THE MOOR OF VENICE, ACT I, SCENE III

Papa was the hardest-working man I ever knew, and he expected us to work as hard as he did. In a family as large as ours, your personality did not count for much, so long as you fit in, carried your load, did your chores. Life on the farm connected us to the hard realities of nature, as well as to the harmony and beauty. Nature was sometimes a companion, sometimes an adversary, and Papa did not spare us any of the lessons nature had to teach.

I followed him all over the farm, around the barnyard, everywhere he went. He had become for me the parent, not the grandparent. I felt a deep connection to Papa, as a boy will to his father, especially after he begins letting go of his mother. Papa made me see everything. Once one of our sows was giving birth to a litter when a piglet got stuck in the birth canal, half in and half out, and would not pass. Papa let the sow walk around a few hours, believing she would deliver. When at last he realized the piglet was dead, he had to pull it with great force from the mother's body. The dead animal tore in half in Papa's hands. He thought nothing of the wasted blood, bone, and tissue. That was life, and he could not—would not—shield me from it.

Papa loved to go fishing and he would take only one of his boys with him at a time. I never understood why until one day he and I were sitting out in a boat in the middle of Lost Lake, a swampy pond nearby. You reached it by traveling an obscure path through a wetland. Nothing was biting that day on Lost Lake, but Papa said he didn't mind. It was then I knew we were out there for more than fishing. Papa did not know how to say, "Let's have a talk," or, "Unload your burdens," but he made himself available for us, one by one, on those fishing trips. If something was troubling you, this was your chance to talk to him in private.

He had a sense of justice, stern but fair. He did not treat his grandsons any better or worse than he treated his sons. Papa was never political, and he never expressed any racism or racialism. (I'll explain to you later what those terms mean to me.) Papa had no enemies, even in the South, and he was not afraid to take a stand when it counted.

The earliest confrontation I remember had to do with a prized and necessary family possession, a child's wooden wagon. It was not a toy for us, but the family wagon, used to haul wood. One day our neighbors, who lived just through the plum grove on the edge of Papa's land, asked to borrow the wagon to haul wood for themselves. They did not stop at hauling, however, but chopped wood in the wagon, chipping the bottom, and returning it badly damaged. They did not apologize or explain or offer any recompense. We were angry about the harm to our wagon, but we were made to know that we did not have the right to complain about it. We had lent the wagon to them. They were white. We were black. There was nothing we could do or say. Not only were we children powerless to redeem the wagon, but our parents seemed impotent, too. Not even Papa could salvage that wagon.

There were other problems with this family in Arkabutla Township. That grove of plum trees straddled their land and ours. The plums fell in their sweet, juicy oblivion on both sides of the boundary line. There were hot disputes between my youngest uncles and aunts and the neighbor's children about who owned those plum trees and their bounty. One day when the children were growing older and the disputes were getting more heated, Papa walked out and laid waste to the plum grove. He chopped down every tree. He could not mediate that perennial dispute over the plums, could not resolve it, and so he ravaged it. This was not an act of anger, but a dramatic and destructive act. Papa denied everyone access to the fruit.

I do not believe this was a racial issue for Papa; I think he saw it as a simple conflict over the bounty of those trees. Mama, to the contrary, saw everything as racially motivated. Every harvest season, she would have led us defiantly into battle over those plums. She would have left that orchard standing as a symbol of her distrust of white people. But Papa's will prevailed in the drama of the plum orchard.

When you were due a whipping, Papa sent you out into the woods to choose your own instrument of punishment. You had to decide whether you preferred the sting of the switch or the pain of the branch. You had to bring your choice back to him for his inspection, and then take your licks from the patriarch. Papa was unemotional about discipline. His sense of right and wrong prescribed the limits, and he was fair. Other than that, nature dictated the rules of life on the farm. The cow *had* to be milked at a certain time or the milk would sour in the udder. The pigs *had* to be fed or they would starve. Eggs *had* to be gathered or they would rot.

Because we had to be hunters, Papa introduced us early to firearms. The game helped to feed us. There were always firearms in the house, and we did not need to be Boy Scouts because our daily life trained us in the way of the woods, in survival, in pitting our skill against and with nature. Papa gave me my instruction in the tools needed to hunt and to work the land, and instilled in me a respect for the intricate rhythms of the natural world.

We wore each season like a skin—the mild gray winters in Mississippi; the soft, moist spring; the stifling summer heat; the dry, hot harvest days of fall. Many months of the year we could sleep on pallets on the porch, to the throb of cicadas, katydids, tree frogs—a din so powerful and constant in Southern summer nights that city folks have been known to come to visit and go home because they could not sleep.

Even after he ravaged the plum orchard, Papa could boast that his forty acres provided almost everything we needed for our daily meals.

He would sit at the head of the table in Mama's fragrant kitchen, smile at us, and say, "I just love to see my children eat."

Besides what we grew, there were wild pokeweed and dandelion greens to pick and cook and savor. There were blackberries, muscadines, and scuppernongs. Sometimes, our bodies craving nutrients we could not name, we ate small portions of clay scooped by the handful from deep inside the banks of nearby ravines. We knew how to dig far back beyond where worms had laid their eggs.

There was the smell of grass drying in the hot sun, of sweet honeysuckle, of supper cooking in Mama's kitchen, of the hearth fire smoke in Papa's house. Some necessary vein tied me to the farm, to the land, to all its energy and permanence and peace. The land could be counted on. I learned that when I was a very young boy.

If the land was Papa's realm, the house was Mama's, and her children's lives were her domain. Maggie—Mama—was always a mystery to me. Part black, part Choctaw Indian, she was handsome and regal with her dark, luminous skin and her straight black hair. She was lean and moody, and taut with energy. She worked as hard as Papa in the field, and then worked incessantly in the house. Maggie gave birth to seven daughters and four sons. One son died, but she raised the others, and then raised three grandchildren. She was always hungry for adventure, and what she wanted she usually got. Once she asked for a piano. It was a symbol of culture and class. She loved music, and if any of her children had a yearning to play, she wanted them to have the instrument. Somehow, Papa got her that piano.

Mama was inscrutable, coiled away inside herself, more so as time went on. Always she was full of drama. At night, from her voice, came vivid reincarnations of hurricanes and lynchings. She told us sagas about men with goat's heads and women with snakes in their bellies. These were Mama's versions of the bedtime story. She lived and breathed legends, fairy tales, spiritualism, horror stories. She also had a clear eye for indoctrination. She wanted to let her children know how dangerous it was "Out There." She wanted to teach us that blacks had to be distrustful of the white man. She tried to indoctrinate us with her own fervent racialism. Mama protected her children and grandchildren from every real and imagined danger just as she had protected me from the Delta and Goofer Dust.

Ruth told me once that when Maggie was only a child she witnessed the seduction of her older sister by their stepfather. Then Maggie witnessed her sister and her mother entrapping him under a car and pulling the jack out from under the bumper. The impact killed him. It was murder. When the sheriff came out, he called the death an accident. The funeral was arranged, and that was that. One of my aunts tells me that one of Maggie's sisters allegedly killed her husband. Maggie and John paid for her lawyer and she was acquitted at the trial. During the hot summer days of the trial, Maggie and John would take the younger children with them, to wait outside the courthouse under the shade trees. The older children would mind the younger ones, and none of them can tell me today what went on inside that courtroom while they played under the trees outside.

This stain of family violence must surely have touched Maggie's soul, must have poisoned her faith in others, and led her to distrust almost everything and everyone in her life. If you cannot trust family, how can you trust anyone in the world? She never spoke of any of this to me.

Likewise, I heard fragments of Papa's history—that he simultaneously had another wife and family, and some say, another career. John Henry, my hardworking, reliable Papa, was said by some to have had once a secret second career as a kind of "Railroad Bill." My mother told me that in a period in John Henry's life, he worked in cahoots with a white freight yard switchman. They would overturn freight cars full of produce, declare them as salvage, and sell the produce at half-price in black neighborhoods. Perhaps it is simply family mythology, a tall tale embroidered into the informal family history. I have never known for sure.

At least once a year, usually at harvest time in Michigan, Mama would end up in a rousing argument with Papa. She would save up all her grievances for months, and then she would let him have it. (I wonder now if she believed that at harvest time, with cash in hand for the year's crops, Papa would send money to his other family.) Usually she would build up to something outrageous—like accusing Papa of copulating with the horse. "Well, you've been with the horse again," she would shout at him.

Then he would explode. There would be that one inevitable night in the fall when the harvest was done and Mama would engineer an emotional accounting. It was as if she said, "All right, John Henry. Before the winter closes in, we are going to let it *all* out."

I remember one of those nights when we children were trying to sleep through this argument. We could hear Mama and Papa, their voices getting angrier and angrier. We hid our heads, covering our ears with the pillows, trying to erase the noise. All of a sudden I had to speak up. I was a lone voice, but I called out, "Will y'all hush?"

"Who is that?" Papa asked.

"It's James Earl," Mama answered. "He's the youngest. He doesn't know any better." And they hushed.

Like Papa, Mama showed little outward affection toward her children or grandchildren. I felt closer to Mama than to Ruth, but closer to Papa than to Mama. But Mama was never afraid to say exactly what she thought about anything, and even if you did not like it, at least you knew where you stood.

"Hallen and y'all! Hallen and y'all! Come here!"

That was my way of calling my siblings, who were really my aunts and uncles. "Hallen" was Helen, my youngest aunt, one of my favorites. Her younger brother Randy was just four years older than I and we grew up as brothers. My cousin Robert Earl was closer to my age, but younger. When he was left with Papa and Mama, too, I dominated him the way big brothers will.

My childhood memories straddle Mississippi and Michigan, the two worlds I lived in as a boy. Often the two places blend. A memory can begin one place and end another. In Mississippi, all the Connollys lived in a community orbiting the Home House. The family gathered there on Sundays for Methodist services in the church-school Wyatt had built. Afterward, there was Sunday dinner for the whole family, with everyone bringing food.

I remember my great-grandmother. I can see her sitting on the veranda of the Home House. I remember her death and burial, for my first fear of dying came when I saw her grave. The family could not afford a gravestone, so a wooden stake had been driven into the ground to mark where the headstone would eventually rest. I burst into tears, fearing the stake would go into her head and hurt her.

My aunts have said that my great-grandparents Wyatt and Sharlett Jeeter always had a house full on Sundays when their children and grandchildren gathered at the Home House for the family dinner after church. Wyatt owned a modest library, and encouraged his family to read his books. Now and then, he allowed the smallest children to touch and hold them, very carefully. He required his children to memorize Bible verses to say at the dinner table. The Bible was a revered and necessary book; all other books were luxuries, also to be cherished.

At Christmas in Mississippi the women in the family would work for days, precooking all the food for Christmas and New Year's. I remember their chatter and laughter as they worked side by side cooking hams, pies, cakes, candies, getting ready for what they called Christmas Cheers. On Christmas Eve, instead of stockings, we put out shoe boxes for Santa Claus to fill with fruit and candy, and, sometimes, a toy. Relatives and friends then passed from house to house for Christmas Cheers, enjoying homemade wine and the feast the women had cooked.

We had few toys, and not much time for play, so I learned early to depend on my imagination to make the most of the time I had. Papa and his sons were obsessed with cars. In the late twenties, they had gone all the way to Michigan to work. There they bought a Model A and drove it home to Arkabutla. We were proud of that car, one of the few owned by black or white people in our part of Tate County. Cars fascinated me early. Later, in Michigan, I would build my own little cars out of sticks, wooden spools or boxes, and spend hours with them until I was called to work or eat.

You are surrounded by animals when you live in the country and you grow up understanding that animals, too, work or die for their keep. But I took a special interest in an old draft horse named Charlie. Somehow I persuaded Papa to keep him long after Charlie was able to work in the fields, and even after Papa had sold all the other livestock in preparation for our move to Michigan. Not only was I attached to Charlie, but I was convinced he was pregnant. I had not quite mastered the facts of farm life, but I was sure that Charlie was about to give birth—to a sheep. Papa humored me, and he let me keep Charlie.

One day Charlie was wandering around grazing, and fell into a deep ravine in the woods near the road we took to some of our sharecrop land. Papa and my uncles found him, and saw right away Charlie had broken his back. They took their pistols from the house and went out to shoot him. I saw Charlie the next morning, when they dragged him out of the gully to leave him in the woods for the vultures. From then on, I was afraid to pass that place on the road, so close to the woods where Charlie's carcass was being eaten by vultures.

Cousin Robert Earl was only a toddler then. One day we had followed Papa down the road to our sharecrop land. As long as I was with Papa, I felt a sense of protection as I walked past Charlie's belly and guts. But later that day, Papa told me to go on home and to take Cousin Robert Earl with me. He was just able to walk then. I knew that, and I knew I was in charge, but somehow on the way home, I lost track of him. Most likely we were each taking our detours on the dusty road, picking up stones. He was probably moving slower than I wanted him to.

As I approached that awful place in the woods where Charlie was
laid out for the vultures, I could not find Robert Earl. I had
neglected him, and now he was not to be found. Suddenly, I started
running for home. I just ran ahead, as fast as I could run, all the way
back. Then I stood in the safety of the porch of Papa's house, and
waited. I remember how, after a long time, Robert Earl ran up the
path yelling and screaming. He may not have known Charlie's body
lay rotting there in the woods, but he knew he himself had been lost
and abandoned.

Mama was rearing two grandsons, Cousin Robert Earl and me,
but she did not treat us the same. He was younger than I, even more
vulnerable, but there was some unspoken history between Mama
and Bessie, Robert Earl's mother, something, perhaps, having to do
with his birth. Never warm and affectionate, Mama was still good to
me, but she treated my cousin with impatience, even rancor. I did
not understand it, and I did not ask questions, but I could not
witness Mama's ways with my cousin without feeling guilt. And
with guilt, I have always remembered that I left him there alone on
that long-ago road.

I knew about death then, too—the stillborn pig; Charlie; my
great-grandmother. I was a child who had already seen death up
close.

My aunts still tease me about being a stubborn child, with a strong
voice. I could dig in my heels and refuse to let them dress me up or
take me to church. I could shout and make myself heard. Papa used
to tell me my child-voice was beautiful, like a bell. I grew up listening
to the music of Southern voices, the rich oral testimonies guised in
stories told on the porch at Papa's or at my great-grandfather's
Home House. The storytellers in the family could mesmerize us with
the high drama of our family tales or with vivid local gossip. At night,
I listened with fascination and sometimes fear to Maggie's epic
bedtime stories. Out in the country, with few books or strangers, and
no such thing as television, we depended on the stories we knew, and

the stories we could invent and tell ourselves. I grew up with the spoken word.

I heard then the story the family tells about our beginnings. Sometime just after the turn of the century—probably in 1908—an itinerant photographer made his way through the back roads out of Coldwater to Arkabutla, and then all the way out to the Home House. Wyatt and Sharlett Jeeter posed for a picture. You can see the fusion of Caucasoid and Negroid genes in Wyatt, and the Negroid and Indian genes in Sharlett Jeeter. The fusion or collision of genetics in this country can be read in Wyatt and Sharlett Jeeter Connolly's family—some genes more evident in this one, others in that one. Bred in all of them was this love for the permanence and promise of the land. That legacy survived Reconstruction and World War I, but the Depression, my time, was testing us.

John Henry and Maggie were planning seriously about this move to Michigan now. We were a big family in a small house. Papa and Mama were trying to exercise their wisdom. I heard them talking about moving the household North. Of Mama and Papa's children, two had died young: the first son, Wesley, and the first daughter, Ruby. My mother Ruth, her sister Bessie, and their brother Henry Lee, or H.L., had already left home, but there were still ten of us to be moved. Papa and Uncle Hubert Berkely, or H.B., had gotten a 1932 Chevy sedan by this time. That was going to be the vehicle for the trip North. Papa and H.B. would be the advance party, for they had bought some land, site unseen, in a place they thought to be a suburb of Grand Rapids.

Papa had heard there were fine schools for black and white people there. In the early 1930s there were only four high schools for black students in the whole state of Mississippi, so you had to travel far and often board away from home to get a high school education. It was too late for Ruth, Bessie, H.L., and H.B. to go on to high school, but Papa and Mama were determined to send their younger children.

After Papa and H.B. got things settled with the new land in

Michigan, the rest of the family would travel North by train. It was going to be a big expense, uprooting the family and getting everybody to Michigan, and settling down again.

When you are five years old, there are questions you do not ask, images and words you cannot interpret. I was listening to my Papa and Mama in the dark, not fully understanding what they said or meant. I believed that Papa and Mama had decided to give up this house, this land, this world—to leave everything behind and go to Michigan.

When the day came, Papa and H.B. and I got in the car. I cannot even now remember—relive—my parting with the family, with the house, with the familiar woods and fields, with the Home House. I just remember that I got in the car with Papa and H.B. It was loaded with luggage, and a mattress in the back. We had no sleeping bags, and the mattress was necessary for the long drive North. Those were segregated times, and even if Papa could have afforded to rent a room overnight on the long journey North, he would not have been permitted to do so.

I remember the long ride to Memphis, and stopping in front of a house with a nice picket fence covered with roses. There stood Robert Earl's mother, Elnora Jones Jackson.

"This is your new home," someone said to me.

I remember Elnora standing there, pleasant and smiling, as beautiful as a Gibson Girl. But she was a stranger.

I could not speak. There were no words exchanged between Papa and me. But I knew I could not live with this stranger.

Instinctively, I did the only thing I could think to do. Silently, stubbornly, I hung onto the mattress, physically protesting this separation with all my strength. I wouldn't turn loose, no matter what. I refused to let go.

I remember that Papa and H.B. finally took me back to the refuge of the farm in Arkabutla Township, and then headed on their way North. I stayed with Mama and the aunts and uncles until it was time to take the train to Michigan. But everything had changed for me, the safety of home, the sense of belonging in the family. Even before we moved to Michigan, a world ended for me, the safe world of childhood.

There are questions not asked, words not spoken. I could not talk to Papa and Mama about their decision to leave me behind in Memphis, and then their reprieve. There was so much I could not ask or say. The move from Mississippi to Michigan was supposed to be a glorious event. For me it was a heartbreak.

And not long after, I began to stutter.

3.

THE PROMISED LAND, SITE UNSEEN

We are bound for the Promised Land,
We are bound for the Promised Land.
Oh, who will come and go with me?
We are bound for the Promised Land.

ANONYMOUS HYMN

When Papa and H.B. reached Michigan, they encountered some surprises that many other people might have viewed as obstacles. Their forty acres of land, bought on trust, site unseen, was not a suburb of Grand Rapids. Not by a hundred miles. It was farmland, far north of Grand Rapids, in Dublin, near Manistee, in Manistee County, Michigan. It was an "improved" property— "improved" by the presence of a big chicken house. But Papa and H.B. knew how to make the best of a bad deal, and they liked what they saw in Manistee.

Papa was looking for better schools, but wherever we lived, he had to have enough land to grow food to feed the family. He could see right away that this Michigan soil was thin and sandy, but the farm was reminiscent in its size and layout of Arkabutla Township, of home. Papa and H.B. saw possibilities in those empty farm fields and that chicken house. They decided to stay.

Their letters back to Arkabutla stirred up everybody in or near the Home House. The family was shocked to learn that Papa expected us to move North and live in a chicken barn.

A remodeled chicken coop, one of his sisters chimed in, after she read the letter. Even Mama's hunger for adventure abated.

To us a chicken house was a flimsy enclosure to keep the chickens penned up so they wouldn't wander away. None of us realized that a Michigan chicken house was a far different matter. What Papa found on his property was a long, sturdy wood structure with a concrete floor, built to house what was once a thriving poultry business and to protect it through the hard Michigan winters. Papa and his sons were skilled carpenters; Papa's oldest brother Ed had a successful construction business in Coldwater, Mississippi, and they all had learned their skills from Wyatt. So Papa and H.B. got to work converting the chicken house into a sturdy, reasonably comfortable house for the family. They even bought cheap old Persian rugs to cover and insulate the cold floor, a well-laid concrete slab.

Much of the Michigan land was already cleared for farming, but Papa could see that it had been farmed out, its strength depleted by overuse. It needed fallow time, so he and H.B. cleared an extra acre or two, cutting back into the brush. They retained a grove of trees behind the house to give us summer shade and a windbreak in the winter. In that grove I have my only childhood play memories. Under the trees, I built a road network for my handmade toy cars. It is the only time I remember playing alone and enjoying it, living in the kind of fantasy world my son, Flynn, now enjoys with Nintendo.

When Papa was ready, Mama and the rest of us packed up our possessions and took the train north to Michigan. I remember part of the trauma I felt as crates and boxes were being loaded onto the train. I remember we kids sang a little jingle at the train station to lighten the departure: "Meatskin, Meatskin, We're going to Meatskin."

Black people were not allowed access to the dining car, so we packed box lunches to carry with us for the trip. Cousin Robert Earl and I played peekaboo games with a dark-faced, clean-cut stranger, also traveling north. That is all I remember of the trip itself.

In many ways, the Michigan house was an improvement over the house we had left behind, but the Mississippi relatives were still appalled to think of us uprooted to that strange, cold place, living in a chicken coop. It took some time, and some pictures, and some actual visits to convince them that Michigan was civilized.

Papa was determined to make our new home work by spring. He took stock of all his land had to offer. Next to the chicken barn stood a farmhouse which had never been quite completed. It belonged to us now, and we cannibalized what was left of the house, taking away timber and boards to help rebuild the chicken house. Soon we had stripped the farmhouse down to its concrete slab. Papa already had a friend, our neighbor George Snoddy, a black man with white hair and a great Stalinesque mustache. George Snoddy was an excellent hand-builder. He and Papa broke up that concrete slab, sliding whole sections of concrete into the excavation which was to form a basement abutting the chicken house.

There was a hay barn where we stabled a horse. Down toward the road, there was another long chicken barn where we kept cows and chickens in winter. Best of all, there was a great terra-cotta silo, inhabited by starlings. It was one of the best built silos I've ever seen in America. We used it for silage when the crops were good. It was scary to try to climb the sturdy iron ladder that soared to the top, a feat of daring we attempted often despite the admonishments of our elders.

With the remains of the pile of railroad crossties which had served as our firewood through that first winter, we built a storm shelter to store potatoes and other foods which needed cooling in the summer. We had an outdoor toilet which we had to relocate every spring because the family was so large. Mama delighted in each new change because she could grow beautiful flowers over each abandoned site. The major Halloween prank in farm country was tipping over outhouses. A few boys could accomplish that with a shove or two.

Mama's piano was one of the first things to go on the freight train taking our possessions to Michigan. Uncle H.B. played by ear, some rolling barrelhouse songs, and later, boogie-woogie. We never had a piano teacher in Mississippi, so anybody who played the piano played by ear. But the instrument was there, just in case—symbolically, as if to say, "If you have any talent, there it is. It's up to you." Later on in Michigan, there were piano lessons for some of my aunts. Besides, the piano was an instrument we associated with church, and the church was important all through the years to my family. The piano was part of the culture.

When we first settled in Michigan, Papa looked around Manistee County for a church. He went over to the neighboring town of Wellston to take a look at the church there, and soon afterward, he took the whole family to the Sunday service. This was our first experience in a church attended by white people. We didn't know what to expect and, apparently, neither did they. The congregation serenaded us with "I'm coming, I'm coming, For my head is bending low. I hear the gentle voices calling, 'Old Black Joe'."

As I look back on it, we really believed that the white congregation meant no offense, that this song was an innocent if awkward gesture toward trying to relate to us as their guests—their black guests. The only appropriate hymn or song they could think of on the spot was "Old Black Joe." Maggie fumed, but Papa simply took it at face value, and did not read anything into it except the great cultural and religious gap in the awareness of this white congregation. We did not indict them for racism. But Papa decided to build his own church, as his father Wyatt had done at the Home House.

In Mississippi, I was taken to the Southern black Methodist church, which was fairly conservative, unlike the black Baptist church was then. I remember the journeys to church, the walk, with the whole family strung out along the road. I remember in the early days, when I was very small, I did not like walking all the way to church.

"I want to be tote [to be carried]," I would insist. "I want to be tote."

For the black people in Mississippi and in Michigan, much depended on whether you had a circuit preacher, who traveled to the Methodist church one weekend and the Baptist church the next. If the preacher had that kind of ecumenical round to make, the distinctions between one denomination and another tended to blur. What counted was the preacher's presence and his fervor.

I remember as a child seeing Maggie—Mama—"falling out," "having shouts," being moved by the spirit, very much like the Holy Rollers. It was both frightening to me and fascinating to watch. Mama rarely expressed much emotion except through the spirituals she sang all day long, and her occasional irrational behavior at home. Yet at church, this woman was suddenly and dramatically transformed from a grandmother, a mother, and a wife into a person in the throes of religious ecstasy. Even then, I questioned whether it was real or pretended.

It didn't matter whether Maggie's rapture was self-induced or induced by the sermon. As the preacher got nearer the climax of what he had to say, really performing, "getting over," swaying his flock, suddenly members of the congregation would leap to their feet, extending their hands upward toward God. Women were freer at it than men. It was called shouting. Sometimes there was only one burst of shouting, and that was all the preacher got that week. Sometimes people would break into a kind of shuffle dance. At the peak of the dance, the extreme would be falling flat on the floor, almost going into seizures. Every other Sunday or so, Maggie would be transported into one of these religious dramas.

Papa tended toward a pragmatic, if not restrained, Methodism: you did unto others, fulfilled your duties, tried your best, sought forgiveness for your inevitable sins, tried to forgive others. Mama's religion seemed to spring out of her fatalistic views of tragedy and doom more than out of any faith in finding the promised land, but she was deeply spiritual, and always searching for the "way, the truth, the light."

Mama embraced the mythic power of religion. When she felt that power of the spirit at church, she turned into a Holy Roller, speaking in tongues, falling into ecstasy. At home she was always singing hymns and spirituals roiling with images of sacrifice, blood, and doom. In them, she seemed to find power and sustenance akin to what they had fed our slave ancestors, for the songs were as much as anything a litany of oppression, and supplication for release:

> Precious Lord, take my hand,
> Lead me home . . .

> Were you there when they nailed Him to the tree? . . .
> Oh! Sometimes it causes me to tremble, tremble, tremble.
> Were you there when they pierced Him in the side?

> Sometimes I feel like a motherless child
> A long way from home. . . .

Soon after we settled in Michigan, I started first grade at a one-room grammar school in Dublin, Michigan. On my first day at school, I could not believe my ears. I had never heard such speech. Even the black kids spoke differently. They rolled their "r's," for one thing. They called me James Earrrrl instead of James Uhl, as it had sounded in the South. They pronounced the "-ing" at the ends of words. We had a regular diphthong standoff. When we got home, Randy and I mocked their strange speech, and fell over laughing. It was mimicry, not derision. "Oh, they speak so properrrrr," we would say, "so fancy." Our ears quickly absorbed this different rhythm and style, and while we kept our Mississippi ways of speaking at home, we were soon talking just like our peers at school.

I was doing far more listening than speaking, however, for it was at that time that I began to stutter badly. I began to find it painfully difficult to talk, to speak what was on my mind without stammering. Long before we moved to Michigan, Randy stuttered, and he suffered from petit mal epilepsy. I loved him like a brother, but I remember mocking him, often to his pain, partly out of warped sympathy and partly out of a mean-spirited childishness. I began to wonder if I was cursed for my actions. I withdrew further into silence, gradually relinquishing the power of speech.

Children do not ask the questions they need to ask. I did not interrogate. I did not say, "Why did you take me to Memphis to be with Elnora?" It is all dealt in silence, and that is part of the tragedy of the silent American family. After a time, I seldom talked at home, except when I had to introduce myself to visitors, and, for the most part, the family tolerated my silence.

I did not even try to talk at school. No one laughed at me there, and my teachers were willing to assess my learning through written exercises. Only in church, in the house of worship Papa built, did people make fun of my stuttering. There in Papa's new church, I was forced to speak. I had to stand up and recite my Sunday School verses, and my classmates thought I was funny, even though I certainly was not trying to be.

Finally, I said to Maggie, "No more, Mama. I'm just not going back there." She accepted that, and in that very religious family, I was allowed to stay away from church. Once again, I had made a major decision for myself, and I think they accepted my choice in part because I was a grandchild. They might not have permitted one of their own children to get away with making up his own mind to leave the church.

For about eight years, from the time I was six until I was about fourteen, I was virtually mute. A child can stutter from the moment he learns to speak. It can happen from the onset of speech, or from a later emotional overload. A stutterer has usually suffered some traumatic experiences, often very early on in life. Stuttering is not unlike narcolepsy or petit mal epilepsy in that there is electrical tripping in the brain, much like stumbling physically, often from some temporary emotional jolt.

My family and friends often accused me of lying about my inability to speak: "We know you can talk. We have heard you talk," they would say. My grandfather was the most devastated by my loss of speech.

During those years of my muteness, I did talk: I talked to my family in basic terms; I talked to the farm animals; I talked to myself. But when a stranger entered the house, I froze. Even to introduce myself was beyond my ability.

There was a blizzard one winter in Michigan. Earlier storms had already left the fields knee-deep in snow, and the blizzard dumped so much more that the total accumulation approached five feet. Powerful winds sculpted the snow into even higher drifts. I couldn't have been more than ten that winter, when the blizzard closed the roads and shut us inside by the fire to wait for the wind and snow to die away.

In the midst of that drama, Randy had an epileptic seizure. I remember seeing him lying on the floor. Mama hovered over him, giving him the remedy she knew from Mississippi, a thimbleful of laundry bluing.

"Put on your snowshoes, James Earl," she ordered. "Run to the store. Ask somebody to call the doctor in Manistee. Run." As I hurried to pull on my snowshoes, I looked at Randy in the throes of his seizure. The blue liquid spilled out of his mouth.

The store stood a mile away through the snow, but I didn't care. All I knew was that Randy was sick, maybe even dying.

I ran as hard as I could. I cut across the fields, hoping to get there faster. Finally, I reached Frank Fortelka's store. I raced inside to give him Mama's urgent message—and I started to stutter. I couldn't get the words out. I felt like Randy's life depended on me, and I couldn't speak.

"Sit down—relax," Mr. Fortelka told me. "You can get it out."

Those were moments of sheer panic. But finally I calmed down, and the words came. The doctor was called. Randy recovered. But the stuttering—that stayed.

I think a stutterer ends up with a greater need to express himself, or perhaps, a greater awareness of the deep human need for expression. Being a mute or stutterer leaves you painfully aware of how you would *like* to say something. And I would know, as an afterthought, how I could have said this or that. But at the moment, you are too busy making the choice to speak or not to speak, to use this word or that word. The pain is in the reflection. The desire to speak builds and builds until it becomes part of your energy, your life force. But when I was a boy, speech became a wall I could not surmount.

At first in that little school in Michigan, there were only three students in my class and there was only one teacher for all eight grades. I was the sole student in my class from second grade through eighth grade, but it was not limiting. Each grade went up in front of everyone else to do their exercises with our teacher. There was no way you could avoid hearing the classes ahead or behind. You were hearing eighth-grade work when you were in the first grade. It was a hotbed of learning, a wonderful open forum. Inadvertent tutoring interceded all the time, and we were one big family. I always got individual attention from the teacher, who found ways other than oral exams to assess my development.

There was another boy in school who stuttered, a little kid with rosy cheeks, new to the community. I took him under my wing, especially when one day the teacher shook him in frustration. I knew that she did not understand him. I never admonished her, because she was my teacher, but I always felt very protective of this little boy.

My first teacher was Mrs. Gardiner, who taught me what expressed affection means. She was a huge, large-breasted woman. I can remember that on one of those first school days I wet my pants, and I started to cry. She called me up to ask what was wrong. I told her, and she embraced me in her great bosom. This was something that had never happened to me before. I am sure Mama comforted infants in the family when they cried, but by the time you were walking, you were on your own. I was overwhelmed by the protection I felt in that embrace.

My friend Eileen Cronkite's mother was the school janitor, and she had a hairstyle very much like George Washington wore in a picture hanging on the school wall. I marveled at this woman who wore her hair just like our first President. She would start the fire and open school in the winter, when the weather was so bitter. That first winter, Papa's hands, used to working in the temperate Mississippi weather, chapped and split open from exposure to cold forty degrees below zero.

Once, when the teacher was late on one of those winter days, we put pepper on the red-hot stove. Plain black pepper on a red-hot stove equals tear gas. We had to evacuate the building, and our teacher threatened to hold classes out in the snow.

In those years, all our teachers were women: Mrs. Gardiner with the wondrous bosom; the spinster Miss Elifson, who chain-drank coffee until her body smelled like coffee and who inadvertently gave us a glimpse of her bloomers; and Mrs. Bahr, who had a figure we boys admired. When I was in the eighth grade, I was having full-blown fantasies about Mrs. Bahr. I thought she was beautiful. On the last day of school, one of my friends ran up and stole a kiss. Mrs. Bahr looked straight at me and said, "You put him up to it." It was the first time I felt that a woman treated me as a male. I saw her years later, when I was nearly fifty and she was nearly seventy, and I confessed to her that I had had a terrible crush on her back in that one-room school. She didn't know what to think of it.

We took our farm produce to the little town of Wellston nearby. There was a brine factory right next to the railroad tracks. We took our cucumbers there to be sorted, and stored in huge vats of brine, then loaded on the train to go off to pickle canning factories. There was also a lumber factory owned by a German family, the only other industry allowed in Wellston. Crystal Lake, deep and spring-fed, was the focus of the tourist industry, as well as the source of the ice supply for all the county. During ice-cutting time in the spring before the thaw, storekeepers would fill up the ice houses with blocks of ice from Crystal Lake.

An old Army camp in Wellston was also the site of a Civilian Conservation Corps Camp, housing boys from urban areas, particularly Detroit. The CCC Camps had been organized during the Depression as part of Franklin Delano Roosevelt's New Deal legislation. They brought an influx of urban strangers to Wellston, and the town's citizens were paranoid about these strange city boys, viewed as hoodlums and gangsters who posed a threat to their daughters.

There were black and white children in our school. Only on "dentist day" was I aware that certain distinctions were made about race. The school district nurse arranged to take all of us regularly to see the dentist. I realized that all the black children were put into one car, and all the white children in another. That seemed to me to be a serious distinction, and certainly an act of discrimination. Parents either did not know about it, or they insisted on it. No protest was made.

Mama would have said, "Well, what did you expect?" Papa would have said, "Things haven't changed much." I felt disturbed by such discrimination, but I left it in silence.

I think our move to Michigan in the 1930s spared me from being the victim of obvious daily institutional racism so that I was free not to have to think about it all the time. Yet when it did occur, it was a shock.

We were used to the long growing season in Mississippi. Michigan winters were harsh and bitter. Papa tried to grow some of the crops he had grown back home—peanuts and tobacco, especially. Like his father, he read and studied. He trusted the *Farmer's Almanac,* and the *Almanac* said you could not grow tobacco in Michigan. Yet Papa stubbornly experimented until he got that Michigan acreage to yield tobacco. He also found many melons that grew for him, and in that short growing season, he produced peanuts galore.

He would hang the tobacco leaves in the barn to cure, and just before they turned brittle and dry, we would twist them into braids, and soak them in molasses, to be used as plug tobacco. Papa never smoked, because he was asthmatic, but he chewed tobacco constantly. Mama chewed, too, but only store-bought tobacco, usually Mule or Apple. Chewing tobacco was something we could all enjoy as often as we wanted to. We would make some cherry wine, but wine was a delicacy for special occasions, not an indulgence. Sometimes at night we would be awakened by an occasional wine bottle exploding with a potent excess of fermentation. We'd say, "Oh, boy, it's getting ready!"

We grew cabbages and buried most of them in furrows in the ground for winter storage. The storm shelter, which doubled as a root cellar, received potatoes. As always, Papa worked us hard. We were his field hands, and we called him our straw boss. He was a good farmer, smart about crops and animal husbandry. Papa used nature to harness our natures, and to shepherd us toward constructive daily living. That was necessary to survive on and off the farm.

Sometime early in the Michigan years, my mother Ruth married Claude Brown and moved to St. Louis. Her brothers and sisters who had not preceded us to the North eventually moved to cities such as Washington, Chicago, Detroit, South Bend. None of them wanted to live on the farm anymore, but the train brought them home to visit.

I always thought Ruth's new husband was confused about his sexuality. Later, she divorced Claude and married her third husband, a photographer and a closet homosexual. We did not think he was good for Ruth, and he would later cause trouble for the whole family.

Ruth would find work in a city, usually as a seamstress, and she would come to visit us during her summer vacation. For weeks before she came, I would repeat the old habit of simultaneously anticipating her arrival and mourning her inevitable departure.

Ruth seemed to have fewer social graces and more reserve than her sisters—Bessie, Annie Bell, Thelma, Ozella, and Helen. They were fairer-skinned, younger, better educated, and more vibrant and outgoing. She was more of a loner, a brooder. I do not feel warmth when I remember Ruth, as I do when I think of Helen and Ozella, for instance. I remember only one time of feeling my mother's warmth. I was sick, and Ruth was visiting and she sought to comfort me.

One summer when Ruth came to Dublin, Papa consented to let his children have a big party. Some of the girls begged him to let them invite boys from the CCC Camp in Wellston, but Papa resisted. He did not approve of those hotshot city boys. He had no problem with their inviting any of the local boys, black or white, but to Papa's mind, those urban strangers were dangerous. Papa was convinced that all the men in the CCC were after his beautiful daughters.

The girls finally wore him down, and he let them go ahead. On the night of the party, Papa's worst fears came true. There was a shooting. Papa was caught in the crossfire between two angry CCC Camp interns. Papa fell, his leg covered with blood. Mama was hysterical, traumatized. Ruth, usually so contained and quiet, leaped into action, a lioness in a fury.

"You let those boys come around," she told her sisters. "This is what happens." For Ruth, life was all axioms: you do this, and that will happen.

The state police could not do enough to convince Ruth that they were going to get to the bottom of the shooting. She was outraged. She wanted vengeance. I never saw such passion in one human being as I saw in Ruth when Papa was wounded.

Later on, Uncle H.B. joined the CCC, for in those Depression days, paying jobs were impossible to find. He got room and board, but no pay, working on a CCC forestry project. Papa had recovered from the shooting by then, but he was even more wary. He gave H.B. a gun to take with him. He knew this farm kid was going to be living with those CCC hoodlums.

Our chicken house began to feel too small to some of Papa and

Mama's children. The girls wanted to escape—by getting married, if necessary, if that would get them into their own homes. My uncle H.B. was ready to get married. He had left a tall, handsome, ebony black sweetheart back in Arkabutla Township, and as soon as he could, he wanted to send for her so they could marry. It was 1936 or 1937, and during those Depression days, even if you had a job, it was hard to find a place to live. After his CCC Camp experience, H.B. came home to look for a job so he could afford to get married. When he applied for work, the county said, "We can only allow one male member of the household at a time to have a job." Papa was working for the forestry department then, and he had to keep his job. H.B. was going to have to move into his own place.

H.B. sent for his bride. Her name was Willeva, and she could have studied at a conservatory, her voice was so beautiful. Uncle H.B. knew how to get music out of the piano keys, and Willeva knew how to sing. I can still hear her plaintive soprano voice singing a spiritual on Mother's Day shortly after her mother's funeral. She sang through her own tears.

Willeva and H.B. made the music in our family in more ways than one, and together, they knew how to laugh. They had to spend their wedding night in our house, with all of us around. Willeva had that beautiful singing voice—and a high-pitched laugh that set everybody else to laughing, too. Papa welcomed her to our house, and to the family, but Mama wanted no part of her. Mama was a very jealous lady. The idea that this black woman would possess her son made for some anxious moments. Maggie was immensely bothered by the sounds of sexual pleasure emitting from the room her son shared with his dark bride from Mississippi, who could sing like a bird.

The morning after their wedding, H.B. and Willeva were having a good time in their own bedroom. Their laughter was spilling out of that room, and Mama got very upset.

"Young children in the house, and them carrying on like that on their wedding morning," she fumed. She made sure they did not stay with us very long.

Soon H.B. and Willeva moved to a little house a mile and a half down the road. I liked it. It was a small cabin built of unfinished, weathered boards, as welcoming as our house in Mississippi. I loved to go there. H.B. and Willeva have always had a home where people like to go. When Papa divided his land among his children, H.B. and Willeva were the only ones to build a permanent house and raise their children there. They still live on their land, eating pure food, breathing pure air. H.B. is still sharp and fit, still working hard. And he still has the company of that good woman, who knows how to laugh and sing.

Living on the farm, we always exercised our voices, calling the cows, calling the hogs, never having to worry about bothering neighbors with our sounds. Papa worried that I was silent most of the time: "Your voice was like a bell when you were a child. I don't know what happened to it."

I suppose part of it was my need to stay quiet, in the background, causing no trouble, giving no displeasure, so that I would be allowed to stay.

World War II took our minds off everything—my stuttering, and other personal matters, and, certainly, the Depression. During the Russian-Finnish War, when the whole nation was largely pro-Finn and anti-Soviet, Mama had held another opinion, and she let everybody know about it. Some of the kids I knew were Finns and Poles. One of my teachers was Norwegian. But Mama was pro-Soviet. She had no training in Bolshevism or Marxism. She had just heard that the Russians were trying to do something she liked. Consequently, she was adamantly pro-Soviet.

Many people in Mississippi and Michigan, including some of the family, considered Mama mad. As time went on, she grew more eccentric and mysterious. She delved far into the esoteric, into mysticism and the occult. If you looked on Mama's bookshelf, you saw books on yoga and Eastern philosophy. She read a lot, but I never saw a book on politics in the house. Yet Mama was vigorously opinionated about politics.

Before her life was over, Mama was surely touched with madness. She wasn't deranged—she was just strangely arranged. But as I was growing up, she was fiercely independent and often misunderstood. In roundabout ways, she educated me. I learned her stories. I saw the drama in her soul. I learned to value independence.

During the time of the Russian-Finnish conflict, I would hear pro-Finn sentiments at school, for there was a Finnish settlement nearby. Then I would go home and hear the pro-Soviet line from Mama. I decided I simply had to make up my own mind. That experience forged my political independence.

Like all of us, Mama hovered over the radio during wartime. Once she heard a program which started by playing Tokyo Rose–type propaganda, pleading that people of color in the United States reconsider their antagonism against Japan, and urging them toward solidarity as colored people of the world. It was the most exciting day of Mama's life during the war. Even though the broadcast was repudiated later, she heard in it the validation of her own opinions. To Mama, Oriental people were colored people, like us. Therefore, Tojo was colored. Mama decided that if Hitler liked Tojo enough to fight with him, Hitler couldn't be all bad. If Hitler would just bomb Mississippi! Anybody who would bomb Mississippi would not be all bad in Mama's eyes. During the war, we couldn't even let Mama go out in public by herself. She was that passionate about her beliefs, crazy as they were. She was never afraid to say what she thought about anything.

Ozella's husband Bob was in the Pacific campaign. When they dropped the bomb on Hiroshima, Ozella was at home with us. Mama turned to Ozella, who was transfixed by the radio, and said, "Don't think it's over. Tojo will win yet."

*   *   *

Maggie—Mama—was by far the most spellbinding person in my life, at least until I met my father Robert Earl. Mama had forced me from childhood to think independently. But perhaps her own outspokenness planted some of the early seeds of my fear about words. You had to edit the words of your mouth. I dared not take Mama's unorthodox views to school, or bring home the different opinions I heard there. Second-guessing others, you begin to distrust yourself. That distrust breeds a fury of its own. It seemed to me that trust in others was a basic human right and expectation.

I look back and see that my stuttering and muteness constituted a form of self-denial. I was robbing myself of any presence. I was denying myself identity.

Most of my aunts and uncles, along with Papa and Mama, held strong views on politics and religion. In Michigan, we would sit around the radio every night listening to Gabriel Heatter broadcast the latest news over WGN. Afterward, Papa would lead a discussion. He would get out the newspaper and read aloud to us. There would be more discussion and argument, a sort of family forum. My aunts and uncles voiced their opinions exuberantly, but I was the quiet one, the observer, thinking hard about what I was hearing, but holding the words in, either by choice or out of fear of stuttering. Without the ventilation of expression, my emotions sat and cooked. That can be dangerous.

I came home from school one day in a fury. The antilynching bill had failed in Congress. It was simply an attempt by the federal government to enact civil rights legislation, to say that if the vigilantes of the Southern states insisted on killing people without trial, the federal government had to take some kind of action. At the very least, they were saying, death by lynching was a violation of a person's civil rights! I felt a powerful sense of outrage—not because of anything I was fed by an angry grandmother, but because of the blind cruelty and injustice. I must have been almost inarticulate, my stuttering intensifying as my emotions boiled. I was angry enough to short-circuit even normal speech patterns.

I exploded. I wanted to kill white people, I raged.

"Write it down," one of my aunts told me. She handed me a pencil and paper. "Write it all down."

I poured my fury onto the page.

My aunts helped me edit it, and we mailed it to the *Grand Rapids Herald.* It was damnation time. To my surprise, the newspaper published my letter. They even gave it a title: "Fire Over the Heads of the Whites."

That was one of my first lessons in taking the words that would not come out of my mouth and making them come out of my hands—supplanting the spoken with the written.

Many years later, I discovered that it can be just as dangerous to write words on paper. When I was being investigated for my Army security clearance, some of my neighbors in Michigan were interrogated about my loyalty and my fitness to serve my country. That newspaper article had surfaced.

Mama and Papa's daughters married to escape the farm, as was the habit then. Some married wisely, and others did not. Most of them, including Ruth, lived in neighboring cities throughout the Midwest. On special occasions, Mama would go off to visit them. She served as the midwife when her grandchildren were born. That was her specialty, and her services were valuable during the war. She had a wanderlust, too, and sometimes she just liked to get away. When she came home, she and Papa would exchange a kiss, rather formally. If it happened to be in front of one of us, Mama would almost fall on the floor with embarrassment. I never saw Papa and Mama publicly express any affection toward each other except at that reunion after one of Mama's trips.

I heard the rumors that Papa had had another family on the side in the South. One of my aunts tells about a beautiful young woman whom my uncles liked. When one of them wanted to get serious with her, Papa and Mama cut it off. There was no explanation; there was just not going to be *any* romance. Conjecture was that this was Papa's daughter from his other family. Nobody ever has discussed the details with me, but there was a time, when I was in college and all Mama's other children were gone, that she left Papa and went off by herself for a long time, abandoning him and the farm. Sometimes you would find Papa sitting alone on the porch, silent and morose, as if he were watching for her to come home.

In the country, we had daily lessons in sex education: you saw the bull mount the cow. You didn't know quite how this was happening, but you knew they were breeding, and that was important to the farm. We grew up, too, with the typical barnyard/classroom sexual vocabulary and jokes, laughing, a little pleased with ourselves, and sure that we were the only ones who understood such talk.

Our church from time to time relied on circuit preachers. Reverend Davis was one of those preachers. He was built like an Adonis, a weight lifter, but with small hips. When he wasn't preaching, he was working on the railroad, tapping in the gravel with a big jackhammer. The congregation respected this preacher, and they knew he was homosexual. While these people in our country church did not necessarily accept his life-style, they did accept him as a human being and as a minister. Without condoning his sexual choice, the grown-ups in the church recognized him as the only minister we had.

This minister also took on the responsibility of arranging the rite of passage for any interested young male in his congregation. When the boys were about fourteen or fifteen, those who needed or wanted sexual initiation would be entrusted to the minister, who would find an appropriate girl, not a footloose girl, but an available girl who was not a virgin, sometimes a city girl from one of his churches in the resort area. He would then arrange for her to be in a cabin at an appointed time so that she could relieve the boy of his virginity.

It was the classic initiation rite, and my grandparents and the other adults in the congregation trusted the minister to take care of this appropriately. When I was ten, I went along the night the reverend drove my fourteen-year-old uncle up to the resort area, where he had fixed him up with a date in the cabin. The preacher parked the car, my uncle disappeared inside the cabin, and I sat quietly in the backseat, waiting.

There was a long silence. The preacher turned around. He reached over and unzipped my fly.

"I want to see how big you are," he said.

I froze. He got that far, and then he said, "If I had more time, I would make you come."

I didn't know what that meant.

"Zip it back up again," he said, and I did.

I was afraid, and very confused. I was on my guard from then on. He was a grown-up, and he was the preacher. I spoke of it only to Randy. I did not tell Papa or Mama. There is shame, even if you do not understand what has happened, even if nothing has happened. But there is that touch, the sense of the taboo violated. There is that first great breach of trust. And those were the days of my silence.

The adults in the congregation expected us to know enough to take care of ourselves. How we were supposed to come by that knowledge and sophistication, I do not know. That was all part of the great unspoken.

Papa always ran the farm very tight, but especially so during the war. He organized the idea of a co-op, although he certainly had none of the Bolshevist leanings that Mama adopted. To the neighboring men who had cattle, Papa said, "You bring your cattle to my land and you can go off to work in the defense factories." And that is what they did.

We had a large herd of cattle for a long time, then, and that is when I had my first contact with shepherd dogs. We had two dogs that were excellent shepherds, and brought the cattle in. That was

Papa's idea, too. He was a very industrious man. Papa taught me industry, and Mama taught me independence. When I was not working hard on the farm, I was working hard at school, still mute, but having a lot of conversations in my head, especially with the books I was reading. I was a careful reader, not fast, in fact, probably dyslexic. But I appreciated books, and worked hard to absorb what they had to teach me.

Ruth came home to the family every summer in Michigan. There was a wall behind the hay barn. I still have a piece of wood from it, kept as a memento. When life got too much, I would go there, and hang my head against the wall, and cry.

By the time I was fourteen, it was too late for Ruth and me to become mother and son. Parenting, parenthood—that happens from experiences shared, from time spent together weaving an intimate web of days. Blood has nothing to do with it. So, as a boy, I had my own wailing wall.

There I had no need for words.

PART TWO

SILENCES

4.

LEARNING TO SPEAK

I have come to see I am a victim of being like my father in form and favor. I had his love, and my mother's love. Then he left us. My mother got so she couldn't stand my presence, I was so like my father. But she did not know what made her feel that way toward me.

ROBERT EARL JONES, INTERVIEW, 1992

Mama and Papa did not allow me to communicate with my father. I was forbidden to write to him directly, but I heard about him from my other grandmother, his mother Elnora. She kept me abreast of his life in little journals she wrote, letters telling me what was happening with Robert Earl—and with Jesus. She was very much a fan of Jesus, and you had to wade through her celebration of Jesus to find out what she was really trying to communicate about Robert Earl.

When I was about fourteen, Robert Earl wrote me a letter sending a one-way train ticket so I could travel to New York to see him. Mama got the word to Ruth, who was living in St. Louis with her husband and working as a seamstress. Ruth was very suspicious about the one-way ticket. She immediately countered with *two* train tickets to St. Louis, one for me and one for Randy. I did not go to see my father, but when summer vacation started, Randy and I got on the train and went to St. Louis to see Ruth.

Papa and Mama held a deep prejudice against Robert Earl and his world. He was a boxer and a troubadour actor. He had started the prizefighting in the early years in Memphis, and kept at it after he moved North. He told me about riding the rods of a train and getting shot at in the freight car switching yards in Jackson, Michigan. That bullet sent him on his way East. He has always been a wanderer. In the seventies, when my half brother Matthew was growing up and Robert Earl was still driving, there were times when he would just take off. There are elements of the Bohemian in him, the prodigal.

Robert Earl was Joe Louis's sparring partner when he filmed *The Spirit of Youth* in 1937. He saw then that acting looked easier than fighting, and began to try acting. He performed a leading role in a movie financed by aviator Colonel Julian, the Black Eagle, but he never got paid and the film was never released.

Robert Earl met the poet Langston Hughes during the thirties in New York, and Langston cast him in the lead in a play he wrote for his Harlem Suitcase Theatre. Robert Earl got some other small stage roles and parts in black movies. He was the understudy for the role of Crown in *Porgy and Bess,* starring Leontyne Price and William Warfield. For an untrained actor, especially a black actor in his time, he enjoyed some unusual success in those days. But Mama and Papa did not see it that way. To them, he was still "no-account." They forbade any communication with Robert Earl, off in New York with a new wife, trying to make it as an actor, instead of doing real work.

Ruth got her visit from Randy and me—her brother and her son, enough alike in age and now in size to be brothers. I called Randy "Duke," and he called me "Todd," after the comic strip character Tipton Todd. We went to St. Louis that summer in high style, dressed in the Dublin, Michigan, equivalent of zoot suits—garish tailoring, gaudy colors, rakish hats—two country bumpkins hitting the streets of the city, at least two years behind the fashion.

That summer's journey to see Ruth had its bliss and its sorrows. At the Forest Park Outdoor Theatre, I saw my first live stage performance—*Naughty Marietta.* Randy had discovered a young lady in Ruth's neighborhood, the ghetto of St. Louis. Randy preferred spending time with his new girlfriend rather than with me, and Ruth was at work, so I was left to my own devices.

I would have money in my pocket to go to the movies, but I never made it to the movie theatre. Every time, one or two or even three or four kids would stop me on the street.

"Give us your money."

My assailants were all smaller than I was, but I would hand over the money—and go back to Ruth's and get some more.

Even though the boys probably had knives, the ghetto streets were not as dangerous as they are now. When I was cornered, I felt an immediate sense of jeopardy, but no real fear. Because there was no consideration of fighting, the adrenaline did not kick in, and I was not afraid. I certainly was not going to fight over a pocketful of change. The fact that I went home and got more change suggests that I did not fully understand that I was being mugged.

I remember hitting Randy once when I was finally bigger than he was. The punishment I got from Papa discouraged me from developing my pugilistic skills. At some point in my high school years, before I was fully grown to my size, we had boxers like Joe Louis for heroes. My best pal Alfred Ogelsby and Randy's best pal Bob Hollis and I would have donnybrooks. I always lost. I remember only one fight when I had intent to injure. It started in grade school in Michigan with a snowball fight. I remember launching into my opponent with all the fury of an animal—a fury so complete and irrational that had I been armed, I could have killed. I learned my own lessons about fury from that encounter.

I have not lifted my fist in anger since.

Papa only whipped me three times that I can remember, although he inspired a fourth whipping. Once during my first year of grade school, Dicky Kroppel put me up to writing a forbidden four-letter word. He did not speak the word, but he dictated the spelling. I had no idea what it meant. Nevertheless, I wrote that word out in a rainbow of colors from my brand-new crayon box. Proudly, I took it home to show it to my grandparents. Papa decided that since it was near the end of the school year and Ruth would soon be coming to visit, she should punish me for this inadvertent sin.

If they had explained this word to me in biological terms, everything would have made clear sense to me. From the time I was eight years old, I observed the breeding of the cows and bulls. Every season, I would go on this wonderful, exciting adventure with Papa. When the female cows started mounting each other, we knew it was breeding time. We would walk the cow in heat about three miles to our neighbor's, where there was a wonderful bull for breeding. I would watch this happen. It was nothing Papa felt ashamed for me to see. This was farm life. This was nature. He called the bull's penis a pistol. When it came to farm animals, I understood sex quite openly and realistically—but apparently, none of this was supposed to have anything to do with people. Sex kept the farm animals alive. But whatever it had to do with people seemed to be taboo, a forbidden secret certainly not to be disclosed in rainbow colors in a school notebook.

Once I called one of my aunts a liar, and got whipped for that. Once I took the Lord's name in vain, and got whipped for that transgression. Three of my whippings had to do with words. The last was for hitting Randy in the stomach. He and I were arguing, and I drew back my fist and hit him, just to see if I could get away with it. But that was not tolerated in our family. Later on, when I was a teenager, Papa punished me when he overheard me say I wanted to be an actor. But he did not spank me then—he clobbered me.

The lessons at home joined the lessons at school to shape the way I looked out at the world. I went from a one-room grammar school in Dublin to Dickson High School in Brethren, Michigan. It was a two-story brick building, with a wing added on the back, and a small bell tower. There were ten teachers on the faculty; five of them taught all the high school classes, and five taught junior high and elementary students. There were good teachers there, with solid training. I loved science, in part because I had good teachers and in part because, for me, science was an adventure. I believed science was closing in on science fiction. Jules Verne was one of my heroes. Following his example, my friend Alfred Oglesby and I were making blueprints for an earth-burrowing vehicle. John Henry discovered what we were up to, and took us seriously, fearing that we would actually undertake this project and the earth would cave in on us.

For me, the pivotal teacher was Donald E. Crouch, a former college professor who came out of retirement to teach us English,

Latin, and history. I was still mute when I entered high school. I had gotten through eight years of school without using the power of speech unless I was forced to.

The turning point in my ability to cope with my stuttering came in Professor Crouch's English classroom. He introduced me to good literature—Shakespeare, Emerson, Longfellow. Because it had taken place in our part of the country, I especially loved Longfellow's "The Song of Hiawatha." In fact, I was so inspired that I started writing poetry, and poetry got me into trouble, and then, ironically, changed my life.

During the Depression and on into the war, the government shipped surplus food around the country, staples and perishables, any overabundance of fruits. We knew when the food train was coming to town, and we could go get our welfare allotment of whatever the train was handing out on that trip. One winter, we got grapefruit, shipped all the way from Florida to Michigan on the food train. We hardly ever had grapefruit in our house.

The taste of it knocked me out, the pure, juicy luxury of grapefruit in winter. I decided to write a poem about it, patterned after the poem I knew best—Longfellow's "Song of Hiawatha." I forced my grapefruit rhapsody into Longfellow's cadence and rhyme scheme. Fortunately, no copy of that poem survives.

I was proud of my effort, however. Somehow Professor Crouch, to his surprise and pleasure, discovered that I wrote poetry. The boy who had written the poems was the same mute boy who had fought with uncontrolled fury. Both fury and poetry poured out of my silence.

"I'm impressed with your poem, James Earl," Professor Crouch told me after he read my ode to grapefruit. "I know how hard it is for you to talk, and I don't require you to do that. Unfortunately, it is hard for me to know whether these are your words. This is a fine poem. Did you copy it from somebody?"

My honor was at stake. Plagiarism was bad business. I had

written every word of this poem myself. I would never copy someone else's poem and claim it for my own.

"I think the best way for you to demonstrate that you wrote this poem yourself is for you to say it aloud to the class," he told me.

It would be a trauma to open my mouth in front of my classmates, who would probably laugh at my poem and my stuttering. But it would be a greater trauma to be disgraced, unfairly charged with plagiarism. Now I would just have to open my mouth in public in self-defense.

I was shaking as I stood up, cursing myself. I strained to get the words out, pushing from the bottom of my soul. I opened my mouth—and to my astonishment, the words flowed out smoothly, every one of them. There was no stutter. All of us were amazed, not so much by the poem as by the performance.

Professor Crouch and I had stumbled on a principle which speech therapists and psychologists understand. The written word is safe for the stutterer. The script is a sanctuary. I could read from the paper the words I had composed there, and speak as fluently as anybody in the class.

"Aha!" my professor exclaimed as I sat down, vindicated. "We will now use this as a way to recapture your ability to speak."

And so, gradually, my powers of speech were resurrected. Throughout the rest of high school, I read Shakespeare aloud in the fields to myself. I remember hearing Uncle Bob Walker, Ozella's husband, reciting Mark Antony's speech from *Julius Caesar.* He was a fine man, not endowed by society or economy with the chance to be highly educated. He had worked in a foundry since his discharge from the Army. He was unpretentious in his speech, but he read Shakespeare with a full appreciation of the English language. I witnessed the joy he took in the words, and found it contagious.

I would have glorious experiences reading Edgar Allan Poe aloud. I could throw back the curtains in the high school gymnasium, step out on the stage with a lighted candle, and read Edgar Allan Poe— and everybody would *listen.* Those were special nights for me.

You could not mount a football team in such a small school, but we had basketball and track. I had the body of an athlete, but not the will. I was pouring all my energy then into learning again to speak. Poor boys of my race have often prided themselves on athletic skill, seeing it as a ticket to somewhere better. I never had that agenda. I played some basketball and ran track, but the time I might have given to honing my athletic skills I gave instead to forensics—public speaking, orations, interpretive readings. That was my extracurricular passion, and it was another of those crucial choices we make in life.

I could not get enough of speaking, debating, orating—acting. I became the school's champion public speaker. During those mute years, of course, my voice had changed, almost without my awareness, so in addition to the novelty of being able to speak, I could now speak in a deep, strong voice. People seemed to like to hear it, and I was overwhelmed to be able to speak aloud, in any voice at all.

Once, I remember, Professor Crouch took me to a regional forensics meet in Traverse City, Michigan. I competed, but any prize I may have won was overshadowed by what happened after. We went to lunch at a fine restaurant in Traverse City. I had never been to such a nice place.

"No colored people will be served here," a voice told us.

Somehow that arbitrary wall always took me by surprise. We left. I do not remember what we did after that.

I remember driving to basketball games with Randy and the Bean brothers from the county below us. Hartwell Bean was tall, muscular, athletic—one of the athletic champions of the school. We were driving to a basketball game one day when the Bean brothers and I agreed we were going to stay virgins until we married. We made a pact, one reason being the seriousness of cross-cultural, cross-racial dating. There was only one black girl in the county—and she was so ugly she didn't even know it. There is no doubt that my experience with the preacher had a lot to do, too, with my remaining a virgin. I had two attractions in school. One was a little Italian girl, really petite, about four feet tall, cute and sweet with great legs. I think she liked me, but we never expressed our attraction. I had a great crush on a bright, pretty girl named Roma McClelland, but not until years later did I confess to it.

There were eighteen people in my 1949 graduating class at Dickson High School in Brethren, fourteen boys, four girls; fifteen whites, three blacks. I do not remember even having a date when I was in high school. I was very shy with girls.

According to the inscription next to my senior class picture in the *Dickson Hi-Lite,* I was a student council officer, a class officer, and editor of the yearbook. I played basketball all four years, wearing the number 42 on my jersey in my senior year when we won eleven games and lost four. I was the only black player on the first team that year, and the yearbook picture reveals me to be the tallest player on the squad. But I remember more about my life on the debating team than on the basketball team.

I had left our homemade church in Michigan because people there made fun of my stuttering. Many of my school classmates were Catholics, and I was curious about their religion. Some of my friends were Polish-American kids, from devout Catholic families. I had learned to be an expert mason during those high school years, serving an apprenticeship which led me to be considered one of the best masons in the township. The priest of the Catholic church in Irons, Michigan, asked me to take on the building of their new church. They decided that I would be their one trained mason, and the rest of the labor would be supplied by the Polish farmers when they got off work in the summertime. That was my summer job, and every day that summer, I worked beside those farmers, who spoke Polish most of the time.

The priest took an interest in how I felt about Catholicism, and offered to give me some instruction, but I wasn't ready for that.

There was only one thing on my mind and that was the problem with the work on the church. Because of the geometry of masonry, I thought we had to first build up one side of the building with thick joints of mortar. After we had finished, I had to go to the priest and say, "I'm not sure if we did this right. I don't understand the chemistry of mortar, whether if we add bricks on top of this, it is as strong as concrete block or not. I just want you to know my concern. I wonder if we should have done it differently."

He said, "Don't worry about it." And I went home, and I didn't worry about it. He accepted what I said. I felt somehow morally absolved. I guess that was my first confession.

Nobody in John Henry's family had ever been to college until Randy and I decided we wanted to go. We knew that as first-generation college students, we would have to choose practical professions. College was for serious business—engineering, doctoring, lawyering.

One day, Papa and I were working in the field spreading manure with pitchforks from a horse-drawn wagon. The wind was blowing the wrong way, giving me a face full of it. I was complaining—not using the profanity Papa wouldn't allow, but coming dangerously close to it.

"What's the matter?" Papa asked me. "Don't you like farming?"

"Not today," I said.

"Well, what are you going to do—be a doctor?"

"Yeah," I said.

And that stuck.

Randy—Duke—knew he wanted to be an engineer. One day, I remember, he and I were sitting on the porch, talking about the future. Even as a child, Randy was very good at mechanics. He had an innate talent for building things and making things work. He always knew he wanted to be a mechanical engineer. He knew Papa and Mama approved.

I admired that. I knew I couldn't top him. I had just recently found a picture of Robert Earl in an old issue of *Look* magazine. He had appeared with Mel Ferrer in 1945 in *Strange Fruit* on Broadway. I just happened to open the magazine and see my father. I felt very proud of that. I had not realized that I looked like him, for I had never really seen him since that one moment when I was a baby. Out of that discovery, I spoke out loud for the first time about being an actor.

"Well," I said, "I am going to be an actor on the stage."

All of a sudden there was a blow. We had not realized that Papa was standing behind the screen door listening. He was still suffering from that image of the irresponsible actor. He did not want to hear that kind of ambition expressed by me. He flew out from behind that door and without a word, gave me a whack on the head. And there was no word spoken in response.

That put a stop to any dreaming out loud about acting. But deep down the idea was set in motion, and for a long time, I kept it to myself. I knew better than to bring it up again with Papa and Mama.

Randy went after his dream before I did, and I missed him. We had been together almost every day of my life, and we are brothers in the truest sense. Randy set out to Grand Rapids to go to junior college and work full time to earn enough money to enroll in the engineering school at the University of Michigan. He earned his degree, and went on to work with Boeing Aircraft.

The first time I actually spoke to my father Robert Earl was in 1949, the year I finished high school. One spring day, I got two unexpected awards—a public speaking championship and a college scholarship.

"This is a wonderful honor, James Earl," our school superintendent told me. "You ought to share it with your parents."

He gave me the coins to make the calls from the drugstore pay phone, knowing that like most country people, we didn't have a telephone at home. In fact, that *was* the first time I had *ever* tried to use a telephone, and I didn't know how. I studied the face of that phone, and I couldn't figure it out. I was not about to ask for help, so I walked back out to the street. I paced up and down that block in front of Sturdevant Market, one of the few businesses in Brethren to boast a telephone—number 9021. I drove all the way to the town of Manistee before I finally got up the nerve to use a telephone.

I hoped Robert Earl would be happy about the news I had to share. I was proud of what I had learned surreptitiously about his achievements. He was pleased, I think, although we spoke just minutes on that strange instrument, the telephone.

In the fall of 1949, with the help of that Regents Alumni Scholarship, I enrolled at the University of Michigan in Ann Arbor. I was *determined* to be a doctor, but when I hit the college chemistry class, I said, "Where am I going to pack all this stuff in my brain? How am I ever going to memorize it all?"

I worked as hard as I knew how, but this science was a far cry from the work I had done in high school—too much like force-feeding a goose. Along came physics and it was just as bad as chemistry. I took a senior anatomy course in my sophomore year, telling myself if I passed it, I would continue in premed.

5.

LONER

I wanted to be a journalist, a strange pursuit for us then. But my choice of profession was no stranger than that of another Negro student, who was going to be a forester, and it was a lot less strange than that of the stiff loner from the West Quad who was going to be an actor. We all knew he was crazy, partly because he never mixed with anybody and partly because everybody knew there were no decent acting jobs for Negroes anyway. Even after we had seen him in a few campus plays, we still thought he was crazy. His name was James Earl Jones.

ROGER WILKINS, *A MAN'S LIFE: AN AUTOBIOGRAPHY*
(NEW YORK: SIMON & SCHUSTER, 1982)

I had little spare time at the University of Michigan. I worked several jobs to stay in school, enrolled in ROTC, and studied hard the rest of the time. My only semblance of a social life came in the fraternity of my fellow ROTC cadets in Pershing Rifles and Scabbard and Blade.

American students were beginning to have strong feelings of antagonism toward the military uniform. That hostility was beginning to be openly, sometimes violently expressed on American college campuses, including ours. I remember being called out with other cadets to serve as an honor guard when foreign dignitaries such as the Shah of Iran visited the campus. Students threw stones at us. Many of us cadets felt isolated by those incidents. We were loners together. As I kept my commitment to ROTC, I was exploring a "road not taken," as I would do often in the years ahead.

When I realized I was not cut out to be a doctor, I changed to the study of drama, with the idea of simply doing something I could enjoy before joining the war in Korea. Technically, because there was not an official degree in drama then at the university, my degree had to be in English.

Until I got to college, I do not remember having any truly deep friendships with anyone other than Randy. There was only one person I remember then who was a very close friend. I had another such close friendship later, in the Army. Both were classic, true friendships. I did very little dating in college. Briefly, I had a crush on a co-ed, a Jewish girl from Scarsdale, New York. As briefly, I dated another co-ed, a black girl. I had a summer stock romance with an actress. When I left the University of Michigan in 1953, I was still a virgin at twenty-two.

I was a loner. I suspect that all those years of muteness had something to do with that, those years when I was observer more than participant, in the background, looking on. No introverted child is happy, and I was very introverted, but if you like yourself, you can like other people. I was beginning to like myself.

Being myself is very complex, even as a racial entity. I am not only African, but I am Cherokee and Choctaw through my maternal grandmother. I am Irish through my maternal grandfather. Contrary to the view of racialists, black and white, a mixed blood black person is not only black. On a certain genetic—if not spiritual and emotional—level, way beyond social identity, there is a competition, at once dissonant and harmonic, as if all these genes are battling for dominance over my soul. This rich, complicated heritage of blood does make for an interesting life, being fought over by so many different, wonderful ancestors.

One summer, between my junior and senior years at Michigan, a group of us from the ROTC program—three or four white students and I—drove down to Fort Benning, Georgia. The route back from camp took us east, since one boy lived in Washington, D.C.

Every time we stopped to lodge at night, no one complained about my being black, for we were all wearing uniforms, and we were all males. We would get a room for everybody, and we didn't worry about whether the motel allowed "colored" or not. But gas station attendants, who didn't have a whole lot of authority to exercise anywhere else, would look at me and say, "You are not going to pee in our rest room, boy."

"Where am I going to pee?" I would ask.

"In the road, if you want to. If you want to risk public exposure, you are going to pee anywhere you want," they would say. "But you are not going to pee in our toilet."

I can hear Maggie now saying, "I told you we should have let Hitler bomb Mississippi."

* * *

Sometime during my student years at the University of Michigan, Ruth, between marriages, decided to move close by so that she could be part of my life, and Randy's. She wanted to rent a place to live and find a job near the university. She wanted us to feel at home in her house. She wanted to cook for Randy and me, and wanted us to visit her and bring our friends to visit her. "I want to make myself useful for these children," she said. That was her endeavor, her fantasy.

The reality is, Ruth decided to wander north. She left her husband Claude Brown after a troubled time. I resented her for using Randy and me for the excuse to leave her marriage. She got on a bus bound for Michigan. On the bus, she met Lucius, who struck up a conversation. They took up with each other, and eventually married. He happened to live in Jackson, Michigan, and she went home with him and made the best of it. Because of him, she wound up in Jackson, and that became the place she offered to Randy and me for weekend visits.

Her presence provoked me to great anger. I verbally assaulted her for entering my life too late, and offering too little. It saddened her deeply, but she followed through on her plans. Eventually, Randy and I did go to see her often, riding the bus over after the week's classes. Her house did become a refuge for us. In that sense, Ruth did fulfill her dream.

I started appearing in campus plays during my last two years at the University of Michigan. Professor Crouch had encouraged me to keep reading Emerson.

"If you read enough Emerson," he promised, "when you go into your adult life and choose your career, no matter what you do, you will do it well. If you understand Emerson, whatever you choose you will be *your* best."

At Michigan, I found it painful to sell my last year's textbooks to buy the new textbooks. I wanted to keep every book because I knew I had not really, really read it, fully discovered all it had to say. I still do that. I have a hard time, even discarding paperback books, thinking that some day I will *really* read them.

When I heard about casting for a drama department production of *The Birds* by Aristophanes, I showed up at the theatre and asked to read for one of the minor parts. After I sat down, the director, a remarkable teacher named Claribel Baird, asked me to audition for the role of Epops, the King of the Birds. They gave me the role. (Claribel, who lives even now in Ann Arbor, encourages me still. "You played him magnificently," she tells me today, "despite the difficulty of negotiating the constructionist set built for the benefit of students who had never seen one.") What Claribel didn't know was that it was a delight for me to negotiate that set. With Gwen Arner, the attractive actress who played the Queen of the Birds, I had to climb up to the top of that platform before the curtain went up. We had to remain there silent and still during the first act. I found it delightful to be in the quiet company of Miss Arner.

I did not realize it at the time, but it was Claribel who chose the next student production, *Deep Are the Roots* by Arnaud d'Usseau and James Gow, so that I could play the lead role of Brett in this play which exposed intolerance in the South. The show went on, despite the interruption during one performance when a graduate student rose and ostentatiously exited to protest a scene between me and the white actress playing opposite me.

I got to be Verges in *Much Ado About Nothing* in an off-campus professional theatre production. During all this time, I did not talk to Claribel or others in the theatre program about my stuttering. Only in recent years, when she read about it in an interview, did Claribel know about my struggle. "This accounts for your occasional over-precise enunciation for which I think I nagged, probably the worst thing I could have done," she wrote to me not long ago. "Why didn't you tell me?"

* * *

I was coming into acting and coming into adulthood, and I had not seen my father since infancy. Suddenly, he invited me to visit him in New York, and this time, being twenty-one, I wanted to go and I was free to go. So on a leg of that trip back to Michigan after my ROTC encampment, I hitched a ride with my buddies for my first glimpse of New York and my first real encounter with Robert Earl.

He and his third wife Jumelle had a tiny apartment in Manhattan, but were staying then out in Far Rockaway, where Jumelle was working. I managed to navigate the huge maze of the city, and to find the train to Far Rockaway. How would it feel, at last, to meet my father? Would the few pictures we had seen of each other be enough for recognition, face-to-face? What did I want from this meeting? What did he expect? Why, now, had he asked me to come?

When I reached Far Rockaway, Robert Earl was waiting there to meet me. There was an awkward, warm embrace, and we walked down the tracks together, he a little taller than I, muscular, vigorous, handsome.

All I really knew of my father's life I had gotten from those occasional letters from his mother, Elnora. He had acting jobs now and then, but supported his wife and himself by working as a floor finisher. The acting jobs had dried up after he got on the blacklist in the McCarthy days, but he did not want to discuss that with me, for my sake as well as his. Consequently, when it came time for my Army security clearance, I truly did not know anything to tell about my father's political activities. In the eyes of the military then, many soldiers who had lived with left-wing parents were probably influenced by them.

Robert Earl had wanted to see me for a long, long time, he told me, and he was hurt by the family's constant refusal to let me come. It was Jumelle who encouraged him to keep on trying. He wanted desperately to make our first visit a good one. He wanted to show me New York, and share the world he loved there. He wanted to introduce me to the theatre, to culture. His treating me to New York was like giving me a grand tour: "We're going to see some opera, some ballet, some theatre."

And it was a grand tour. *Tosca!* I had seen the Ramsdale Opera House in Michigan—but the Metropolitan!! *This* was an *opera* house! Yet the opera itself didn't mean much to me.

Then the ballet, *Swan Lake!* That meant a lot to me—great legs, not just pretty legs, but legs whose extraordinary motion seemed to go on forever.

Next the musical *Pal Joey.* I am not a fan of musicals even today, but from the moment the lights came up on *Pal Joey,* I was powerfully attracted to the theatre. Except in paintings, I had never seen a setting in which people were lit that way. The electricity simply knocked me out, the warmth of the lights on the stage, those lights that burned with the radiance and mystery of the golden birth light.

We went to see Arthur Miller's *The Crucible,* where the effect was just the opposite of *Pal Joey.* I garnered no warmth from the performance, but I was deeply impressed by the play, the drama of it.

Then, for the finale, Robert Earl took me to meet his friend Paul Robeson. In later years, Moses Gunn and others suggested that Robert Earl was a Robeson protégé. Although he was not the singer that Paul was, Robert Earl shared many of Robeson's attributes and interests—in theatre and in politics.

Robert Earl wanted to take me to a black-tie concert where Robeson would be singing, and afterward, to present me to this man he so intensely admired. I had arrived in New York dressed in my ROTC dress uniform, having nothing else formal to wear. Robeson had spoken out vigorously at the Congress of World Partisans of Peace in Paris in 1949 about the role of black soldiers in a foreign war. Robeson had said that American wealth had "been built on the backs of white workers from Europe . . . and on the backs of millions of blacks. . . ." He called for wealth to be equally shared, and for peace to be protected. "Our will to fight for peace is strong,"

Robeson said, but he did not want to see black soldiers fighting
Oriental soldiers in any unjust war. "We shall not make war on
anyone," he had asserted in Paris.

It seemed certain then that I would wind up fighting in Korea. "If
you don't serve in Korea, I'll love you forever," Robert Earl told me.
From the outset, he tried to bargain his love.

"After Paul's statement in Paris, I don't think it would be
appropriate," he insisted.

"But this is all I have to wear," I answered.

The concert hall was sold out, so I stood in back. Even at that
distance, when Robeson opened his mouth to sing, I felt my body
vibrate, at once jolted by his energy and soothed, as if I were being
rocked in a cradle. The magnetic power of his voice hit me physically
as well as emotionally. I had encountered such magnetism only once
before in my life. Our University of Michigan ROTC instructor
Sergeant Kelly was a father figure to all of us cadets. I was on night
watch duty at one of the campus dormitories when someone came to
tell me Sergeant Kelly was dead. I felt my body vibrate with emotion.
I felt his presence. When I heard Paul Robeson sing, I felt that same
energy.

Robert Earl took me backstage after the concert to introduce me,
and to his surprise, Robeson embraced me, uniform and all. I could
tell that for Robeson the issue of black soldiers fighting yellow
soldiers was an international political issue, not a personal issue. To
my gratitude, he accepted me as I was, as the son of Robert Earl
Jones.

I did not go to visit my father that first time seeking to know him. It
was a visit, not a quest. I found it as wonderful and as uncomfortable
as he did.

My father professed to be an atheist, but I think he has always
been deeply religious. He was engaged in left-wing politics, but I

think he has always been deeply conservative. Robert Earl was black at a time when there were no other outlets for his activism except left-wing politics. He took the only avenues open to his energy in the thirties and forties.

Very early as a child, by my choices, I killed my parents off, my absent father, my distant mother. But now my father and I had met.

I went through four years of college, but I did not leave with my degree. I did not even go to my final examinations at the end of my senior year. Why bother? With the Korean conflict intensifying, I thought I would be dead by fall. With my ROTC commission almost in hand, I knew I would be shipped straight to Korea in the spring of 1953. But as peace negotiations went forward at Panmunjom, assignments changed for fledgling officers.

As I waited for orders for active duty, I went home to the farm, and found myself a part-time job, with low pay, but irresistible opportunities. I still had my skills as a mason, and I had some training as a carpenter, so I joined the crew at the Manistee Summer Theatre, a summer stock theatre in the business of entertaining the summer tourist crowd. I built and struck sets, worked lights, and worked as a stagehand, and later, as stage manager. I loved being part of a small fraternity of people doing something unusual together, creating something impossible out of something unseen. As a stage crew, we worked in privacy, at night, with no fanfare. What we did we did not advertise. I loved this community in the theatre.

With my experience in college and community theatre, I had the confidence to try out for some small roles—and worked in six productions, including *Father of the Bride* and *Philadelphia Story*. Summer nights, Mama and any of the family who were willing to drive her would pile in the car and ride to town to see me on stage. Papa was still skeptical and unhappy about this theatre idea of mine; he always associated it with Robert Earl. Mama hated Robert Earl, but she loved the theatre. She had drama in her bones, like it or not, and she was the first in the family to affirm this emerging passion of mine.

One summer night—July 27, 1953—in the green room at the theatre, we heard the welcome news of the truce ending the conflict in Korea. But the war had ended without me, and I had already left Michigan without my degree. By summer's end I had my Army orders and my commission as a second lieutenant.

Originally, I was assigned to Fort Leonard Wood in Southwest Missouri, but my orders were changed before I arrived there, and our unit was sent to Colorado. There, the Army planned to establish a Cold Weather Training command at the old Camp Hale near Aspen. Our regiment was established as a training unit, to train in the bitter cold weather and the rugged terrain of the Rocky Mountains. I took to the physical challenge, so much so that I wanted to stay there, testing myself in that awesome environment, mastering the skills of survival. I loved the austere beauty of the mountains and the exhilaration of the weather and the altitude. I didn't mind the rigors of the work or the pioneerlike existence. I thought it was a good life.

I had time and solitude for reading, and I read most of Shakespeare's plays during that Army interlude. But I concentrated on the work we were doing in the Training Command, and soon after I made first lieutenant, I had to face another decision: extending my tour of duty.

"Are you going to go for another two years?" my commanding officer asked me. "Are you ready to make captain?"

I told him I wasn't sure.

"Well, is there anything you feel like doing 'outside'?"

He gave me some fatherly advice. "We in the Army always have trouble with things on the outside we want to do and do not try."

"My father is an actor, and I have often thought about acting," I told him.

"Why don't you go out and try it," he said. "You can always come back. March. Go climb that mountain."

There was nothing to lose, I thought. I could use my GI Bill to go to acting school, and if it didn't work out, I could step back into my

Army career. I had saved a little money, but not enough to get me through. I was on my own now, and Papa might not approve, but Mama, caught up more and more in her own interior world, was no threat to my dreams. Besides, she liked to see me perform. Ruth would not know how to help me even if I would ask, which I wouldn't do. But Robert Earl was in New York, and he was in the theatre. I could at least turn to him for advice.

I worked during the summer of 1955 at the Manistee Summer Theatre, glad to be back in expanded on-stage roles in popular summer stock fare—*Green Grow the Lilacs; Dial "M" for Murder; I Remember Mama; Mr. and Mrs. North; The Caine Mutiny Court-Martial.* Another actor and I lived in the theatre, in a supposedly haunted bell tower. Mama was my fan club, and I could feel my confidence grow.

I fell in love with Pam Printy, a bright, lovely actress in the company. She and I were innocent, both virgins, and our romance went unconsummated, but we caught the attention of our elders— and, once, the local law enforcement officer, who stopped us on a summer day when we were driving out to Papa's farm in Pam's car. He wanted to be sure this white woman welcomed the company of the black man in her car, and Pam made that emphatically clear. Her grandfather came out once from Indiana, carrying a gun. He did not approve of our interracial romance, and he wanted to be sure that I was treating her well. When word reached the theatre board that there was romance between a black actor and a white actress in their company, the chairman of the board took Pam and me out for a drink one night.

I don't know whether he called Manistee an uptight or an upright community. "We rely on tourists to keep our theatre alive," he told us. "I don't know what is going to happen with you two, but any interracial romance is controversial. You know that. I know that. Please be as discreet as you can."

* * *

Madge Skelly, the managing director of the Manistee Theatre, urged me to finish my degree at Michigan through an extension program. She also encouraged me to study at the American Theatre Wing in New York, and with her help, I applied for admission.

My childhood nickname had been Todd, for Tipton Todd, the cartoon character. The name gathered even more resonance when I discovered the work of that fine black actor and singer, Todd Duncan, who was, in my opinion, right up there with Paul Robeson in stature. So I assumed Todd Jones as my stage name, and under that name, I was accepted by the American Theatre Wing in 1955. I was elated.

Robert Earl and Jumelle invited me to stay temporarily in their cramped apartment in Greenwich Village, so in the fall of 1955, I moved to New York. My GI Bill paid my tuition at the American Theatre Wing, but in that time of economic recession, I had to work several jobs to pay my other living expenses. Robert Earl and I often worked together sanding and refinishing floors. Sometimes we worked alone or together as janitors. I got up before dawn and made hundreds of hero sandwiches at Morris's Sandwich Place in Little Italy, for half a dozen peddlers to sell to businesses or to vend in the streets. Then I went to school. After my classes, I came home to take a nap before my night work. The next day, I started all over again.

I was twenty-four years old. I had given up all the certainty I had ever known—farming, the university, the Army. I knew acting was risky business. I did not let myself dwell on the difficulties all actors face.

I simply set to work, as hard as I knew how to work, at the acting classes, and the menial jobs that kept me fed while I studied. I did not know what else to do but to work, and trust that with work and time, any talent I had would come out.

6.

JOURNEYMAN APPRENTICE

Unfortunately, there is no other way to cooperate: the technique of acting can never be properly understood without practicing it.

MICHAEL CHEKHOV, *TO THE ACTOR:*
ON THE TECHNIQUE OF ACTING
(NEW YORK: HARPER & BROTHERS, 1953)

Acting can never really be taught. It must be learned in a thousand ways, over and over again. Learning to act is ongoing, a lifelong process, and the responsibility rests with the actor. It does not rest with any teacher or director.

There is one book on acting I have found helpful. It is Michael Chekhov's *To the Actor: On the Technique of Acting*. "It is well known that the realm of art is primarily the realm of feelings," Chekhov writes. "A good and true definition would be that the atmosphere of every piece of art is its *heart*, its *feeling soul*. . . . All you experience in the course of your life, all you observe and think, all that makes you happy or unhappy, all your regrets or satisfactions, all you love or hate, all you long for or avoid, all your achievements and failures, all you brought with you into this life at birth . . . all are part of the region of your so-called sub-conscious depth."

Chekhov also says that the first reading of a play yields the purest knowledge an actor will ever have of the drama. He confronts the play on every conscious and subconscious level that first time. The play resonates afresh in each mind that reads it. You won't replicate that experience on your second reading. All the play asks for is a fresh mind to bombard—and then it explodes with knowledge and insight. A similar thing happens to an audience, too, the first time they see a play.

Acting is not something you can learn like calculus or history. It is a nonintellectual process, and that first reading of a play is nonintellectual. The challenge is not intellectual, but emotional: how deeply in tune you are with the emotional, imaginative planes of being. The key lies, I think, in the "heart, the feeling soul."

For years I had been nonverbal. I was coming at drama having been devoid of language. A nonverbal person beginning to speak is not unlike an illiterate person beginning to read: what captures the imagination is not the twisting and turning of ideas, but the flooding of feeling. I discovered that graceful language was fluid with sounds. Passion graces itself.

I studied in New York for the next two years, returning to the farm each summer to work at the Manistee Summer Theatre from June through August. Our summer theatre had its home in the old Ramsdale Opera House, built in Manistee back during the lumber baron days. People who had made their fortunes cutting prime timber and stripping the rich forest lands of Michigan built the opera house with its elaborately decorated painted ceilings, adorned with angels. Opera companies came from Chicago and elsewhere to perform at the opera house, which survived, then fell on hard times, and was eventually converted into our summer theatre. There, I played parts of varying range, and style, and importance in thirteen productions.

This was good grounding, not highfalutin. This was real stuff, strong footing for a young actor. This was staying up all night, learning lines, hammering real nails, building sets. We did virtual "slave labor" in those months at the theatre. Only lead actors were left free to study lines. The rest of us worked in the daytime rehearsing and selling tickets. Sometimes we worked all night painting flats or striking sets. We worked on a small budget, and advertised in the community for the props we needed. People would call in and volunteer—pots, pans, sofas, a chiffonnier, or chifforobe. We acted, painted, worked as carpenters and stagehands. This was our apprenticeship.

Here, I got some on-the-job training, and as at the University of Michigan, some insight into the community of players. I found that I enjoyed the company of actors. It was fun painting flats with attractive women dressed in overalls! I liked being part of a group of people working with great dedication on something that would not last, giving energy and commitment to something that would close the next week. We found a relationship with the larger community, and a fellowship within the company. We were apprentices, and the master was the theatre itself. The play had to go on. Even when there was a strong director, the production was a communal experience.

I believe in a journeyman period in any profession. It was so in the Army. It was so in farm life. You apprenticed with your elders, your parents, and learned how to do the work. It should be so in theatre.

One of the forces which has shaped my life as an actor has been the weak muscle of speech, the *lost* muscle. The dancer Gwen Verdon had leg problems as a child, and in the process of exercising, found a strength that led to dancing. The orator Demosthenes filled his mouth with pebbles and practiced his speeches to overcome his stuttering, so becoming a great orator. The weak muscle can become the dominant muscle, either out of obsession with the weakness or a genuine endeavor to correct it. Consequently, the weak muscle can define a life and a profession.

I began my training that fall of 1955 in New York with some teachers who were schooled in the Method, what I later called experiential acting. That is, you share the character's experience by building a parallel track. You are true to a character to the extent that you can construct an experience parallel to his. I cannot fathom what Othello really went through, for instance. I have not had his journeys and his battles. All I can do is build an imaginary parallel track that James Earl has experienced. You commit to the role emotionally more than intellectually. That requires enormous energy, but when you are young, energy seems fathomless.

Robert Earl has said that he never had the driving commitment to be an actor, but I see that he faced the barricades of his times, first as a black actor and then as a blacklisted actor. There was little in Robert Earl's experience to encourage me. It had been a hard, frustrating job for him. He has told me in recent years that he never expected to make much of a living in theatre. But he says now that when he saw the meager standard of living I set for myself, and the tenacity with which I worked, he began to think it might be possible for him to make more of a life on stage, too. I am glad to say he has.

When I told him I wanted to study acting, he said, "Come and stay with me." He never said, "I want you to be an actor," or, "I don't want you to be an actor." He only pointed out the realities: "I have not been able to make a living in the theatre."

There were day and night classes at the American Theatre Wing, and I chose the day schedule. I went to classes and workshops most of the day, and worked most of the night, when Robert Earl and I went out to clean theatres or office buildings, or to refinish floors. When I could get a student ticket, or otherwise scrape up the money, I went to the theatre to watch real, working actors. Often, I would read a play first so I would know what was happening, and go into the theatre in the second act, hoping to find an empty seat.

At the Theatre Wing, I took classes in fundamentals of acting, in speech, voice and diction, in fencing and dancing, and in special fields—radio, television, stage, period theatre. There was even a course called "Acting as a Business." Of the teachers I studied with, there were three great ones in particular—the late Mary Hansen, from whom I probably learned more about acting than from anyone else then or since; Will Lee; and Nora Dunphee, who began as my speech teacher and is still my speech coach to this day.

At first I threw myself into the emotional approach to the work, but I learned to be very careful about how I identify *through* a role. I learned never to totally relinquish my own identity. I deeply admire Marlon Brando as an actor; I do not know how he does what he does. Likewise, I have immense respect for Al Pacino and Robert De Niro. It seems to me that when they perform, Brando, De Niro, and Pacino maintain a rare equilibrium of self and character, of personal identity and dramatic identity. Yet how they can go so far into other characters without losing themselves is beyond me. I have been able to achieve that experience of character on occasion, but not so consistently as a style as these actors do. When it has happened to me, it has usually come with elemental men—Lennie in *Of Mice and Men*; Boesman in Athol Fugard's *Boesman and Lena*.

During classes at the American Theatre Wing, we were cautioned that if you lose yourself in a role, you go over the edge. In one early workshop, a young actress was playing Medea. She grew more and more agitated as we progressed, and the dagger scene became so vivid for her that one day she actually ran the dagger through her hand.

The teacher stopped the rehearsal. "What happened?" he wanted to know.

She answered, "It was just an accident."

"No," he said. "That was not an accident. You stabbed yourself in the hand. You inflicted pain on yourself. That has nothing to do with acting, or with achieving that character." That mishap actually tainted her entire career: it was a sign that she was in deep trouble personally.

I ran that risk myself. In my second year at the Theatre Wing, we were all young and reckless. We were working once on a scene from a play in which my character carried a gun. I decided to carry a loaded .45 Army pistol. I wanted to make it really frightening—bristle the hair on the back of your neck.

Finally, at the end of one day, our teacher sat us down to talk.

"You know this is just a play," he said. "This is called acting. Loaded guns can cause danger far beyond the actor's prerogative. And, besides, some of you are smoking pot. That is going to make it very expensive—if not impossible—for some of you to be actors. First you will inevitably have to bail yourselves out of jail. It is destructive and expensive, not to mention illegal. I don't think you people can *afford* to be actors—not this way."

*   *   *

My father and I had to compress into that small apartment and those few months a stormy spectrum of emotions—regret, resentment, hope, anxiety to please, rebellion, struggle for dominance. Once he invited me to step outside, but I avoided the fistfight.

"Oh, no," I said. "If I walk out there, the sky will fall on me." He had been the prizefighter. I wasn't walking into doom. There would probably have been other near-fights had I not found my own nineteen-dollar-a-month cold-water flat in the winter of 1956.

Robert Earl needed and wanted to be the father, the patriarch.

We worked together well cleaning offices and reading Shakespeare. In truth, that was far simpler than the undone work between us as father and son. It was too late—too late for Robert Earl and me. Six months in my father's house in New York were not going to make up for those twenty-one years of absence. In our first months together in New York, we were not going to resolve the issues of a lifetime. There is not enough magic in a bloodline to forge an instant, irrevocable bond. Robert Earl hoped the magic would happen, but I could see long before he could that magic was not going to do it. In those close quarters, I could only say, "I don't even know who you are."

I began to believe that the best we could do was to become friends, and to hope we could achieve even that.

I think you are destined to follow in your father's footsteps, or to obliterate them. I was becoming an actor, and despite the tensions between us, I decided to reclaim my real name. What's in a name? I had chosen Todd Jones in part because I thought James Earl Jones was just too ordinary. "Todd" was a gesture toward the past, since it was my childhood nickname.

Robert Earl Jones—Earle Jones—was well known in theatre circles in New York. Even more than I had, he had played with his name over the years. But I did not think that my father's name would get me work; that is not why I returned to my given name. Becoming

James Earl Jones, once and for all, was a simple gesture toward affirming my lineage. Todd Jones ended his career. James Earl Jones began his.

All Mama and Papa knew about actors and acting they had learned by example from Robert Earl. They believed that because he was an actor, actors must not be trustworthy. They harbored a distrust of actors and acting, even though Mama started coming to see me act on the Manistee Opera House stage.

Yet Maggie—Mama—was the woman who had told me bedtime stories about lynchings and murders, about women cursed to wear the heads of mules and men who had bellies full of writhing snakes. And this was the woman who could not resist watching the much tamer dramas we acted out on the stage of the summer theatre. In her convoluted way, Mama had taught me to think for myself.

I first became aware of Robert Earl's politics when his mother wrote me a letter after his first confrontation with the House Un-American Activities Committee. He had been called up because of his involvement with the leftist movement in the late 1930s. Elnora wrote to me, "Your father has been called to bow down before the rulers of the land."

I was aware that when the Army was doing my security clearance, I had not been declared guilty by association because Robert Earl had not raised me. I was cleared for Secret. From that time on, I did not want to be political. When I met Robert Earl in New York, we talked only briefly about his politics. We agreed that the less I knew about his past activities, the better. I did not know whether he was a Communist or not. He denied that in public. I didn't want to know anything that would require me to compromise myself in any way with the government. In 1991, when I sought my FBI file under the Freedom of Information Act, I was told that the government does not have a file on me.

*   *   *

Robert Earl and I had knocked heads during the course of our first few months together, but he was a good actor, and he knew his Shakespeare in particular. He gave me my first understanding of Othello that year, and I respected his insight. We could talk about acting with more ease than we could talk about anything else.

"You read Iago, and I'll read Othello," he told me.

Robert Earl felt a spiritual bond to Othello. We had spent hours during the winter and spring in New York reading the play, taking it apart, probing the characters, usually with Robert Earl reading Othello to my Iago. He took an organic approach to the role of Othello, warning me that you could not do Othello if you were thinking like Iago in real life. You have to "straighten up your act" spiritually to do justice to Othello.

Othello, like me, like my mother and like my father, was a stranger in a strange land. Perhaps that is what Robert Earl and I recognized in Othello most of all.

My father has never played Othello in a major production, but as I studied the role with him, I was apprenticing to a master, although an unfulfilled master. I am sure I learned more about Othello in spite of Robert Earl's lack of fulfillment—and maybe even because of it.

Aspirations can be even more haunting than achievements, more urgent than accomplishments. There is something to be said about fathers and sons standing looking out over the landscape of potential life, and one father saying to his son, "I did this; I did that; I traveled here, and there," and another father saying to his son, "I wanted to achieve this but I didn't. I know I could have, but I didn't." Perhaps because Robert Earl aspired to play Othello and did not, I wanted even more urgently to do it, not to try to do it better than he could, but simply to do it.

And on those nights when he and I worked together over Shakespeare's text, voice to voice, some words of Iago's struck home:

How poor are they that have not patience!
What wound did ever heal but by degrees?

PART THREE

VOICES
DISCOVERED

7.

VOICE LESSONS

Eliza, I know you're tired. I know your head aches. I know your nerves are as raw as meat in a butcher's window. But think what you're trying to accomplish. Think what you're dealing with. The majesty and grandeur of the English language.

It's the greatest possession we have. The noblest sentiments that ever flowed in the hearts of men are contained in its extraordinary imaginative and musical mixtures of sounds. That's what you set yourself to conquer, Eliza, and conquer it you will.

HENRY HIGGINS, MY FAIR LADY

POLONIUS: What do you read, my lord?
HAMLET: Words, words, words.

HAMLET, ACT II, SCENE II

During the next year, I worked hard with my speech teacher, Nora Dunphee, who made me concentrate on articulation and voice control. Nora had studied with Margaret Prendergrast McClain, who had studied with the linguist who was the model for Professor Henry Higgins in George Bernard Shaw's *Pygmalion*. McClain had also written a respected textbook called *Good American Speech*, which we used in our class. McClain encouraged purifying the actor's voice of any regional or ethnic influence, which meant that Nora had her work cut out for her as far as I was concerned: she had to help me work against my leftover Mississippi inflections, and more than that, against the obstacle of my stuttering. She inspired confidence in me, not only by her patience and her manner, but by that strange link through her to Margaret McClain all the way back to Shaw.

Nora was coaching me to use my voice as an instrument, and to produce clarity of sound. She wasn't trying to teach me to interpret a role. Instead, she continually drilled me in the rudiments of clear speech, much as a piano teacher would have drilled me in scales, technique, and theory. Only with mastery of those fundamentals could I hope to get inside the language of a character in a play.

I studied that year, too, with Will Lee, who went on to be recognized by millions of children who watched "Sesame Street." Will had worked with Elia Kazan and Morris Carnovsky, and he believed that acting comes out of your own life experiences. I had often frozen or stammered or turned mute when problems confronted me in real life, and sometimes it seemed that the harder I worked, the murkier my speech would become in class. As I probed the emotions of a character in a scene, my voice would betray me, bogging down as if swamped in the sounds. Sometimes my speech would accelerate with emotion, and my words would race with each other, rapid as heartbeats in a footrace. Will taught me to confront the reality of that emotional overload and to begin to harness the emotions to the voice.

He also urged me to tone down my natural instincts toward power in a scene and to control that energy. "Never use your total power," he told me. "Use three-quarters of your power only, and let the rest of it bear you up."

He was giving me a sense of proportion, and some valuable experience in working *with* rather than *against* the emotion and passion I brought to a characterization.

Because of my muteness, I approached language in a different way from most actors. I came at language standing on my head, turning words inside out in search of meaning, making a mess of it sometimes, but seeing truth from a very different viewpoint. In those years I spent in virtual silence, I developed a passion for expression. I do not believe that speech is a natural function for the human species. Therefore, any barrier to speech—stuttering, for instance—only intensifies the difficulty of an essentially unnatural process, the futility of words. But as I regained my powers of speech and began to use them as an actor, I came to believe that what is valid about a character is not his intellect, but the sounds he makes.

I had come to the American Theatre Wing wanting to act, but without any real knowledge of the different schools of acting. One strategy which made sense to me, and which has stayed with me, is the attempt to discover the motivation of the character. Chekhov called it seeing the inner life of the character as well as the outer appearance. And I wanted to discover the character's voice.

My training at the Theatre Wing was now finished. I really needed a job, so I took a position at the local YMCA as a desk clerk. I told the director of the Y that my ambitions were to be a clerk at such an establishment, and that I hoped for a future in hotel work. Soon after,

I read a casting notice in *Show Biz* magazine for an off-Broadway play called *Wedding in Japan*. I went to the audition, and while I didn't get a leading role, I got a part. I came back to the Y and told the director I had the job.

"You lied," he said. "I should have known you are an actor. Only an actor can lie like that. You really fooled me, and if I could blackball you with everybody in this city, I would."

My hotel career over, I set to work in rehearsals, playing the small role of Sergeant Blunt in Ted Pollock's *Wedding in Japan* at the off-Broadway Graystone Hotel Theatre in New York. It was a drama about the occupation in the Army, with an underlying story of a romance between a Japanese girl and a black Army sergeant. She has chosen the black man over the Southern white lieutenant who loves her. The two soldiers become embroiled in a court-martial battle. My role was insignificant, but one night, in that understudy's dream, I got to play the lead when Ivan Dixon could not go on. After the performance, an agent named Toby Cole came backstage. "I am not sure if you know how to act, but I like what you were doing up there," she said, and asked if I needed an agent. I jumped at the chance. Toby worked for literary and theatrical agent Lucy Kroll and they represented me from that time on.

Wedding in Japan did not last long; I settled back into part-time jobs, and into my acting workshops. I was tackling roles of every kind—Othello, Big Daddy in *Cat on a Hot Tin Roof.* We were not allowed to be limited in our roles or our imaginations by ethnic or cultural definitions. I wanted to take advantage of that freedom to get as firm a grounding as I could playing characters of different cultures, different "skins."

I played as many as possible of Shakespeare's characters in those workshops. I knew that I would not get to do them in commercial productions—or, if so, only rarely—but that was not true at the Theatre Wing. There, I could be Hamlet, Othello, King Lear, Macbeth. Race did not matter.

I think black actors have to come into the theatre with an awareness of our reality. We are the minority culture. Most of the plays are about the majority culture. But you never accept the negative thought: "I can't make it because I'm black." You can't concede defeat before you even start, any more than Marlon Brando could have.

Brando's style is so great that no matter where he came from, the doors would eventually have had to open to his talent. I believe that all of us have to look at ourselves that way. If the talent is heightened enough by hard work, then there is no barrier.

After I got my diploma at the Theatre Wing in 1957, I auditioned for Tad Danielewski's acting workshop. Tad had done some workshops at the Theatre Wing while I was there. I knew his reputation as a teacher as well as a television director. He had studied at the Actors Studio, but his practical, challenging workshop was independent of any of the acting schools in New York. He only accepted professional actors in the workshop after they auditioned successfully. He focused on the individual actor. He set me to work on scenes from three memorable plays—*Othello*, of course, which, because of Robert Earl, has obsessed me from the earliest days; August Strindberg's *Miss Julie*; and John Steinbeck's *Of Mice and Men*, adapted by Steinbeck with the help of playwright George S. Kaufman.

Now I gained further insight into the components of the craft of acting, especially voice control and diction. Tad was Polish; and with his accent, he was not trying to teach me language: he was teaching me something else that precedes language, something that makes language on one hand unnecessary or irrelevant, and on the other hand desperately urgent.

There is something that rages in every human being. It does in me; it does in you. It rages in the best of dramatic characters. I am talking here about universal rage—that voice screaming in the wilderness. Language exerts a pitiful attempt to harness it, to define it. It is hard enough for writers and composers to "define" life and experience with language, but actors must then take that definition to the stage and try to give it another definition. The challenge of being in touch with that voice in the wilderness makes acting interesting and also dangerous. Drama should always take us to the edge, where we don't know what is going to happen, or how far it is going to go.

When you communicate honestly, whether in your real life or your stage life, you have to actually inhabit the words, touch the core of their meanings. You have to enter the character, penetrate his spirit before you can honestly utter his words. Hard labor stretches muscles, no matter what kind of work you do. Sometimes, just before you break through to new possibilities in your work, the muscles resist. They hurt. They balk. That would happen to me with my speech. I would stretch so far—and speech would crash. But I learned to wait, and try again, and again. The muscles began to grow.

In October 1957, I had a stroke of good fortune and got my first chance to be in a Broadway production. I understudied for Lloyd Richards, who played the role of Perry Hall in *The Egghead*, starring Karl Malden and directed by Hume Cronyn at the Ethel Barrymore Theatre. This began a long association with Lloyd, whose advice I often sought. No understudy's dream came true this time, but in January 1958, I got a speaking part on Broadway, playing the valet in Dore Schary's *Sunrise at Campobello*, a drama about Eleanor and Franklin D. Roosevelt, starring Ralph Bellamy. Vincent Donahue directed me in the small part as Edward the valet.

One night on stage, my worst fear sabotaged me. Here I was, acting in my first play on Broadway. I only had three lines, but one of them gave me trouble: "Mrs. Roosevelt, supper is served."

"M"—the Mama-letter—the overload Mama-word.

"M-m-m-m-m-Mrs. ———" I said during a performance.

Mary Fickett, the actress playing Mrs. Roosevelt, just stood there and let me get through it. That was the only way. I recovered, and we went on. Miraculously it never happened again.

I have not yet solved the mystery of Othello, and I have played him many times, at different ages in my life. My work with Tad gave me at least a piece of the Othello puzzle, and it sustained what has been a lifelong interest in the brooding, majestic Moor, troubled by his betrayal at the hands of his trusted friend Iago, obsessed with his wife Desdemona, torn by the dark conflicts of passion and revenge.

With Tad, as with Robert Earl, I talked over possible personal scenarios for Othello. Who was this man? Where had he come from? I was trying to come to terms with this complicated man, trying to figure out how he rose to the heights so I could understand how he fell to the depths.

Another fascinating character, almost diametrically opposed to Othello, was Lennie in Steinbeck's *Of Mice and Men*, a man of primal simplicity, with raw instincts and no social conceits. Unlike Othello, Lennie was unelevated, with no means of protecting himself. These two characters have fascinated me for nearly forty years.

I was learning, but barely surviving financially, working at any odd job so I could eat and sleep somewhere and keep on studying, experimenting with roles, seeing plays. I certainly was not getting any paying work in the theatre. Two other teachers at the American Theatre Wing had at least noticed my presence there. One was Joseph Papp, a man of great ingenuity and energy. The other was the famous acting teacher Lee Strasberg. Strasberg was much in demand then as a teacher at the Actors Studio in New York, and I thought he was the most important entity in the American theatre at that time. I wanted to study with Strasberg. To get into his classes at the Actors Studio, you had to audition, and the competition was fierce.

I auditioned seven years running and was never accepted. I was invited, however, to audit and observe at the Actors Studio, and when I discovered that Lee gave private classes, I managed to scrape up the money to enroll.

Ruth Connolly Jones and her son James Earl in Mississippi in 1932. "My mother was looking away, perhaps because she was having a picture made to send to my father, and she did not want to be a part of the picture."

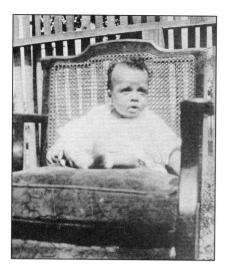

James Earl Jones, 1931.

James Earl Jones's great-grandparents Wyatt and Sharlett Jeeter Connolly and their sons, daughters, daughter-in-law, and grandchildren, at the "Home House" in Arkabutla Township, Tate County, Mississippi, about 1908. From left to right, first row: Mary, Wyatt, Lillian, Sidney (little girl in foreground), Sharlett Jeeter; Ed and his family, daughter Purlie, wife Mary and son Sam Eddie; second row: James Carver, Esseck, Ira, Nimrod, John Henry (James Earl Jones's grandfather) and Lenna. Wyatt and Sharlett Jeeter's oldest daughter, Eliza, is the only one of their children not in the photograph. Photo courtesy of Terry Connolly.

James Earl Jones as a boy in Mississippi.

James Earl Jones as a boy at the family farm in Michigan.

James Earl Jones, his mother Ruth, and his uncle Randy, about 1944: "I could not really appreciate her presence without at the same moment mourning her departure."

Front row, left to right: James Earl Jones, Cousin Robert Earl, Uncle Randy;
second row: Aunt Helen and Aunt Ozella, in Michigan about 1941.

James Earl Jones's "Papa" and "Mama"—John Henry and Maggie Connolly, on the front porch of their homestead in Mississippi, about 1933.

James Earl Jones's grandmother Elnora Jones.

The Connolly sisters, daughters of John Henry and Maggie, in Michigan:
Left to right (seated in order of age, youngest to oldest): Helen, Ozella,
Thelma, Anna Bell, Bessie, and Ruth, James Earl's mother.

James Earl Jones (back row, number 27) on the Dickson High School basketball
team, Brethren, Michigan, 1946, 1947, or 1948 (he wore number 42 in 1949, his
senior year).

James Earl Jones and Mr. Daniels, school superintendent, at James Earl's high school graduation.

James Earl Jones, in his early twenties.

* * *

After I enjoyed some success, and got to know Lee, he told me that he, Cheryl Crawford, and Elia Kazan shared the consensus that there were actors such as George C. Scott and me who, by following their own particular drumbeat, had already found an effective technique. Rather than pull them back and teach them the Method, they said, "We'd better let them go on their own paths." That is how Lee put it to me, years later, when we spoke of those seven failed auditions.

Theatre critic and director Harold Clurman has called the Method—short for the Stanislavsky Method of acting—"the grammar of acting." The Russian actor and director Constantin Stanislavsky developed this method about 1909 at the Moscow Art Theatre. What came out of the nature of the Russian people, not dissimilar from the nature of the American people, was an organic association with language which could express human behavior. I think the whole style of acting called the Method came out of Stanislavsky's own insight that there is nothing more interesting than human nature itself, and what is next most interesting is an actor who can evoke the same pattern of behavior that one finds in nature, having the same ring of truth. It was that simple.

Few people in nature sound like they come from Oxford. More people in nature sound like they come from wherever Marlon Brando came from. People heard him and said, "Yes, that's a human being. That's the way I am." Brando gave us the shock of recognition of ourselves.

At the Actors Studio, Lee Strasberg "taught" the Method to actors such as Brando, Montgomery Clift, Paul Newman, Geraldine Page, Marilyn Monroe, James Dean, Shelley Winters, Kim Stanley, and Julie Harris. In essence, the Method propels the actor toward the organic, toward plumbing your own deepest experiences, your emotional memory, and finding there the energy and vision to shape your interpretation of the role on stage.

Almost every Method teacher, director, and actor has put his own

stamp on its meaning and manifestation. I found Stanislavsky's books
and essays difficult to read, and I do not know if I have done
anything with what I learned from them. Stanislavsky the man
fascinated me, however, since the day I first saw a photograph of him.
I worked for a time as a clerk in a French bookstore in New York,
filing and filling bookshelves. I enjoyed the job, and one of the
"perks" it provided was a copy of *The Russian Theatre* written in
French. There I saw my first photograph of the great Russian. What
a handsome, self-conscious rogue he looked. I knew when I saw that
photograph what he was really about. He could have stepped out of
that picture into the dark, malevolent role of Iago.

Curiously, I never found Lee Strasberg effective as a director. He
was a great teacher, in my opinion. He rambled, but if you were
attentive enough, you gathered something from what he said. Lee
loved students fresh out of Las Vegas, girls who had a flair for
entertaining on stage, but who had no acting experience at all. He
loved to teach them when they were shy and frightened, trembling in
their boots. The chorus-girl types were his favorite students, not just
because they were pretty and a bit used. What he loved was the raw
talent, someone who had no presumptions about acting, only the
desire to project herself in some way as an actress.

One day I came into Lee's class and sat down. I noticed behind
me an attractive girl. Her hair was scraggly and she wore no makeup,
but I kept looking back at her.

"Hi," she said at last.

"Hi," I answered.

"I'm Marilyn—Marilyn, the actress," she said. It was Marilyn
Monroe.

I was too shy even to look at her again, much less to say another
word to her.

"Good morning, Lee," you would say. He would just look at you. He
did not indulge in social amenities. Somehow you understood that he

was working on another level, a deep, unconscious level. He would just look at you. There was something at once genuine and odd about him. He was hard to figure out. I did not really know Lee as a man. One eccentricity intrigued me. Lee was terrified of electronic equipment. He had no shame about it: he asked other people to change the record or whatever it was. He simply did not know anything about the world of technology.

Lee stressed memory exercises to awaken and deepen the five senses. I responded most to Lee's song exercises, designed to fuse voice control with emotional release. We would have to stand before the class and sing the melody of a given song, holding on to each syllable and each note for several seconds each. "The Battle Hymn of the Republic," for example, would be sung with no attention to its rhythm or tempo, but with sustained, equal emphasis on every note-syllable. The result—always a flood of emotion.

While you put yourself and your classmates through this exercise, you were not allowed to move. You had to look into their eyes. Needless to say, you felt deeply awkward and self-conscious—and almost every time, intense emotions welled up to the surface. You might tighten up and squelch the emotions—or give in to them, let them flow, giving you a sense of physical and emotional release.

I do not believe that Lee's class had any lasting impact on my acting because I did comparatively little work with him. But it did leave me more awake to strategies of acting. Lee evoked in all of us the wonderful awareness of acting as an art, and of the importance of theatre as an art. Life is enhanced by art, just as it can be illuminated by it.

My first breakthrough opportunity as an actor came in a chance meeting on a New York sidewalk. It was a spring day in 1960 when I bumped into Joe Papp. He was getting a new project underway, and as we stopped to chat on the street, he offered me a job that coming summer, playing Michael Williams in Shakespeare's *Henry V.* There, on that noisy, bustling Manhattan sidewalk, in all its infinite variety, I had the chance to join in at the beginning of one of the most important, landmark theatrical endeavors in the history of the theatre, Joe Papp's New York Shakespeare Festival, "Shakespeare in Central Park."

8.

THE BLACKS

One evening an actor asked me to write a play for an all-black cast. But what exactly is a black? First of all, what's his color?

JEAN GENET, *THE BLACKS: A CLOWN SHOW*
(NEW YORK: GROVE PRESS, 1960)

All of a sudden, after no work at all, I had two jobs—the summer commitment to Joe Papp's Shakespeare Festival and my first leading role on the New York stage. I got the part of the black composer in Lionel Abel's play *The Pretender*, to be directed off Broadway by Herbert Machiz. My character, Jessie Prince, moves from the North to Mississippi and tries to adopt the mores of the Old South. But the dramatic conflict centers around the alleged rape of Prince's wife by a white man—and Prince's struggle for revenge. He attempts to rally the black community around a plan to lynch the rapist.

I was disappointed in my work in *The Pretender*. I fared better with the critics than the play did, but not by much. I was "first rate," one reviewer said, but I was pompous, according to another. But at least I had finally made it to a leading role in New York—and that was a milestone for me. And, as I have done often since, I got into some disagreements with the director. I was needed to begin rehearsing for *Henry V* while *The Pretender* was still running. Herbert Machiz wanted us to keep rehearsing *The Pretender* after the opening, and the schedules conflicted. Machiz thought his play took precedence over *Henry V.* Moreover, he told me that I should stick to one thing if I expected to develop as an actor and establish a career. It was frustrating to have to respond to directions to "act like Cary Grant." I felt *The Pretender* was a lost cause and a waste of time.

Instinctively, I thirsted for variety. I had to have intense stimulation to stretch and grow. I have always had to work that way, migrating from one role to another, coming back to some of them time after time, as with Othello, Lennie, and *The Blacks*, but taking on one new challenge after another. That habit I formed early.

I was going step by step then, but I was rapacious. I was out there all over the place, aiming to cut off as big a piece of the off-Broadway pie as I could. I would often do the first act of one play and the second act of another. I was just approaching acting as I have approached language and speech, upside down and "standing on my head," trying to listen to my own drumbeat. It was not a gesture of defiance at all. It was just my nature to explore, to seek new pathways. If what I was working on was not feeding me, I would move on to something else.

So I was sure that *Henry V* would nourish me far more than *The Pretender.* After four weeks of rehearsal with Joe Papp, we opened at the New York Shakespeare Festival on June 29, 1960, outdoors at Belvedere Lake Theatre in Central Park.

Shakespeare himself would no doubt have saluted Joe Papp's innovation in taking his plays not only off Broadway, but into Central Park, where people could see them for free. Broadway theatre tickets were selling for the then exorbitant price of $9.90 apiece that summer of 1960. People stood in line for hours to get free tickets to see Shakespeare in Central Park.

Critic Arthur Gelb called *Henry V* a "vividly beautiful and rousingly paced pageant . . . all dash and splendor and spectacle— just what Shakespeare ordered." Performing outdoors was a challenge, with the distant horns of traffic drifting into the park, and the occasional overhead roar of an airplane.

At one point, after I had been in New York for quite a while, I auditioned for roles time after time without success. It was then that I began to wonder if I should seek another kind of career. I even went to the New York University vocational guidance center, and was assessed as having talent and ability in architecture. I was accepted at the Parsons School of Design, but before I began my studies, my father and I got roles in *Of Mice and Men* at Purdue University.

So instead of giving up, I chose to live a very Spartan existence.

Sometimes I would joke that I was a privileged person, that I came from a wealthy family and had never had a problem in my life, and was living this way "for the experience."

I decided then to dedicate myself to the work without letting concerns about making a living overwhelm me. There were actors who of necessity took on double careers, especially if they had spouses and children to support. I stayed free so that I could live as austerely as I had to.

In the spring of 1961, when I was thirty years old, producer-director Geraldine Lust asked me to audition for Jean Genet's *The Blacks*. She had secured the rights to the controversial drama, which had been a huge success abroad after its Paris debut in 1959. Genet's *The Balcony* was still enjoying a successful run at the Circle in the Square in New York. Gene Frankel was asked to direct the American premiere of *The Blacks* off Broadway, with an all-black cast.

I have always loved the wilderness, and frontiers, and if there ever was a play on the edge of the frontier, it was this one. Deceptively ironic, the play offers an intricate structure of ceremonies to a counterpoint of anarchy, chaos. Before an audience of masked figures—a queen and her valet, a judge, a governor, a missionary—a group of blacks perform a ritualized murder. When the authority figures—representatives of white colonialism—set out to punish the murderers, they themselves are killed. This violent action is a ploy to divert the audience from a more somber offstage drama: a black is being tried and executed for betraying his people.

"Genet's play is a drama of the absurd," Geraldine told me when we first met. "It is not written in everyday, naturalistic, realistic speech or behavior. Sometimes there is the soaring, poetic speech that you find in Shakespeare. Other times, the language is violent. The characters are allegorical. This is volatile drama. Complex technique is required. I'd like you to audition. But I am worried about finding black actors who can handle the stylistic speech of this play."

Her comments put me so on the edge that when I looked at the script, I thought, "I don't know how to handle this sort of off-the-wall stuff."

The sections I read for the audition were not close to each other in the script, and seemed disjointed. If you read or heard the dialogue in fragments like this, it would make no sense at all, for the unorthodox structure of the drama made it hard enough to grasp its coherence in the first place.

For instance, in early passages of the play, Village says to Virtue (Cicely Tyson):

> Madam, I bring you nothing comparable to what is called love. What is happening within me is very mysterious and cannot be accounted for by my color. . . . Oh, if only I hadn't been born into slavery! I'd have been flooded with strange emotion, but we—you and I—were moving along the edges of the world, out of bounds. We were the shadow, or the dark interior, of luminous creatures. . . . When I beheld you, suddenly—for perhaps a second—I had the strength to reject everything that wasn't you and to laugh at the illusion. But my shoulders are very frail. I was unable to bear the weight of the world's condemnation. And I began to hate you when everything about you would have kindled my love and when love would have made men's contempt unbearable, and their contempt would have made my love unbearable. The fact is, I hate you . . . I know not whether you are beautiful. I fear you may be. I fear your sparkling darkness. Oh darkness, stately mother of my race, shadow, sheath that swathes me from top to toe . . . I know not whether you are beautiful, but you are Africa, oh monumental night, and I hate you. I hate you for filling my black eyes with sweetness. . . .

I took a shot of vodka and launched into the audition. Somehow the character and I were in sync: I got the key role of Deodatus Village, and signed a contract—at forty-five dollars per week. And Geraldine did indeed find a cast who could handle the play. Several careers were launched in the process. Cicely Tyson played Stephanie Virtue Secret-rose Diop. Cynthia Belgrave played Adelaide Bobo. Roscoe Lee Browne, the first to be cast, played Archibald Wellington, the master of ceremonies. Lou Gossett played Edgar Alas Newport News, the gunman who kept running in and out, the messenger/courier. Raymond St. Jacques, Maya Angelou, and Abbey Lincoln, who joined later, and comedian Godfrey Cambridge were also in the cast, among others.

This enclave of characters suggested militant revolutionaries, the kind of movement which was evolving in Europe at the time, and their white adversaries. But Genet took the colonial situation as applied to European whites and African blacks and flipped it upside down. On the upper tier of the stage stood the colonial whites and on the lower tier, the blacks they suppressed. The lower group were African-American actors, with no makeup, just ourselves, with our kinky hair and our dark faces. We all wore tuxedos or tails for the ceremonial burial of a white victim Village had raped. We gathered there in our formal clothes to give this person a decent burial.

The upper group tier symbolizing the court that intended to judge us were black people wearing stylized white masks. They did not look like people, but like stark, surrealistic creatures dressed in the trappings of empire, entities of the European colonial apparatus—the queen (played by Maya Angelou); the general, the priest, etcetera.

The Blacks opened on May 4, 1961, at the St. Marks Playhouse, not so much as an experiment in technique as an experiment in haranguing the consciousness of both the audience and ourselves.

Genet was saying in *The Blacks* that we are doomed unless we rid ourselves of the damaging myths of religion, race, and sex. Our on-stage drama was only a hand mirror of the real dramas being enacted all around us—protests against segregation and for the civil rights movement. Nineteen sixty-one was the year that the CORE Freedom Riders sought to integrate buses and trains and confronted angry hands of Birmingham mobs. With Martin Luther King's urging, we were trying to deal with the problems of integrating the South. Those were sensitive, painful times for America. We as members of the theatre community, and our theatre audiences, were willing and ready to sit and listen to Genet, to find in his brutally stylized conception of colonialism the light it might shed on the real-life drama confronting us as a nation.

The Blacks would not work today as it did thirty years ago. We as a society are too cynical now to embrace the pure conscience evoked by the drama. But in the early sixties, the play was right for the times. It was one of the most perfectly timed productions I have ever been involved in. I have seen it since. Recent productions necessarily resorted to style and symbol. But when we performed the play in 1961, it provoked a raw, almost religious appeal to conscience.

Because black actors were involved in the theatre, the play got all kinds of militant political attention. Maya Angelou had arrived at an extreme position, and was vocal about it. Abbey Lincoln was even more vocal about her political position. She was dating Max Roach then, a famous drummer, and an outspoken militant. Max had designed our drum orchestra for some of the ceremonial parts of the production. During the rehearsal, all the focus was on the acting. That was going very well—but the whole political undercurrent built and built.

Gene Frankel was a Jewish director. Members of the cast often challenged him. "What do you know about being black?" Gene would say, "What do you know about Genet?"

I liked working with Gene. He encouraged me to go far out in my work. He trusted me to find my own way of creating the role of Village and told me to let my instincts guide me more than my intellect. Gene had a good way about him, and he kept control of the production, even when James Baldwin came on board as "commissar." He was not part of the company, but he was around a lot, allowed to monitor rehearsals.

Jimmy Baldwin had even then a way of going abroad to write and live his personal life, and then of coming back to America only when he perceived a crisis—and then he came on as the self-appointed spokesman. He did not speak for me. I resented his spokesmanship. I resented his need to politicize our drama more than it was already.

Until I worked in *The Blacks,* I felt fairly free of racial conflict and frustration, but when I stepped into the shoes of Village, I had to walk through the hatred, distrust, and disaffections that can split blacks and whites. I came to see the black man in America as very much the tragic hero, an Oedipus or Hamlet or Willy Loman.

I remember one discussion when Jimmy Baldwin asked, "What do you see when you wake up in the morning? Do you see a black person or do you see a person?"

"Hell, my ego is strong enough," I said. "I see *me.*" The rest were saying, "No, you see a black." That was the point at which the company began to fragment. There were geological fault lines. But still the job at hand kept us all committed to the play.

Genet was a radical in his own right with strong social and moral points of view, which all became evident once the play opened and the critics and the audiences started coming. Because of politics, *The Blacks* went through some strange changes. In that volatile time, too, the theatre was being challenged to deal with the problem of representative images. It was inconceivable to most people in New York, for instance, that there could be a musical comedy called *Subways Are for Sleeping* with no black members in the cast. Working class people, Puerto Ricans and blacks, dominate the subway. It was the day of picketing at lunch counters in the South, and it was the day of people picketing Broadway shows such as *Subways Are for Sleeping* to protest the casting.

Genet's *The Blacks* was being performed by our all-black cast, and the play itself was vigorously critical of racial issues. The fact that it was a big hit calmed everybody down and we were able to let the play speak for itself. The play worked, and it did what everybody needed it to do.

The race issue has always been a problem in theatre. At the same time that *Subways Are for Sleeping* was being picketed, there was an embarrassing Broadway production, *Mandingo,* the story of black slaves brought in from the same region of Africa where the Czar of Russia procured his court guards. These were genetically very tall, strong, muscular people, prized by slave masters and always used for breeding. In *Mandingo,* when the white mistress of the plantation learns that her husband has been dallying with black women, she seduces one of the slaves. It was an indulgent and exploitative production, with nothing serious to say about the extremely painful subject of slavery. Only in Alex Haley's *Roots* has slavery been dealt with calmly, sensitively, and with any kind of clarity.

The time of *The Blacks* was a rich, fiery period in New York. It was my first major role after *The Pretender.* Roscoe Lee Browne and I had worked together then and we enjoyed working together again. We have quite different life-styles and choices, but I admire him very much as an actor, an intellectual, a master of poetry, a remarkable person all around. For the most part, he was able to handle adroitly all the political hysteria swirling around us in the production.

The history of the more than three-year run of *The Blacks* is interesting in that many of us were deeply fatigued before it was over. It was more than just physical weariness—it was spiritual fatigue. There was a constant harangue. It was wearing, and it was a relief to leave the production, which I did several times. I always lost weight while I was playing in *The Blacks.* The theatre was usually too hot. Our clothes were soaking wet after each performance. All told, I was in and out of the production seven times from 1961 until late in 1963.

The production gave all of us a home base, however. One by one, we would leave to work on other projects, and come back again. One critic suggested that the constant change of cast in the show was a problem because the chemistry altered so frequently. What the audience saw in 1962 was not what the audience saw in 1961, and that was a serious problem. I realized each time I returned to the show that I was not capable of giving exactly the same performance I had given the previous season. I was a different person, and slowly, painfully, the South and the United States were beginning to change.

I was still working out some of my own issues of racial politics. I had come out of the Army with all my personal firearms and a part of my mind ready to accept the possibility that there might be overt racial conflict. I even expected that I might be called on to use my Army training in that kind of struggle. I did not want to join any militant organization. I was not politically inclined. But I accepted the idea that I might be drawn into violent racial strife. In a race war, the neutral cannot remain neutral.

I deeply believed then as now that there are solutions to social problems which the theatre can address. The theatre itself can contribute to understanding. Later on, when I acted in several plays by Athol Fugard, I learned that you cannot tell anybody anything. You cannot lecture. You cannot mandate a message, you can only *evoke* an experience. The theatre can show better than it can tell. Drama can reveal political experiences. The drama and the actor can meet the audience and help them experience a problem. Theatre offers the chance of deeper understanding.

I found myself in a career that was an alternative to the body politic. I did not have to render my energy or my life to a militant group, and I have been determined not to do that. I have always thought politics are personal. I think one's politics are determined by something deeply personal, rooted very early in one's life. Often the people who get into politics have their own axes to grind. They cloud the picture rather than clarify it. There are very few people in politics, especially militant politics, who do not operate on hidden agendas.

The Blacks had been a lightning rod for political and critical controversy. Richard Watts of the *New York Post* (May 5, 1961) called it a "fascinating and disturbing dramatic experience," a "stunning production . . . violent, complex, subtle, mocking, devious, cryptic, forthright, perverse, terrifying, shocking, beautiful, ugly, illuminating and confusing," less a play than "a kind of snarling ritual" with unforgettable theatrical power. Norman Mailer and Lorraine Hansberry carried on a debate about the production in the pages of *The Village Voice.* Seymour Stern, in the May 3, 1961, issue of the *New York Daily Mirror,* described the play as a "plotless cacophony," an "acting out of a ritual by a group of embittered Negro actors before a court wearing white masks to symbolize the white world." To James Davis, in the *New York Daily News* on May 5, 1961, the material of the play was "vulgar," bordering "on the psychotic and always grotesque," "freakish," a "pretentious bit of sham intellectualism."

In *The New Yorker,* Whitney Bailliet wrote, "James Earl Jones is tall, graceful, and weightless, and spins magically through shouting anger, fear, and sweet talk." Jerry Tallmer, writing in *The Village Voice,* saw the debt I owed to our director, Gene Frankel, noting that I played Village with "vigor, virility, and a kind of catlike lyricism, all in one package, pulling it intuitively from his own roots as Frankel urged him to."

Gene himself called the drama a "hate therapy" play which stimulated people in the audience to examine their own racial prejudices. He said that he deliberately played on the white sense of guilt, striving for an emotional rather than an intellectual confrontation of racial themes.

Joe Papp offered me a change of pace that summer when he and Gerald Friedman cast me as Oberon in *A Midsummer Night's Dream* at the New York Shakespeare Festival. Central Park was the perfect place for this play in particular with its setting in the woods.

I began to get small parts on television in 1961—that breakthrough year—roles on "Playhouse 90," "The Brighter Day," "The Catholic Hour," "Camera Three," and the popular "Phil Silvers Show."

I left *The Blacks* again in the fall of 1961. It had been a landmark experience for me, one of those pivotal moments in a career, and I was grateful. But I was spent and I needed to return to a more realistic setting and characters.

9.

OFF BROADWAY: THE PATHFINDERS

Replacing the old star system are groups of actors working together in studios, ensembles, institutes and institutional theatres—communities of artists who are turning their backs on Broadway, the West End, and the Boulevards.

TOBY COLE AND HELEN KRICH CHINOY,
ACTORS ON ACTING (NEW YORK: CROWN, 1970)

Our search for a true theatre should not make us unduly harsh with modest efforts of the moment. It is not altogether helpful to demand that all plays or performances be "masterpieces." Heaven protect us from the museum mind which dismisses all present work on the grounds that it is inferior to the best of another day or another place! Art alone does not create art; our living experience is what matters most. I am hospitable to all forms of theatre which spring from a life-inspired and life-giving source.

HAROLD CLURMAN, *LIES LIKE TRUTH*
(NEW YORK: MACMILLAN, 1958)

The avant-garde theatre is fun; it is free-swinging, bold, iconoclastic and often wildly, wildly funny.

EDWARD ALBEE

Just as you can feel an earthquake and not know where the epicenter is, you can live and work in the middle of a movement, feel it exploding around you, and not, at the time, fully understand its cause or its repercussions. Off Broadway was that earthquake for me.

Broadway had become narrow, rigid, conventional, and expensive. Off Broadway was not about commercialism; it wasn't about money. Many wonderful renegades were hard at work in the ferment there. In the general public, young people were going downtown to the Circle in the Square or to the Living Theatre, or dozens of makeshift, improvised stages in warehouses, nightclubs, or basements. Off Broadway was a firmament to itself.

The tremendous explosion in the theatre paralleled the explosion in politics and civil rights. We lived in a milieu of discontent, about class, race, and sexual identity. Off Broadway mirrored that. It was often rough-hewn, and always affordable. It dared to take risks.

The political and social revolutions of the sixties ignited change everywhere, including the theatre. The fifties had bombarded us with Korea, McCarthyism, and the Cold War. Volatile countercultures struggled over issues and ideology in the decade that followed. Martin Luther King, Jr., was leading us in the civil rights struggle. The whole establishment was being shaken to its foundation. Broadway could no longer contain all that life and energy, or absorb all that turbulence, even to exploit it.

The seeds of the off-Broadway movement were probably planted in the late 1940s, in ground prepared in the thirties by such groups as the Federal Theatre Project and the Group Theatre to protest Broadway's commercialism and conventionality. Off-Broadway theatres began to introduce new plays, or to revive existing ones that had not been successful on Broadway—Tennessee Williams's *Summer and Smoke* in 1952; Eugene O'Neill's *The Iceman Cometh* in 1956. In the sixties, off-Broadway houses welcomed new playwrights such as John Guare, LeRoi Jones, Lanford Wilson, and Edward Albee (who had four plays off Broadway in 1960–61—*The Zoo Story, The Sandbox, The American Dream,* and *The Death of Bessie Smith*). A luminous roster of actors trained in and "graduated" from off Broadway—Jason Robards, Dustin Hoffman, Al Pacino, Colleen Dewhurst, George C. Scott, Geraldine Page. The off-Broadway theatres were physically innovative and different—intimate spaces sometimes holding no more than 199 people. (If you seated 200 or more, you had to comply with stricter city building codes.) Many theatres found their homes in spaces never designed to be theatres; ingenuity and necessity produced imaginative, often minimal staging, in theatre-in-the-round, or on thrust or arena stages.

Edward Albee noted with interest that "if an off-Broadway play has a substantial run, its audience will begin young and grow older; as the run goes on, cloth coats give way to furs, walkers and subway riders to taxi-takers. Exactly the opposite is true on Broadway."

There were famous avant-garde theatres such as the Living Theatre, founded in 1946 by Julian Beck and Judith Malina, who produced Brecht, Lorca, Pirandello, Gertrude Stein, Strindberg, Cocteau—and Jack Gelber's *The Apple* in which I got a role. Samuel Beckett's *Waiting for Godot* opened in London in 1956 and quickly made its way across the Atlantic. Circle in the Square imported Jean Genet's *The Balcony* in 1960.

Joe Papp was committed to "people's" theatre, and so started the New York Shakespeare Festival in 1954 and Shakespeare in the Park in 1957. Of course, many off-Broadway productions moved on to find success on Broadway, and as off Broadway grew more successful and, consequently, more mainstream and high-priced, off-off-Broadway was born. It has been estimated that between 1960 and

1965, more than four hundred new plays by two hundred new playwrights were staged off-off-Broadway. At Ellen Stewart's courageous La Mama Experimental Theatre Club, 175 plays by 130 writers found homes and audiences.

In those Kennedy days, off Broadway was the new frontier of theatre, and whether we realized it or not, we were part of an international movement. In this vitality there was room for pathfinders. Here, I could push to the edge of yet another frontier.

The Blacks was for me a contradiction. I busted my butt to do my role. I did not want a hysterical political climate to keep me from my focus on my work. On the other hand, I knew that I was part of a play which could never have been produced before. I hoped that by being a good actor—who happened to be black—I was carving a bit of a clearing in the woods. I was helping to open the way for actors and plays that came later. The best way to be political was to make the production as exciting as possible. For me, what was "political" was to do my job well. If the production of *The Blacks* had been bad, we would have been crucified. My own personal politics are something else.

When I left *The Blacks,* playwright LeRoi Jones told me, "Now it's time for you to come work with me."

"No," I said. "I'm going to do Shakespeare at the Public Theatre."

Despite how hard jobs were to find, I was a working actor. For almost all actors, regardless of race or sex, jobs are few and far between. Yet, oddly enough, a few black actors broke the barriers, and off Broadway helped us do it. Black actors played a special role: we certainly never worked on Broadway the way we worked off Broadway.

I could cut across the "pie" from Shakespeare to the avant-garde. I was able in a relatively short time to move my career along. Ironically, in those few years, I probably "integrated" more productions than many actors who set that as their agenda. I, too, got to be one of the pathfinders.

Sidney Poitier inadvertently played a role in the path I took then. If he had access to movies, a black actor could easily be drawn away from his theatre training because there were so-called street roles you could play that didn't require anything except "doing what comes naturally." Sidney said to me, "If you're not hungry and you don't have kids to feed, don't rush to Hollywood because they will only ask of you what you are, and not that you grow."

In that special off-Broadway world, the black actor had as much of a chance as anyone else. It was the democracy of the frontier. The off-Broadway social consciousness gave me and other black actors, as well as black directors and writers, an unexpected freedom to work at our craft, to find our own pathways. The Greenwich Mews Theatre had been home to actors regardless of race, practicing "color-blind casting" as early as 1952. It was for me, I see in retrospect, a stroke of great good fortune—that confluence of a new kind of experimental theatre and my own commitment to the stage. In the off-Broadway theatre, I received the gift of vital material and colleagues, and receptive audiences. All of that allowed me to tap deep into my energy, and if, as someone said, I dazzled off Broadway, it was because off Broadway nourished me and gave me a place to do my work.

I had left *The Blacks* in the fall of 1961 to play a featured role in Josh Greenfield's new comedy, *Clandestine on the Morning Line*, at the Actors Playhouse off Broadway. We opened to mixed reviews on October 30, with general praise for the cast but criticism for the play—"some likable characters interrupted by a story," as the *New York Post* said on October 31, 1961. We didn't last long, and when we closed, I got a role in another experimental drama, Jack Gelber's *The Apple*, which opened at the Living Theatre in early December.

"Experimental theatre with a vengeance," Howard Taubman wrote in his *New York Times* review. He said the play seemed "to stagger along the thin line that divides comprehensibility from gibberish." Gelber was unabashedly avant-garde.

"I am a failure," Walter Kerr wrote in the *New York Herald-Tribune*. "I did not hate 'The Apple.'" Acknowledging that Gelber wished to "alarm, shock, revolt and emotionally inflame" his audience, Kerr went on to say that "there is a case to be made for the effort. Most of our theater is conventionally dull, and we go to it as placid dullards. Hate is at least an emotion. To hate is a verb. Something active might happen."

The Apple did not last long either, but the experience fed me, even though I perceived a good deal of chaos in the play itself and in the working atmosphere. Where Gene Frankel had been a subtle, encouraging director, Julian Beck and Judith Malina intentionally allowed a "freedom" which sometimes bordered on anarchy. But I felt then as I do now that you play each scene of a play for itself, for all it is worth, and if you can do that with concentration, energy, and commitment, the scene works itself out.

I had played a range of characters that year, and I was willing to take chances. I had nothing to lose, although I knew that I had to watch myself very carefully. I was getting into characters so far out that I was not sure I could still create a believable human being on stage. I had to balance one type of drama with another, and I was beginning to get more steady offers for work in the theatre, so my range of choices expanded at the same time.

Early in 1962, I auditioned for a role in a new play written by the West Indian playwright Errol John and directed by George Roy Hill. I got the part of Ephraim in *Moon on a Rainbow Shawl*, Errol's play chosen by Sir Alec Guinness, Peter Ustinov, and other judges as the best of two thousand entries in a competition in England. The predominantly black cast was exciting to work with—Vinnette Carroll, Ellen Holly, Bill Gunn, Cicely Tyson, Melvin Stewart—and Robert Earl Jones. The program notes did not mention that we are father and son, but did cite Robert Earl's professional debut in *Herod and Mariamne* with Katharine Cornell and his Broadway debut in *The Hasty Heart*.

Robert Earl and I already had a history of jinxes when we set out to work together in a play. We both had small parts in a musical until I was fired because I couldn't dance. We both had gotten parts in *The Pretender*, which was written with many compact, dense, rhetorical speeches. Robert Earl had a problem with the complexity of the language, and Herbert Machiz let him go and replaced him with Roscoe Lee Browne, who is a master at languages and speaks several fluently. Roscoe is a diminutive man who does not evoke the power my father has, but he was ideal for the role. Robert Earl and I both got parts in *Taffy*, and managed not to get fired, but the producer ran out of money before the play even went into previews.

The shadow of the blacklist days blotted out some chances for my father to work then. When I got my first television role, there was a part for a father, and the director said, "Why don't you take this script home and let Dad read it. See if he wants to play the father."

We were both cast in *Infidel Caesar*, a modernized production of *Julius Caesar* set in Castro's Cuba, with Caesar embodying Castro. The production was quite a mess, despite some wonderful actors— John Ireland and Ramon Navarro. I felt blessed, not jinxed, when the production closed prematurely.

Before I even got home with the script, there was a telephone message retracting the offer. The director had checked the *Red Channels* and learned that my father should not be hired.

Thankfully, the jinx was broken with *Moon on a Rainbow Shawl*. I thought it was a wonderful play, and so did almost everyone who saw it. The setting was Port-of-Spain, Trinidad. I played a bus driver trapped in my life. Ellen played my girlfriend; Vinnette, my mother;

Robert Earl a cricket player, my boyhood hero. He and I had one scene in which age and youth clash, and we had to confront the way changing times affect the realities of the black man's burdens. Robert Earl got fine reviews for his performance, and he well deserved them.

I remember one night Robert Earl went blank on stage. He lifted his hands in a beautiful gesture, as if he were clearing cobwebs from his face. The gesture was organically connected to his acting, but I knew he was in trouble. We got through it, and afterward, the director asked me if my father had a drinking problem.

"I don't know," I said. "He has and he hasn't." Robert Earl is still a health fanatic. He has run the New York Marathon successfully three times—in his eighties. He is essentially a teetotaler, but when he does drink, he does not handle alcohol very well. Every once in a while he will indulge and drink sometimes as a refuge. But he has no way of dealing with it. I think that is what happened to him that night on stage.

The play was a successful experience for him. Originally, Claudia McNeil was cast as the leading lady. She was fresh from her success in *Raisin in the Sun*. I never knew why she left our show, but she was the only actor to show up for rehearsal in a genuine fur coat. Perhaps her ego was a bit out of place. Eventually, Vinnette Carroll took over the role. She worked so beautifully with Robert Earl that later they were hired to play together in *The Sting*.

Moon on a Rainbow Shawl had run for a year in London, but not nearly that long off Broadway in New York, yet our short run was not because the play was a failure. It got unanimously good reviews. For the producer, it was a bit of an economic experiment. He had set out to prove that you could produce an off-Broadway show with the petty cash budget of a Broadway show. Once he had achieved that, he had no interest in putting money into publicity, and the production died.

Back in those days, I nervously read some of the reviews. It was a surprise, even a shock, to find my name and picture in the newspapers in New York. My agent, Lucy Kroll, began to keep press books on my career, and years later I sat down in her apartment in New York and showed those books to my mother Ruth as a belated way of sharing my career.

Walter Kerr praised Errol's writing, and the cast's performance. Ellen and I played together "magnificently," he wrote. There were richly deserved raves for Vinnette and Cicely. The *New Yorker* critic found me "magnetic," but puzzling— not "entirely at ease on the stage or entirely in the play, possibly because he has not yet learned to handle his own dramatic power, or possibly because so far no director has shown him how to handle it. I think he is a potential star but not yet quite an actor." Jerry Tallmer wrote that our company gave the best ensemble performance then in New York. He had liked my work in *The Blacks*, Tallmer said, but with reservations. He thought that I had grown as an actor since then. He suggested that I was the most "dynamic young talent now at work in New York." All this was rewarding and discomfiting at once. The chemistry of cast, director, and material deserved the credit for our success. Howard Taubman correctly noted that Errol had "charged his play with the truth and pathos of life. . . ."

I won the first award of my career in 1962. The Theatre World Awards, set up to "give deserving young performers a helping hand," were announced in May. Names on the list included, among others, Robert Redford, Elizabeth Ashley, Brenda Vaccaro, Sandy Dennis, Peter Fonda, and James Earl Jones. At about the same time, I was given the Obie for best actor of the 1961–62 off-Broadway season.

I knew then, and know now, the continual insecurity that an actor feels, despite prizes and awards, for I was never sure when I finished one role that there would be another. We had made a modicum of progress, but there were only 168 black actors employed on Broadway during the 1963–64 season, and only 116 black actors working off Broadway. I wondered then, in a newspaper interview just after the Obie was announced, why Arthur Miller or Tennessee Williams had not written about black people. I was even quoted as saying, "The actor, white or Negro, isn't done right by; he is not considered an important part of our society. . . . Actually, the Negro has something the white actor doesn't, a lever, an opening. He can holler. He can say to a producer: 'Do you mean you don't have a job for me because I'm a Negro?' If the white actor can find a lever he should and he should use it. And that goes for all actors, the midget, the one-armed actor, I don't care. They should coerce, yell, and use any weapon they can find. And this is not just to get jobs, but to get plays written for them."

The summer of 1962 found me back in Central Park, playing the Prince of Morocco in *The Merchant of Venice* with George C. Scott brilliant as Shylock; and Caliban in *The Tempest*, with a wonderful cast including Charles Durning, Abe Vigoda, Kathleen Widdoes, and Mitchell Ryan. In the fall, I joined a new off-Broadway ensemble company, the Writers' Stage. Our purpose was to discover and produce new works by American writers and to build an acting company which would nurture writers, actors, directors, and designers. We took over a small theatre on East Fourth Street, and set to work on our first production, *P.S. 193*, a play by David Rayfiel. I played a terrorist, an angry, frustrated veteran of ten years' service in the Army and combat in Korea. The play sought to examine the personal as well as national repercussions of the violence of war. It was not a success, although the critics were kind to our director, André Gregory, and to several of us in the company. Deric Washburn's *The Love Nest*, our second effort, was even less well received, but at least we were pioneering. We happened to open on the night of the "missiles of October," at the peak of the Cuban crisis. People, critics included, were more interested in whether there would be a world left tomorrow than in an angry little anti-war play.

Somebody called me a one-man stock company in those days. I was testing myself, trying every different kind of role I could get. In 1963, film director Stanley Kubrick had come to see George C. Scott

play Shylock in Central Park when he was casting *Dr. Strangelove.*
Kubrick also saw me playing the Prince of Morocco: "I'll take that
black one, too." I got the role of Lieutenant Lothar Zogg.

Not only did I have my first part in a movie, but I got to make my
first trip to Europe. It was wonderful to live briefly in London, but I
was homesick. Eva Weith of the Lucy Kroll Agency kept watch for
theatre parts for me to step into once the filming was completed
abroad. There was a chance to go back into the company of *The
Blacks* for a run in Chicago, and to play the lead in *Othello* at the
Corning Summer Theatre in Corning, New York. Joe Papp and
Gladys Vaughan offered me the chance to play in *The Winter's Tale.*
By overseas letters, there was discussion of my playing the part of
Polixenes, King of Bohemia.

I really wanted to play the role, but I knew that it had "socio-
ethnic illogicalities," as I wrote in a letter to Eva and Lucy. Joe and
Gladys would have to decide if casting me in that traditionally white
role would stretch the idea of unorthodox integrated casting too far.
Here is some of what I said:

> There are two major problems [in casting a black actor as
> Polixenes in *Winter's Tale*]: the racial purity of Perdita [daughter of
> Hermione, wife of the King of Sicily] and the question of whether
> Florizel [son of Polixenes] is cast Negro or not. On the first—since
> Perdita is obviously white this hangs up Leontes' jealousy logic.
> This can be viewed as weakening the jealousy aspect *or*
> strengthening it. It weakens it in that it makes Leontes' logic
> flimsy—makes him more a madman. In staying he could not *look* at
> the child. But therein lies a possibility of strengthening the truth
> about jealousy—a father in a maternity ward who suspects his wife,
> has become sick over the prospect that the child is *not* his, *would*
> dread looking, would rather have the truth buried rather than know.
> His suspicion is easier to bear than the truth, *should it be so.*
>
> The question of Florizel (if he is cast white, the point of
> Polixenes being Negro is negated—the audience is being asked to

ignore colors altogether) has more ramifications, if he is a Negro son of a Negro Polixenes, when it comes to his relationship to Perdita. I've discussed this with Gladys. She is a bit afraid it would look as if the Festival were promoting inter-racial relationships between teenagers (which, I agree, is a big bugaboo). There are problems of social illogic: it is valuable to have Bohemians, racially different from Sicilians, but, historically, "Bohemia" was Slavic. Besides, would one bother to cast all Bohemians as Negroes? Hardly.

One thing causes me to favor this, however. Illogical as it was, when I did MacDuff this spring, it made a great deal of difference to the non-white students of greater New York. They "dug" it. And the New York Shakespeare Festival has some obligation to non-white New York. Shakespeare, after all, is public domain. All in all, I'm making one final appeal in *favor* of a Negro Polixenes. I'd love to play it with an eye, cynical though it is, to the social hypocrisy that we are all prone to.

I did not get to play Polixenes. I was assigned the role of Camillo instead.

Before I returned to the United States, I had a memorable experience in a theatre audience. I went to see Paul Scofield play *King Lear.* Elated, I wrote to Lucy about it:

For the first half hour I was worried. Everyone, including Scofield, poked about finding their characters. *Then,* when Lear is rejected by Goneril and he *up-ends* the banquet table in a childish rage, it all began to happen and I was completely *"had"* from that point on. His Lear is an ass, an old fart with nothing to do but cavort with his hoods! This takes the onus off the two bad daughters' usually unmotivated meanness. I didn't sympathize with Lear, but I thoroughly believed him. Scofield's careful, methodical, moment-to-moment building of the character allowed Lear to breathe the same air I was breathing. Scofield is almost detached as he works, never "involved" in the sense we know, but constantly *presenting* reality. He was never bound by or limited by his own involvement. Some people see this as laziness on the part of the actor, but, as an actor myself, I find the man profound.

After another summer in Central Park, I went back to *The Blacks* with most of the original cast to help celebrate the one-thousandth performance of the play. In the fall of 1963, it was the longest-running off-Broadway play in New York. Roscoe Lee Browne was there in fine form, telling the press the story of how one night a man in the audience stood up menacingly and threatened to punch him in the nose. Roscoe started to remove his coat, and then put it back on. "I like to look chic when I fight," he said disarmingly. The audience burst into laughter, and the would-be assailant laid down his anger.

I had been in and out of the cast probably seven times by 1963, and I found the play even more relevant than when it first opened. It had been hailed as a "record-smashing off-Broadway show" which moved "its shocked audiences to tears [and] terror." Many of us in the cast thought the significance of *The Blacks* was heightened by the 1963 March for Freedom in Washington. This drama truly resonated in its time. Critics in 1963 found the show "better and even more timely than when it opened in 1961."

One horrible Sunday that year, four little black girls died in the bombing of a Birmingham, Alabama, church. We were scheduled to perform *The Blacks* on the afternoon of that tragic event, and the show went on. I had a line to speak: "In my eye I trotted out a big parade of our warriors, diseases, alligators, amazons, straw huts, cataracts, hunts, cotton, even leprosy and even a hundred thousand youngsters who died in the dust." When the time came, I took a liberty with the text, saying, "And even four little girls who died in a Birmingham church."

Someone there remembered that the audience sat, shattered.

I enjoyed my first significant television role that fall on George C. Scott's television series, "East Side, West Side," on CBS. One positive experience with another actor could lead to other roles. George and I had already played together on stage and in the movies. A wonderful script and cast brought us together now on television. The script was *Who Do You Kill?* by Arnold Perl, and Cicely Tyson and Diana Sands were in the cast. It took network courage in 1963 to air a "message" drama about racial issues, and this script was designed to reveal the harrowing reality of life in the ghetto. Diana played my wife. Our child, bitten by a rat in our one-room slum apartment, suffers a cruel death. The episode was reviewed as "a moving love story set in the Harlem slums, a story of Negroes caught in the cross currents of today's struggle for better housing, better jobs, a more dignified way of life. It was a tragic story and a humanizing one. . . ."

I closed out that richly productive year in an Equity Library Theatre production of Norman Rosten's play *Mister Johnson* and James Saunders's play *Next Time I'll Sing to You*, with Estelle Parsons. There is an interesting bit of history attached to *Mister Johnson* and me. A couple of years earlier, I was cast in the play to double as a village native and a young native African policeman in cutout trousers and a pith helmet. This was actually the first Broadway show I was ever cast in. Earle Hyman played the lead, and I was going to be his understudy. As a village native, I was part of the chorus line and would have to do a lot of dancing. The choreographer called a meeting of all the young men up for parts as dancers. As she walked in front of the line, she stopped and looked at me.

"You can't dance, can you?" she said. I confessed that I had never had any training. "Thank you," she said, and that was it. I was fired. Now, in 1963, I got the lead in the play—and without having to dance a step.

Neither of our plays succeeded in running for long, but I found my face looking out at me from the pages of *Newsweek* in the issue of December 2, 1963. "The Dynamo," they called me. The article pointed out that I had worked in eighteen plays in thirty months. I don't know whether this fact came from me or from their research department, but they also reported that, at age thirty-two, I earned "less money than the average off-Broadway stagehand." I had never, the article said, "in any one year earned as much as $4,000." The reporter correctly noted that I lived within my means, in a cold-water flat on Manhattan's Lower East Side. My rent, according to *Newsweek*, was $13.80 a month. I remember it as $19. Then they had this to say about my daunting, exhilarating struggle off Broadway:

> Jones has never been guilty of underplaying; he invariably comes on strong, often effectively, but sometimes too strong. In play after play, he tromps on stage like a wild pony and, with a broad, irresistible grin, communicates his own pleasure at being there. Then he pounces upon the audience with his thunderous voice. . . . Up to now, most of Jones' best work has been in comedy. "I'm beginning to accept that I'm funny in spite of myself," he says. . . . Offstage, Jones is totally different, serious, quiet, controlled. He even looks smaller than his 6 feet 1. [Actually, I'm 6 feet 2 inches tall.] "I tend to come off much more civilized," he says. . . . On the GI Bill, he studied at the American Theater Wing, then began playing spear carriers in Central Park. After several walk-ons on Broadway at $125 a week (he has since studiously avoided making so much for so little work), he was called to read for "The Blacks," and bulled his way to success.
>
> Asked to project himself into his future, he stretches his imagination, smiles, and says: "I might even become a star." Then with a shrug, he adds: "But I'll never be a rich actor."

10.

OTHELLO

OTHELLO: Speak of me as I am; nothing extenuate. . . .
OTHELLO, *OTHELLO, THE MOOR OF VENICE,*
ACT V, SCENE II

I first met Othello in New York in my father's house. I was twenty-four then, a man grown, I thought, but a stranger to my father, as he was to me. We were trying to find each other. The father-son dialogue was not working. He could not find the words to talk about the past, about his life or my childhood. It was clearly too painful for each of us. It must have seemed uncanny to him, this twist of fate, that the son he did not know at all, this stranger from an old world had chosen to take up his "business."

The Moor had come to watch over us. That character was to be the one thread of reconciliation between us—not Mississippi, or the farm, or Ruth. There was no dialogue about these, but only about Shakespeare's *Othello*, which gave us a scripted language we could share.

Othello stood there waiting for me one afternoon when I came home from the American Theatre Wing with an assignment to work on Hotspur's speech in *King Henry IV, Part One*. "Read it to me," Robert Earl said. He got very excited as he listened. What impressed him was not my ability to speak the lines—language was one of his own weaknesses—but I think he saw me striking flint with the character's emotions. That was his forte. When he saw me working that way, Robert Earl immediately introduced me to the man standing there in the shadows, and started to fill me with his visions of Othello.

Although Robert Earl has himself played Othello only twice that I know of, both workshop productions, he understands Othello better than anyone I know. The character has been an obsession for him, the greatest challenge imaginable for an actor. Yet ironically, the standards he has set for himself have held him back. Robert Earl has never found the director who could take him far enough into the heart of this enigmatic character without tripping him on the snares of language. Directors have forced him to step back, to surrender his innate emotional awareness of the role.

I sometimes wonder, too, if Robert Earl has not let his overidealization of the role keep him from moving on to do other roles.

My father's strength is his intuitive, emotional understanding of Othello's character, caught in what critic A. C. Bradley calls the "most painfully exciting and the most terrible" of Shakespeare's tragedies.

Robert Earl has always been convinced that *Othello* cannot work unless Iago masters the art of persuading the audience that he is believable, that this complex, seemingly evil "split personality" is really, after all, a good man somehow gone wrong. The audience must say, "Yes, I see, Iago is a good man. He is not really a villain." Iago goes through something terribly painful—not contrived, not mock pain—when he tells Othello that Desdemona is not what she seems. The audience has to say, at least momentarily, "Iago is playing the devil's advocate here." It is as if Iago says, "Everyone around me talks about love, love, love, nothing but love. What is this love? I do not believe in it. I must challenge them, protect them from deluding themselves." We must be led to believe that from the depth Iago is trying to serve, to do something useful.

Robert Earl sees that the odds are against Othello because, unlike Iago, he never speaks directly to the audience. He speaks only soaring poetic soliloquies from his heart to God. Iago, on the other hand, speaks directly to the audience, confesses to them his secret self. He says to them, after he has convinced *us* otherwise, "I hate the Moor."

My father spoke to me in those early days about Othello's nobility of presence and soul. "If you are going to play Othello," he would tell me, "you have to come to him strong and clean." I believe it has been said that Othello "has greater dignity than any other of Shakespeare's men." If you understand that, you will come to understand the character—and your *own* role in life. In a way, this was the most fatherly thing he ever said to me about moral and ethical responsibility, on or off stage.

I intensified my assault on the mountain of *Othello*. It was a daunting task, full of false starts. It was a trial by fire. I could see the possibility that this play would always be as unresolved for me as my relationship with Robert Earl.

I have played Othello at seven different times in my life in the theatre, beginning in Michigan in 1956, when I was twenty-five. The last production opened at the Winter Garden Theatre in New York in 1981, when I was fifty.

At Manistee Summer Theatre we had only one week of rehearsal. I was fresh from my beginning year of study at the American Theatre Wing. We all knew it made no sense to try to produce a Shakespearean play during tourist season in a summer stock theatre, but our director, Madge Skelly, liked to try. I had the reckless daring to try it, too. We naïvely assumed that we would come to the first rehearsal with our lines learned. I remember that Pam Printy— Desdemona—came prepared, but I had memorized only my major scenes, and not the connecting speeches.

We put our hearts into that summer production of *Othello*. Don Garner, the resident leading man, played Iago. I was the stage manager and stage carpenter, as well as Othello. The set designer was a truly gifted young woman to be found in a summer stock company. I remember walking into the theatre one day to find her working on a cutout of the spires of Venice.

"Well," she said. "This has got to serve as Venice and Cyprus. I want to give the look, also, of a Moorish temple dome. These spires look like penises, too. I hope the people of Manistee County don't come in and sit down in their seats and say, except subliminally, 'Ah—penises.' All that great animal energy between the characters gives rise to the horned beast, the green-eyed monster of jealousy, the flames."

I have vivid memories of that first *Othello*. I fell in love with Pam Printy, my Desdemona, and I got to wear the suede boots that William Marshall had worn when he played Othello in 1953 in New York. Bill Marshall was tall and handsome, one of the most visible black actors of the fifties. He had a deep voice, a powerful stage presence, much sound, less fury. He considered himself the heir to Paul Robeson's mantle. Robert Earl would have made a better Othello, even though Bill's success in a New York production of the play led him to Stratford, England, to replace Paul Robeson, who had been denied a passport. When Paul was finally granted permission to make the trip, Bill withdrew. So I was wearing the boots of the man who almost wore the boots that Robeson wore. The boots didn't help a whole hell of a lot.

My high school teacher, Professor Crouch, had been such a man of poetry, including the poetry of Shakespeare, that he couldn't imagine someone not enjoying speaking those great words. "Read Emerson," he told me. "But speak poetry." Two other things he could not imagine: one was going blind and not having memorized vast portions of beautiful poetry surely enough to recite them from his heart, and the other was not being able to speak poetry out loud. It was that second concern that drove him to the insights which so encouraged me to recover my powers of speech.

In the early days, I was still grappling with the harsh reality that when a role on stage evoked intense emotion, a speech "overload" could bring on my stuttering, or resurrect the Southern inflections of my childhood voice. I had my struggles with what Whitman called the "barbaric yawp." It always threatened to sabotage me. Still there is that tendency, if you find yourself with a weakness, to muscle it until it becomes your strength.

Othello's language is a soaring challenge, but I should not attribute my difficulties solely to my fear of stuttering. It is far more complex than that. The true test lies in unraveling the meanings of the words in the play.

I once heard the director Tyrone Guthrie say that no matter what an author writes, no matter how extensive his research or how brilliant his characters, the play itself is only the tip of the iceberg: a dynamic character in a play is a creature of the natural world *within* that play. In the larger universe of the drama, an actor may be able to go way beyond what even the author conceived.

When I had worked on Othello again in Tad Danielewski's workshop, Tad drew me deeper into Othello's complex psyche. But he encouraged me to probe the evidence of the text, and like Robert Earl, was more interested in the organic workings of character than the trappings of language.

"Forget the political argument about whether Othello is a barbarian or a blackamoor or Semitic," Tad told me. "Just deal with the evidence Shakespeare has given you."

Othello came from a fine life. As he tells Iago in Act I, scene ii:

> . . . *I fetch my life and being*
> *from men of royal siege; and my demerits*
> *May speak unbonneted to as proud a fortune*
> *As this that I have reach'd. . . .*

With Desdemona, Othello has regained that lineage for a moment. What happens here is a reenactment of the theme of paradise lost, paradise regained—and paradise is a key word for the Muslim people. Othello was born in paradise in another world. But then "chaos" descended. Through Desdemona he has rediscovered this paradise. He cannot risk losing it again.

What is Othello up to? What is his purpose, his motive? An actor's first task always is to assess the character's intention. "To build Othello, you first have to unbuild him, according to the clues in the language of the play," Tad told me. "Othello is a great general, but that is not what he set out to do with his life. His purpose is not to be a great warrior. He desires peace and love, respite from chaos. He desires progeny. That is in the text, often totally ignored, because people have other agendas. 'The fountain from the which my current runs,/or else dries up . . .' That is one reason he marries Desdemona. He seems to say, 'This woman and I will create a new generation.' It is part of his life's mission."

There are times, at least by implication, when Othello has been presented as a neutered male. And most productions of *Othello* lead to discussions of his sexuality. To what extent is he the aggressor? Has this been a wooing—or a seduction? Is the marriage consummated? Is Othello too old to be virile? Even I dallied at one time with the nonsensical theory that Othello was a virgin. I think the racial undercurrents make it uncomfortable for some directors and critics to confront the reality that Othello is a sensual, sexual black man married to a white woman.

Othello, Tad showed me, is living through a phase of his life which seems to resurrect some earlier one. "Perdition catch my soul," Othello cries. "But I do love thee! and when I love thee not/Chaos is come *again*." He has gone through this before in some other time and place, before the play ever begins. A man of privilege and order is thrown into slavery—which for him is turmoil. He climbs out of slavery by becoming a warrior and survives the destruction of war. He becomes a general, finding bonds and brothers in Cassio and Iago, expert killers, mercenary soldiers. Where is our next war, they want to know, for war is their way of making a living.

Suddenly, Othello finds himself in the house of a cultured man in Venice, a man who likes to hear him tell his stories. He is invited back; he sees what he has been missing since he left the palace as a child. There is a fresh revelation: Othello does not like killing. He does not want to be a warrior. He desires the bliss of this civilized life. What he fears most is being thrown back into chaos. Desdemona and her love are the epitome of this bliss. To lose her is to relapse into turmoil. To lose her is, ultimately, to lose himself.

In the summer of 1963, Dorothy Chernuck directed me in *Othello* at the Corning Summer Theatre in Corning, New York. I was still too slow and heavy with the words. Sometimes my concentration on the language overwhelmed the other aspects of my performance—movements, interactions with the other characters. Again I realized that Othello demanded all the skill I could summon. I had a new appreciation for that wise old tale that Shakespeare might have told to Richard Burbage, "I am going to write a play that is going to bust you."

In Corning, Dorothy Chernuck worked hard with us; we had only two weeks to rehearse, which was far from enough. She set the production in modern times, in modern dress. We gave a kind of Green Beret version of *Othello*, and it was distracting. When I later saw Richard Burton's modern dress production of *Hamlet*, I finally realized what critic Elizabeth Hardwick was getting at when she said of an earlier play I acted in, *Danton's Death*, that to overlook the culture and context of the times is to do the audience a disservice by denying them relevant. It is not that Shakespearean plays were always costumed authentically, even in Shakespeare's time, but today, with the art of design so highly evolved, it is possible to re-create accuracy of time and place. Whatever you gain by placing period drama in modern context you lose on a larger scale.

"This is the castle of Otello." My gondolier, speaking surprisingly good English, pointed out an ancient structure straddling the bend of a canal in Venice. This was late in 1963, my first trip to Venice, but I had not come here in search of Othello. Other work had brought me to this beautiful city, but Othello suddenly overtook me.

"Otello's castle," the gondolier repeated, in case I had not heard.

"Oh, *sure*," I muttered. What better way to garner a bigger tip from a black Yankee tourist than to suggest he is seeing the home of black Othello.

"No, really. Otello," he insisted. "He was a character in an Italian novella. The novelist patterned Otello after a Moorish general who used to live here. Otello—little Otto."

Fortunately, Venice is a city fixed in time. Still so much as it was when Othello lived there. I now wanted to absorb the spirit of the place. I wanted the smells and sounds of it. I stayed away from group tours after that, and wandered around by myself, in constant motion, constant exploration. On one corner, there was a political rally. On another corner, there was a beautiful German artist peddling her paintings. I even bought one, just to get to meet her. The city's energy pulsated against the backdrop of its history. I had not come looking for Othello, but that first encounter with Venice brought me closer than ever to the Moor.

I was also getting an education in Shakespeare then thanks to regular work in Joe Papp's New York Shakespeare Festival. By 1963, I had worked in nine productions with him. The Festival gave young actors a steady continuum of work. It was Joe's dream to have a company return each year to work together, shape new productions together. Joe's lofty dream of Shakespeare in the Park could not offer major actors salaries that would tempt them to stay. Joe realized that very early, but for those of us not pinned down by heavy responsibilities, he offered a place where we could work each summer.

Often I turned down more lucrative work in the theatre so I could keep working with the New York Shakespeare Festival. Late in 1963, I gave up the chance to play my father's son in the movie *One Potato, Two Potato* because I wanted to play in *The Winter's Tale*. Robert Earl did not argue with me about this decision, but it did not seem to make sense to some of the other people in my life then. The film, one of the first serious, sensitive screen treatments of interracial marriage, was honored at Cannes. I would have played the lead opposite Barbara Barrie, with Robert Earl and Vinnette Carroll playing my parents. Bernie Hamilton played Robert Earl's son, and I stayed with Joe Papp. He was giving me better and more meaningful roles, and I did not want to interrupt that.

Once in a class at the American Theatre Wing back in 1955, an instructor asked me to identify Ira Aldridge. I had not then heard anything about that great nineteenth-century black American actor. He performed Othello to rave reviews in Great Britain and Russia in 1827, and audiences all over the Continent saw his interpretation of the role. He was never permitted to be Othello on any American stage. Only in the twentieth century would black actors in the United States be able to pour their energies into the challenge of Othello.

Since Ira Aldridge in the nineteenth century, the only black actor to portray Othello and make the play work was Paul Robeson back in 1943, in a production that ran longer than any previous Shakespearean play in America. (Actually, Earle Hyman played Othello shortly after I arrived in New York; I did not get to see him. William Marshall performed as Othello in 1953.) Although he did not play Othello for an audience on a Broadway stage, Robert Earl knew how to breathe life into him. Aware of this roster of actors who had engaged the Moor, I wanted to continue to grapple with Othello on my own.

December 25, 1963, brought me a wonderful Christmas present. The phone rang and it was Joe Papp, offering me the chance to play Othello in the summer of 1964. Immediately, of course, I said yes.

11.

OTHELLO IN THE PARK

This season has produced two major Othellos, *one in London with Sir Laurence Olivier that is justly celebrated, the other in New York with the Negro actor James Earl Jones, that is unjustly neglected. . . . On the one hand, we have the far-famed and lavish London production—on the other a modest, obscure but truly remarkable show that began in Central Park last summer and moved downtown.*

The American Othello, *for better or worse, is affected by our own contemporary state of history. The ancient story of a dark-skinned Moor married to a fair Venetian noblewoman has special meaning to us in 1964 as a drama of miscegenation. It reminds us, if only subliminally, of civil rights and race relations. . . .*

James Earl Jones, a fine actor, takes on the title role with an obvious sense of responsibility. He is representing the American Negro in a great role at a crucial time. As the Moor, he is tender, strong, jovial, patient, and, above all, intelligent. . . . I think Jones would do better, in the play's climactic scenes, to pull out the stops and blast forth as the powerful actor that he is. . . . My admiration for Olivier in no way lessens my admiration for James Earl Jones . . . within the limit of his historical circumstance, he is immensely moving. . . .

TOM PRIDEAUX, *LIFE*, DECEMBER 11, 1964

"*Suspiro del Moro,*" the Spaniard told me. We had just finished filming *Conan the Barbarian* in 1980. We were driving away from Córdoba, past the procession of hills beyond the city. The driver said again, "*Suspiro del Moro.*"

"We call the hills 'The Moor's Sigh,'" he explained. "The last Moorish king had to relinquish the keys of the city to his conqueror the Spanish queen. He was allowed to return to Africa after the defeat of his army, but when he got to the top of these hills, he turned back and looked for the last time at his beautiful city. He gave a deep sigh and wept. *Suspiro del Moro.* The Moorish queen mother, riding out of the city with the exiled king, saw the tears, and said in her language, 'You jerk!'"

Shakespeare created three characters who were Moors—Othello in *Othello,* the *Moor of Venice*; the Prince of Morocco in *The Merchant of Venice*; and Aaron the Moor in *Titus Andronicus.* The Prince of Morocco is pure fun. "Mislike me not for my complexion," he begins, and then he goes on in great detail about how he got so black and beautiful. Aaron the Moor is pure villain, a black Iago with less to say and more lives to wreck. These two are much more readily understood than Othello, who was, I like to think, a mystery even to Shakespeare.

Othello, the Moor, is a Muslim whose people came from Mauretania in North Africa, crossing over into Spain in 711. They conquered the Visigoths and established a lavish court at Córdoba. Moorish culture in all its splendor spread to Toledo, Granada, and Seville. The Moorish courts were marked by great wealth, culture, and learning. Córdoba fell in 1236 and, in 1492, Ferdinand V and Isabella took control of Granada.

Othello stepped out of this rich culture, then, a Moor in service to the Duke of Venice. He married Desdemona, daughter of a Venetian senator. Unknown to him, his most dangerous adversary is his trusted aide-de-camp, Iago, who seeks to disrupt Othello's marriage. Iago is the most dangerous adversary precisely because he is the man Othello trusts most.

Othello is, first and foremost, a stranger. He is not at home in the culture of Venice and Cyprus, the landscapes of the play. He is not a "noble savage," deficient in language and culture. He is much more comfortable in the filigreed walls I saw at the palace at Cordoba. He is a foreigner, a newcomer to a strange land, bringing with him his own culture and history and sophistication. His native tongue is Arabic, his second language, Spanish. Yet he is in Venice, where the language is Italian. Once, trying to get inside Othello's experience, I read the play in Spanish, a language I myself do not know at all. I read it without understanding a word of it, but it was of great value. I had studied Latin in high school, so I knew where the stress and emphasis should be. I wanted simply to hear the sounds and to hear the rhythms.

Every human being, I am willing to bet, has had the profound experience of being an outsider in some strange land. The experience is universal. I remember the pain it gave me as a child in those days of muteness in Michigan when I was called upon to introduce myself to someone I didn't know. You do not have to travel to a foreign country to be a stranger. That can happen to you at home, in your daily life.

Othello was quite literally a stranger, a Moor among Venetians, set apart by his culture as much as his skin. Western literature has often trivialized the experience of the foreigner, transforming it into some sort of romance or adventure, as pictured, say, in the story of Columbus landing on alien soil. The Western attitude is often chauvinistic: the civilized man feels superior to the native culture he encounters. Yet inevitably there is that moment when he has to become dependent on the will of strangers; no matter how superior he feels, or how superior historians might want him to be, at some point he has to depend on the actions and hospitality of his hosts.

Columbus came with the idea that his Christianity and his color gave him and his people superiority. Othello could have approached the Venetians with the same air of superiority. Yet he didn't; he became almost totally dependent on Iago, his lieutenant and his "host." Iago was his guide in this strange country, his interpreter in this new language.

So Othello brings with him a past, a persona, a world view, layers of experience. He is a noble Moor. He brings with him an instinctive gentility. Chauvinism aside, he has to assume that these Venetians are possibly of lesser manhood or culture or station. In addition, they may be less generous than he is, less aware. Othello does not walk into the world of strangers feeling dependent on their grace; he walks into it expecting them to be dependent on him for wisdom, for knowledge, for experience. When Othello speaks of all the places he has been, he is really speaking to a deprived people, saying, "I have had such privilege, to have been all over this world. If this experience I have been privileged to have does not give me the grace to be gentle with you, then life has wasted all these experiences on me."

That is what I began to understand about Othello. He is kin, on a heroic scale, to the giants. The chemistry of his experience and his character have made him so. He is a superior human being, but not a superman who would exploit others. He possesses grace.

My son Flynn once got lost in the woods in the country, and survived. That raw, private, personal experience made Flynn a better person than the child he was before he got lost in the woods. This was not because a badge was put on his breast, but because he survived and transcended that experience. Othello was a superior man because of his raw, private, personal experience. I am convinced this is a crucial element in understanding Othello's character: if you do not come out of your life experience with overflowing grace, then it all has been a waste. You have not really lived; you are but a ghost.

That 1964 production of *Othello* brought explosive clarity to my vision of the role. I remember hearing producer Joe Papp say, in that time of racial tension, that Othello should be tough and militant. He never said *angry*, but that was a popular concept of the militant black male in the sixties. Joe wanted me to play Othello tough, to meet hostility with hostility. The phrase "black rage" studded so many dialogues then. That did not define black people for me, but it was a popular concept—black rage and anger. You certainly heard it in political rhetoric then, and you heard it in music; as you hear it in rap now you heard it in jazz in the early days.

Our director, Gladys Vaughan, on the other hand, fought very hard to keep me from imbuing Othello with contemporary hostility. She saw him as a civilized, graceful man. She kept fighting for me not to hit "whitey" hard, but to overwhelm him with gentle speech, to overwhelm the Senate with gentleness.

Joe would say, "You are going to make him look like a milksop, like an Eisenhower with no balls. You are going to make him look like an appeaser. That is not going to make a very exciting dramatic hero." He argued for the militant, aggressive black male.

I found Joe's argument tempting in those volatile days of the sixties. It would have excited the contemporary audience of blacks and liberals to see such an Othello strutting his stuff up against "whitey." So my new surrogate mother and father figures confronted me with their conflicting visions of Othello—but I decided to try Gladys's interpretation. From the outset of our work together in the early spring of 1964, she directed me to avoid the trap of creating a character so defensive that he would never have fallen for Iago's duplicity.

"Then there has to be something more," I said. "If Othello is not hostile and defensive, what is his power?" Gladys, the daughter of a

Mennonite minister, expanded the conception in a crucial way: "You don't have to be religious about it," she told me, "but think that Shakespeare intended Othello to be a sun god. Think of Desdemona as the dis-demon, the antidemon, and think of Iago as Lucifer, the beautiful fallen angel."

Othello, then, became for me a sun god, open, expansive, strong, generous of spirit—Akhenaton, fourteenth-century B.C. king of Egypt, artist and pacifist, husband of Nefertiti and father-in-law of Tutankhamen, and prophet of monotheism, one god, the sun, who led him to build a "flower culture," a new capital where art and culture flourished, to the discontent of priests and warriors. Gladys led me to see Othello as that vibrant, benevolent, superior entity. There is no need for him to be defensive or physically threatening, or petty, or mean-spirited. He possesses immense inner strength and humility—grace. He chooses to live democratically with people. He does not seek to abuse his power.

I learned early on that you have to be in the hands of a good director. If you are going to do a tragic play that takes you and the audience on a painful journey, as all tragedies must, you have to be in such good hands that you know you are going to come out safely at the other end. It is much like a good sermon, if you want to compare the theatre to church, because sermons can deal with horrible, dangerous, threatening ideas and images. But if your minister is good, he will enlighten you in the end. That is what you count on. You need to be able to count on that enlightenment in the theatre, too.

Gladys was such a director. I have come to believe that a production of *Othello* and plays such as *Measure for Measure*, in the context of American culture, required a woman's sensibility and sensitivity. Women have directed this play far more effectively than men have. Women seem to perceive, and with more sensitivity, what the issues are, who the characters truly are. There are archaic laws and values at work in Shakespeare's plays, too, and women seem better able to cut through to the universal and timeless themes. Gladys saw clearly that Desdemona is the third and equal pillar in the structure of the play. Usually she is seen as merely an object, the prize people are fighting for. Most male directors do not latch on to the vital concept of Desdemona's equality.

Why does Othello kill Desdemona? "Get a divorce," most men would say. "Go on to something else. Why kill her—and yourself? It isn't worth it." For Othello, age is a factor in his response. For Othello, marriage is for life. "I have waited a long time to be married," he would say. "There is no other marriage for me."

We began to rehearse regularly with Gladys in March of 1964. Mitchell Ryan, a strong member of the company, was cast as Iago, the beautiful Lucifer; a newcomer to the New York Shakespeare Festival company, a Juilliard-trained musical comedy actress, just out of Bert Lahr's production of *Foxy*, was offered the role of Desdemona. Her name was Julienne Marie. Gladys led us deep into discovering the intricate relationships between Othello, Desdemona, and Iago. I had never worked in such profound detail on a role, and it was my best preparation yet for Shakespearean drama, or any other role until then.

As I look back, I see I had been working hard for eight years since I had played that first rough Othello back on the summer stage in Manistee, walking in Bill Marshall's suede boots. Now, between Gladys's skilled direction and the catalytic performances of this Iago and this Desdemona, my first real Othello was born. At last, I felt I had gotten inside his language, and into the interior chambers of his psyche. And the success of this summer festival production propelled us to a short engagement in Philadelphia, then to the Circle in the Square for an off-Broadway run in the fall of 1964.

Gladys had urged us from the beginning to probe the dialogue for all possible meanings, to let our behavior on stage grow out of our understanding of the feelings undergirding the language of the play. She enabled us to open up to each other and to the play, and to come to our own realization of the selfhood and motivations of our characters, each leaning on the other and threatening each other.

Desdemona leans on Othello, who leans on Iago, whom he trusts absolutely. His trust makes Othello vulnerable at many levels, and that vulnerability is essential to an understanding of him. He does not possess a modern Western black man's defenses against bigotry. Racism, even as it evolves in this play, is new to him.

By his insinuations, by his propaganda, Iago raises a question: Is Othello a savage? He deliberately utters slurs for Desdemona's father to hear:

> *Even now, now, very now, an old black ram*
> *Is tupping your white ewe. Arise, arise;*
> *Awake the snorting citizens with the bell,*
> *Or else the devil will make a grandsire of you . . .*

Iago goes on to tell Brabantio that his daughter and the Moor "are now making the beast with two backs." Brabantio, who has loved Othello, is the first to fall for Iago's intimations. Until that moment, no one has thought of Othello in this way. Iago's attack, fueled by panic, takes like quicksilver. Brabantio suddenly perceives Othello as a monster threatening his daughter. His paranoia is infectious, soon permeating the whole society, and leading to Othello's trial in the Senate chamber.

Is Othello a savage? All I had to do was go to the Alhambra in Spain to know that it could not be so. Ironically, the Alhambra is probably the one architectural treasure left in the Western world from Othello's time, when the Moors were strong warriors and conquerors in their own right. Whereas the Crusades wrecked the architecture and artifacts of the Moorish world, even in Islam, Spain preserved the Alhambra. When you walk into it, the answer to Iago's challenge is clear. From the moment your eyes rest on those exquisite filigree artworks and lattices, you see that this was whatever paradise meant to the Islamic people. This was a paradise on earth; Othello came from this rich culture, this sophisticated civilization. This is not a matter of embroidering history or of reinventing Shakespeare; it is simply the truth.

Othello and Desdemona reach out to each other across the chasms of color, culture, and age. There is a spiritual bond between them, and you have to find it in the play. Not only is Desdemona the most refined creature on the stage, but she has to be the strongest. And, conversely, not only is Othello the strongest general of all the armies, but he must also be the most refined. Consequently, when Othello and Desdemona meet, a kinship takes root and blooms.

I came to see a painful conflict in Othello. Here is a man torn, split down the middle, coming to feel that he has two wives—the good and lovely woman he cherishes, the Desdemona he knows; and the seductress and betrayer Iago describes to him, a Desdemona who is distant, unknowable. The madonna—or the whore. This clash leads Othello to anguish, and feeds his confusion, his pain and his rage.

I contend, in disagreement with other interpreters, that Othello is never a jealous man. Mere jealousy is an oversimplification. It is Iago who is jealous because of the twist of fate which renders him deprived. If Othello is seen as the jealous husband, the play is reduced to mere melodrama; instead, you have to create the dilemma which splits him: "I know exactly who Desdemona is; yet Iago claims to know another Desdemona." Only good/bad Iago could even conceive of a good/bad Desdemona.

When Othello begins to be confused about the truth, the dilemma overpowers him. Othello kills Desdemona not out of jealousy, but out of a tragic confusion verging on insanity. It is confusion enough to drive him mad. Dostoevski confronted such a split in his real life: he distrusted his wife, but he realized that the moment you accuse her of infidelity, the moment you announce your suspicion, you have demonstrated total lack of faith. If she is innocent, then you have betrayed her.

I had confronted this in my own life when I was playing Othello in summer stock in 1956. My Desdemona and I were in love. We had not consummated the affair—I was still shy, and a virgin, and so was she. But we became lovers in every other way. There was a party. Afterward, an attractive older man who had been there told me that my Desdemona had flirted with him.

"She tickled my ankles under the table," he said, reading provocation into that alleged gesture. I could never bring myself to ask her about it, but once that seed of mistrust was planted, I was profoundly confused. I never found a way to resolve that confusion and disillusionment.

If the truth be known, this other man was Robert Earl. What was heartbreaking was that I did not have doubts about my girlfriend so much as I had now doubts about my father. My disillusionment had primarily to do with him—the Iago in this piece. The victim, as we know from human nature, is most vulnerable to the person who is trusted most. That, in all its greater agony, was Othello's dilemma.

There are two classifications of distrust: one is when someone tells you he suspects someone whom you trust; the other is when you suspect someone yourself. Shakespeare's Leontes in *The Winter's Tale* is ridden with self-inspired jealousy. Othello is poisoned by someone else.

As we moved toward our October off-Broadway opening, Gladys Vaughan had to hire an understudy for me now that we were mounting a commercial production. She chose a young black actor to play a brother Moor. Every time Othello walked on stage, he was accompanied by this silent Moor. The audience wondered who he was—a younger brother who signed on as Othello's aide? A servant? A confidant? His presence was mysterious—and an intriguing reminder that Othello is in strange waters.

At the end of the play when Othello devises a way to commit suicide, we had this sidekick hand him the sword. The gesture fit the play, for as Cassio says after Othello dies, "This did I fear, but thought he had no weapon; /For he was great of heart." In the shadows stood that haunting enigma, the other Moor.

I have also tried to look at this drama through Iago's eyes, as well as Othello's. I began to see that the key to the deepest tragedy of *Othello* is that Iago feels dispensable, expendable. He feels worthless. He might be mumbling to himself, "Othello, the man who has the power, relies on me to be his guide, to interpret for him. Yet when I try to help him through his life, I am nothing. I get nothing. I get screwed." The bitterness grows and grows. It is a bitterness every modern person has got to understand—to be on the wrong end of the social pole, to be without privilege, on the shit end of the stick.

Iago is from the beginning a split personality. In one moment, he is a truly good person; in the next, something is eating away at him. Iago is like a Hamlet gone bad. It is curious that Laurence Olivier and other actors have explored the possibility that Iago is a latent homosexual. Mitchell Ryan got Gladys's permission to go full bore in that direction in our rehearsals, but discarded the choice. Legend has it that once when Ralph Richardson was playing Othello, the Iago character reached out to give him a kiss to open up the issue. Richardson shouted out, "What the bloody hell is going on?"

I do not think homosexuality is the key to Iago, nor do I think the play supports this theory. Like Gladys Vaughan, I still see Iago as a Lucifer figure, the beautiful fallen angel. You ask, then, why is he so corrupt? I do not make of him a Machiavellian villain. I do not see Iago as a man without remorse. Quite the contrary, I think he is full of remorse, burdened by the heavy yoke of conscience.

* * *

Yet for all this, Cassio is my favorite character in the play. He represents a certain finesse, culture, education. Cassio, Othello, and Iago are three brothers in the play, a formidable team in battle. Nevertheless, Iago and Cassio are not whole, not complete human beings. The only two complete people in the play are Othello and Desdemona, and they are only complete together. Together, they become one organic entity. Without each other, they stand alone, equally lonely. She cannot find a soul mate in Venetian society; he cannot find his soul mate anywhere else in the world.

Othello, I believe, was revered in his own world where there was no racism. He has no sense of inferiority as the Western black man sometimes has. This, in a way, invalidates Laurence Olivier's famous approach to the role, patterned after a Western black man he knew with all the paranoia, suspicions and defensiveness of a victim of racism.

I have always tried to learn from other actors and from directors. When I heard that Olivier was preparing Othello for the National Theatre in London at the same time that we were rehearsing for Joe Papp's 1964 production, I tried everything to get there to see Olivier, but was unable to. I had heard he played Othello in blackface and was fascinated by the dynamic of the defensive Western black man. He did not want to be upstaged by Iago, and he searched for all the bravado which would give his Othello the edge.

I am sure that his portrayal worked on stage. It was praised around the world. But it did not work on film. In film, the camera, not the actor's energy, determines what you see. While Olivier's individual creation is glorious, Frank Finley's transparent, Machiavellian Iago undermines the whole story, and Maggie Smith would have been more effective as Emilia the maid than as Desdemona.

I did get to England to see my friend Errol John do a production of Othello at the Old Vic. The production was lambasted by the critics.

Errol and I talked about the problem, about how the critics had dealt with him. He was convinced that the critics in England did not want to yield to an Othello who was a black African. They were willing, he thought, for Othello to be a Moor, a Semitic, a North African, but not a black African, sub-Sahara. Any purely black-skinned human being playing Othello, Errol believed, went against the grain of British sensibility, although I must admit, he himself was one of the most uptight, defensive Othellos I had ever seen.

Paul Robeson had three great advantages to his Othello—his magnificent person; the great director Margaret Webster; and the fact that in that war-torn world of the early forties, the warrior was clearly and universally perceived as hero.

I lived in Othello's skin most of that year. He brought me insights and a certain amount of notoriety as an actor. He brought me new and valued colleagues. We opened *Othello* in Central Park July 14, 1964, for nineteen scheduled performances. The production was booked into the Martinique Theatre in New York, to open October 12. We gave 224 performances there, and I was honored to receive the Drama Desk–Vernon Rice Award.

Joe brought Shakespeare to the Park and to the people by taking away the elitism often connected with the theatre. And the people loved it; they made it their own. The audiences were wonderful, coming back over and over again, even little children who should not have been out at night. Our audiences worked with us. Many of them had stood for hours in line in the hot sun, picnic baskets in hand. The tickets were free, first come, first served. They were getting an experience they did not have to pay for, and somehow seemed to feel more obliged to contribute to the experience. When they pay, you owe them. When they come in free, they owe you. They listened. Rarely did you hear the derisive laughter that often comes in the theatre when the audience cannot handle a certain moment of revelation or tragedy. These were genuine audiences engaged in genuine playgoing. They were fans of the whole company, not a single actor. They made us feel truly welcome, and we reciprocated.

Backstage, we worked prodigiously hard, and we often disagreed. Gladys and I argued one whole night long about the ending of the play. Why does Othello not take vengeance on Iago, I wanted to know. Shakespeare did not want that for some reason, Gladys observed. But even though Shakespeare did not write vengeance into the play, I contended that in the current atmosphere, it did not work for a black man to be forgiving. "You'll get yours—Leave you to heaven—" That attitude did not wash in the midst of the civil rights tensions of 1964, despite what Shakespeare may have intended.

I remember the Orson Welles film production. He showed us society, not heaven, taking vengeance. The film opens with Iago in a cage, subject to ridicule and trauma. The people carry him to the town square, taunt him, poke sharp sticks into his cage, humiliate him, and hang him. Welles could do that on film, but you cannot do that on stage. Gladys wisely chose not to try it.

Her direction resulted in a wonderful success for all of us, one of the most successful productions of *Othello* New York had ever seen. Joe Papp relished the success, but he would often try to take over a production, even from a director as effective as Gladys. Out of his responsibility as a producer, Joe tried to reclaim the production and impose some of his vision on it.

I appreciated the affirmation given our company by Tom Prideaux in *Life* magazine in December 1964, and his comparison of my Othello to Olivier's. "I've never heard Shakespeare done with more suspense and clarity than it is here under Gladys Vaughan's direction," he wrote, "with meanings, like meat from a nut, being pried out of every line." He thought our production was "on the whole better acted, perhaps better directed than the London *Othello.*"

12.

BEHIND THE SCENES

I think, on stage, actors are more vulnerable to one another. When you laugh and cry you see right into the other person, so it's almost natural to fall in love.

JAMES EARL JONES, INTERVIEW, 1968

What is more fun—to deny a myth or to admit it? I have always resented the implication and resisted the myth that I marry all my Desdemonas. But I have also rather enjoyed the fuss. I will concede that I have had a way of falling in love with my Desdemonas, but I've had more than ten Desdemonas, for crying out loud, and not all of those on-stage relationships led to consummation or marriage. Let me tell you the facts.

By 1964, at the age of thirty-three, I was, although not a man of the world, a much freer spirit than I had been at twenty or twenty-five. But I was not seriously involved with anyone when we set to work on that Gladys Vaughan production of *Othello*.

From the beginning, everyone in the cast was in love with Julienne Marie. We were all smitten. Julienne was married, so we could all safely indulge our fantasies. Mitchell Ryan was smitten—and he was as big a rogue as I was. His Iago was so effective in part because he respected Julienne so much. Later on, Judith Crist wrote that our production was a good one, and that what made it almost great was Julienne's performance. The critic noted that for the first time, Desdemona occupied her rightful place in Shakespeare's tragedy.

Julienne's talent and spirit made that true, and our adoration of her spilled over into the work. We loved her talent, grace, beauty, charm, voice—it was a spiritual phenomenon for all of us.

There was between Julienne and me an undercurrent that we did not for a long time acknowledge. Others saw it long before we did. Friends of hers came backstage after one of our performances. "What is going on up there between you and James Earl Jones?" they asked her.

"Nothing is going on," she said truthfully.

* * *

Gladys Vaughan had gotten us to find within ourselves the realities of whatever love and tenderness and caring meant to each of us. We all knew the complications for a production when cast members become romantically involved off stage. One problem that fellow actors who become lovers face is that the night after you first sleep together, you become so immensely self-conscious that it tears your performance apart. Suddenly new issues are at stake: the freedom to play lovers on stage is often richer than any courtship off stage, often deeper in expression and openness of feeling. You can allow yourself more vulnerability because you feel safe within the boundaries of the play; you do not really have to live the life to play it.

Long before Jane Alexander and I played together in *The Great White Hope*, we talked about what happens when two actors playing lovers on stage act it out off stage. We promised each other we would never do that. It was clear to us that we would jeopardize something on stage if we tampered with the relationship off stage. Yet we had to play it to the hilt on stage, and we did it so plausibly that Jane's mother was convinced, although it was far from the truth, that I was the man who had broken up her marriage.

One night, far into our production of *Othello*, I arrived at the theatre early to find Julienne sitting in the auditorium. The crew had not arrived yet, nor had the other actors. We were alone. I went over to say hello, and found her crying.

"What's wrong?" I asked her.

"I've just left my husband."

I was surprised. I thought, "We all have loved her. One of us has gotten closer to her than any of us thought was possible." I assumed she had left her marriage for Mitch.

"Do you love him?" I asked.

"Yes," she answered. "Can we go out after the show for a drink and talk about it?"

And we did. When we sat down to talk, I said, "Okay. Which one is it?"

"What do you mean, which one?" she asked me.

"You've left your husband. For whom—Mitch?"

"For you," she said.

I was stunned. I had never imagined that. That began our affair. I think Gladys honored it and was quite accepting of it, but our new relationship became a problem for some of the members of the company: it made them uneasy.

Julienne left the production later on to do a musical with Sergio Franco. When I look back at the publicity photographs of that 1964 *Othello*, I find something very curious. In the scene when I am strangling the Desdemona who was Julienne's replacement, Flora Elkins, it is clear that I am murdering her. Yet in the same scene when Julienne is my Desdemona, you cannot tell if I am killing her or if we are making love. The artist Ted Jacobs saw those photographs and did a large oil painting of Julienne and me in the death grip. "What is this?" he asked me. "Is this love—or is this death?"

Julienne and I began seeing a lot of each other during the time of her separation and divorce. We were comfortable together, but even when she was free again, I did not feel ready for marriage. For one thing, despite the success of *Othello*, I was by no means sure that I could earn a living in the theatre, and support a wife and family. So, for now, we were happy to be in love and together. As Othello said, "I cannot speak enough of this content;/It stops me here; it is too much of joy. . . ."

After the production began to wane, Gladys proposed keeping all of us together and decided to create a repertory company. She decided to keep us going by adding Bertholt Brecht's *Baal*. A big dilemma: Who should play Baal, Mitchell Ryan or me?

We discussed it democratically, despite the fact that Gladys and Mitch were in the midst of their own affair. I wanted the part of the renegade Bohemian poet Baal, as sensual as he was homely. He was lusty, bawdy, defiant, often idealistic in the midst of his depravity. But in the end, Gladys gave the role to Mitch and I didn't mind. We were a company, meant to function as a company, and I was happy to play Ekhart. Taking a supporting role, however, made it difficult, when there were larger roles available elsewhere. Lucy would say, "Why would you stay in this production playing a secondary role, after the great success of Othello?" But I played Ekhart through the spring of 1965 at the Martinique.

That summer we were back doing Shakespeare in the Park. I played a tribune in *Coriolanus,* and, then, with Joe Papp as director, appeared as Ajax in *Troilus and Cressida.* I also had a taste of soap opera, playing Dr. Jerry Turner on "As the World Turns."

Julienne and I had been living and traveling together for nearly three years when in 1967 I got the part of Dr. Magiot in *The Comedians,* a film based on Graham Greene's novel. Elizabeth Taylor and Richard Burton starred, with Sir Alec Guinness, Peter Ustinov, and Lillian Gish. We filmed in France.

From the beginning, racial issues made no difference to Julienne and me, although her family had their problems with our liaison. We fell in love with each other not because of or in spite of our color— but because of who we were. The theatre world was more welcoming of interracial relationships than society at large. We could come and go comfortably as a couple. Yet Julienne and I were suffering from the stress of two fledgling careers. It was inevitable that more and more often, our jobs kept us geographically far distant from each other. I knew I loved Julienne, but I still had great insecurity about supporting a family on the fruits of my work as an actor. I had early come to understand the urgency of focus and concentration in my work, and I did not want to jeopardize that discipline. I was still working on the unfinished business of my early life. For many reasons I was not ready to become a husband and father.

Nevertheless, we started talking about marriage while we were in Europe, and decided to have a small wedding in England. It would be unorthodox—beginning with the witnesses. We decided that each of us would ask a taxi driver to come and stand up for us before the English equivalent of a justice of the peace. We were all set.

But on the wedding morning, I woke up and said, "Julienne, I am just not ready for this."

She just stood there and listened to me. Then she said quietly, "Would you like to see what I would have worn to our wedding?"

She had chosen to wear a white lace miniskirt. She held it up in front of her, and we both cried.

With great sadness, we left each other. I went to Scotland, where we would have spent our honeymoon. She flew home. I tried desperately to reach her back in the United States, but she did not want to talk to me. Finally, I got through to her.

"What do you want now?" she asked me over the long-distance wire. "What do you want now that you've ruined the big moment?"

"Let's see each other and try to get this straight," I begged her. But I was working next in Europe, and then in Africa. She was working in the United States. It was hopeless, this geographical barrier. We had to say good-bye.

It took my baptism in the play *The Great White Hope* at the Arena Stage in Washington, D.C. in 1968 for me to accept that I was strong enough to handle leading roles, and therefore capable of earning the kind of living to support a family. I began to court Julienne again. I got her to visit Washington, D.C. after *The Great White Hope* closed, and I was doing a less demanding two-week reprise of Athol Fugard's *The Blood Knot*, with Robert Foxworth.

She said, "I have a chance to play Desdemona in the musical version of *Othello* with Jerry Lee Lewis and Bill Marshall in Los Angeles."

I said, "I have a chance to play *Othello* in a student production at the Goodman Theatre in Chicago with Len Cariou."

"That means more separation," she said. "I'm not promising to return to you if you expect us to be together after our journeys." In other words, she was telling me to make a commitment or get out of her life. I heard her, and I did not want to lose her again.

We were married by Judge Cornheim at the Criminal Court Building in Washington, D.C., with Don Grady and his wife, Svetlana, standing up for us. After we exchanged vows, we temporarily went our separate ways.

With Len Cariou as Iago, I went to Chicago's Goodman Theatre to take part in a student production of *Othello*, in 1968. John Reich was to direct Len and me in this *Othello*, and the student actress playing Desdemona was young, of course, with little life experience yet. She had such difficulty engaging the emotions of the character that the director chose to slap her one day to try to make her cry. I knew we were in trouble. From then on, Len and I just concentrated on making sure our scenes worked. The production had obvious weaknesses, and the designer created a kind of jungle gym setting which hampered us, but next to Mitchell Ryan, Len gave me the best time I have ever had in this tragedy.

I tried Othello yet again at the Mark Taper Forum in Los Angeles in 1971. This time I felt the production was profoundly flawed in spite of our director, John Berry, with whom I had worked successfully in *Claudine, Les Blancs,* and Athol Fugard's *The Blood Knot* and *Boesman and Lena.* John had been blacklisted during the McCarthy era, and had spent years as a result making films in Europe. *Othello* marked his reentrance into the Hollywood artistic community.

The recent film *Guilt by Suspicion,* starring Robert De Niro, was based on John's experience. During the blacklist days, when he learned that authorities were coming to arrest him for contempt of

Congress, he literally leaped over a fence and disappeared. He surfaced in the small French village of Haut-de-Cagnes where he was befriended by Ainge (Angel), the local shoemaker, who gave him a job and a place to stay. John eventually became a highly acclaimed film director in France and in the theatre in London and Paris, where he directed *The Blacks*.

John chose an interesting cast for *Othello*. Jill Clayburgh, still recovering from her breakup with Al Pacino, played Desdemona. She needed the kind of adoration and affirmation from her fellow actors that Julienne had enjoyed in our 1964 Central Park production. Somehow—probably because the director was not a woman—that did not happen for Jill. One of the premier classical actors of the time was cast as Iago.

John wanted a strong yet cooperative Iago. He considered Stacy Keach, but thought he might have an ego problem since John had not reaffirmed his strength in the Hollywood community. He consulted me about it, and said, "How would you feel if I use Tony Zerbe?"

"Fine," I said. "I like Tony." I knew Stacy to be a fine character actor; he and I had worked together in 1970 in *End of the Road*. But I thought of Tony as an equally effective classical actor and consented.

John was married to Margie Goldsmith, who had been Gladys Vaughan's assistant in the *Othello* production in Shakespeare in the Park. John considered Margie an authority on that production. I don't know if the success of that earlier *Othello* intimidated John, but I know he wanted to transcend it. He buried himself in his wife's notes, and before long, John became somewhat paranoid that I was not going to be able to give him an Othello different from the one I had achieved with Gladys. He was also worried because Tony Zerbe had done an earlier Iago in San Diego. I think John felt caught in a vise between the two of us. I don't know the extent to which he was right. I am sure that I wanted to hang on to some of the concepts I thought were valuable that I had discovered about the character. It made him uneasy, and I think Margie was feeding his paranoia.

Just as the production was about to open, John posed an alternative portrayal of Othello, making a good argument that one can harbor cynicism, thinking it but never saying it. He suggested giving Othello a sharp edge of latent cynicism, not expressed, but there. You are aware that he can cut and slash— but he exercises the grace of restraint. This conception of Othello harkened back to Joe Papp's defensive Moor, but John acknowledged that you have to find the subtle balance within the character and without, in his relation to Desdemona and Iago. You are aware of this sharp inner edge that can rip you apart, but the man has enough grace to spare you. The richest conflicts occur when one opponent does not push the other over the edge: he allows him to stay in the ring. That is the act of grace.

It was a fascinating possibility. It gave Othello one foot in the cynical world Iago occupies, but I knew it was troublesome. Unless you have the right Desdemona, you have to play Othello straight. Without the right Desdemona, what happens to love? And without love, what is the play all about? So the idea got lost.

Jill was vulnerable, but in the wrong way—more fragile than vulnerable. John ended up with three actors who terrified him in that he did not know how to get control of us. Soon the production fell apart. I remember stretching out on a bench in rehearsals one day. I had gone into psychotherapy by this time—mainly, I think, to sort out the scars of my childhood and resulting obsessive behavior. I thought, "If therapy taught me anything at all, I should stop this right now. I should get out of this mess." I remember lying on that bench and considering leaving. I thought, "What Shakespearean production could this cast do wherein we would all be happy, and the director would be happy, and we could keep our obligation to the theatre?" But I couldn't think of one.

There were many other problems. I could not believe that I went from the Chicago production with a "jungle gym" to a Los Angeles set with a modern ramp contraption just as cumbersome. True, John was an adventurous, daring director, eager to experiment. He allowed the set designer to build a ramp so that Othello could stride on stage as the conquering hero. The designer created complicated machinery. We had to live with this maze from the moment the play began until the arrival at Cyprus. In the opening scene, we walked on girders. Once Othello made his grand entrance, we went to interior domestic scenes—yet hemmed in by those girders and that machinery.

Tony and I liked each other, and we got along on stage, but unlike Cariou and me, we did not really help each other in performance. We did not lean on each other as strong pillars, the way Mitchell Ryan and I had done. Mitch and then Len and I energized each other in those earlier productions. In Los Angeles, Tony and I gradually pulled into isolated individual performances.

We opened to negative reviews, and Jill Clayburgh got the worst of it. But ironically, the young people of Los Angeles came to see the production, and through word of mouth, it became a sellout. One critic, hearing that the production was a success, re-reviewed the play, commending us for revitalizing, reexamining, and redirecting the play when actually, we had not changed a thing.

By the way—did I kiss Jill Clayburgh beyond the confines of that set? Not once.

PART FOUR

VOICES
CHOSEN

13.

THE GREAT WHITE HOPE

Man, Ah ain't runnin for Congress! Ah ain't fightin for no race, ain't redeemin nobody! My momma tole me Mr. Lincoln done that—ain't that why you shot him?

JACK JEFFERSON, IN HOWARD SACKLER'S,
THE GREAT WHITE HOPE (NEW YORK: DIAL, 1968)

"Jack Johnson would drive up and down the boulevard in his convertible, a black beret on his head, a cigar in his teeth, and two blond, blue-eyed women sittin' next to him. He was one bad man." So one world heavyweight boxing champion talked about the audacity and hubris of another.

The speaker was Muhammad Ali in Galveston, Texas, in 1985. He paid his own tribute to Jack A. Johnson, America's first black heavyweight champion, at a banquet put together by a white man, Johnny Valentine. Valentine organized the Jack A. Johnson Foundation in Galveston in 1984 because he considered Johnson the greatest fighter of all time, and he thought it was a shame that the people of Galveston Island, where Johnson was born in 1878, had not recognized this native son.

Johnson always loved fast cars. He died an ironic death from injuries in a car crash near Raleigh, North Carolina, in 1946. In the sixty-eight hard-packed years of his life, he had fought 113 recorded fights, the first in 1897 when he was nineteen, the last in 1945 when he was sixty-seven. In Sydney, Australia, on December 16, 1908, Johnson won the world championship by beating defender Tommy Burns so badly that the fight was called in round fourteen.

Johnson called his autobiography *Jack Johnson—In the Ring—and Out.* "My life, almost from its very start, has been filled with tragedy and romance, failure and success, poverty and wealth, misery and happiness," he wrote in 1927. "All these conflicting conditions that have crowded in upon me and plunged me into struggles with warring forces have made me somewhat of a unique character in the world today." He said he hoped his life story would be interesting of itself, but that it might "also shed some light on the life of our times."

His life is high drama indeed. As Jack Johnson told it,

... never in the wildest moments of my boyhood imagination did
I vision myself the champion fighter of the world, and the first man
of my race ever to attain that distinction. Never did I imagine myself
in the picturesque costume of a Spanish matador, a victor in the
bullfighting arena. . . . How incongruous to think that I, a little
Galveston colored boy, should ever become an acquaintance of kings
and rulers of the old world. . . . What a vast stretch of the
imagination to picture myself a fugitive from my own country . . . a
voluntary exile. . . . How utterly fantastic would have been the
thought that I should some day be plunged into romances and love
with white women in defiance of a treasured and guarded custom.
How far removed from my thought was . . . the tragedy of a prison
term in one instance and the death by suicide of one whom I greatly
loved. . . . These are but a few of the unusual events that have come
into my life. . . .

The drama of Johnson's life shed continual light on the society he
lived in. His parents, who had been slaves, were illiterate, and
struggled for economic survival in the rough port town of Galveston.
Jack had to leave school after the fifth grade to work wherever he
could, usually around the Galveston docks. There he learned to fight
out of necessity. Prizefighting was against the law in Texas, but so
popular that the law was only sporadically enforced. It was
paradoxically good and bad luck for twenty-three-year-old Jack
Johnson that he got arrested after a prizefight at the Galveston
Athletic Club on February 25, 1901. He lost the fight, and was
locked up in jail for nearly a month with the victor, Joe Choynski, an
experienced boxer. Choynski spent those days of incarceration in a
dank Galveston jail teaching Jack Johnson the rudiments of his sport.
The rest, as we say, is history.

After he won the championship in 1908, an event which set off
national race riots, Johnson was a flamboyant, highly visible

international figure. His signature was a wide grin, glittering with gold-capped teeth and a diamond inset in a back molar. And his appetite for those fast cars, dapper clothes, and beautiful women enhanced his notoriety. People offended by the reality of a black boxing champion searched for a "white hope" to reclaim the crown. Jim Jeffries, who had retired undefeated, emerged from retirement after seven years, at age thirty-five, to fight Johnson in the "battle of the century" on July 4, 1910. Johnson knocked him out in the fourteenth round of the fight.

In 1913, Johnson was convicted of violating the Mann Act, charged with transporting a woman across state lines for "immoral objectives." He chose to flee the country, exiling himself for seven years, and living openly in Europe with his white mistress. At last he came home to face his punishment—ten months in the federal penitentiary in Leavenworth. His 1915 fight with "the great white hope" Jess Willard was fraught with controversy: in an arena in Havana, Cuba, Willard knocked Johnson out in round twenty-six; Johnson would later contradict that outcome, claiming that he had been forced to throw the fight.

Playwright Howard Sackler wrote about Jack Johnson's turbulent life and career in *The Great White Hope*. For legal reasons, Howard named his boxer Jack Jefferson. He gave him a black mistress named Clara who represented several women of color, and a white mistress named Eleanor, who represented several of the white women in his life. He set the drama just before and during World War I.

In May of 1967, I was in France completing the motion picture *The Comedians*. Coincidentally, I was living in Haut-de-Cagnes in a flat over the shop of the shoemaker Aigne, the very same man who had befriended John Berry in his expatriation. Director Edwin Sherin forwarded to me the script of *The Great White Hope*. He and I had never worked together, but he had come backstage once during the 1964 production of *Othello* and we made a connection.

He treated me as if he had found a gold mine, had discovered a source of energy. Later on, he determined that that was the energy he needed in the character of Jack Jefferson. He offered me the part. He thought that my classical training would help me take on this monumental, epic role.

I knew immediately that this was a role I had to play: here was explosive drama, and poetry, and complex tragedy. Beautifully drawn on the page was a role of a lifetime. Lucy and I had a problem, though. She thought the play was old-fashioned, not avant-garde enough. We had just come out of the off-Broadway movement and the theatre of the absurd. "Are you sure you want to do this?" she asked me. "The play has to justify itself," I told her, "but this is a character I want to do."

As soon as I could, I traveled to England to meet Sackler and talk to him about the script. I was overweight, and Sackler introduced me to the trainer who had brought Olivier into shape for his Othello, a gymnast who prescribed exercises that were to begin my physical metamorphosis into Jack Jefferson. If I was going to play a boxer, I was going to have to look like one.

I heard that there were people who wondered if I was right for the part, thinking that because I was quiet and reticent in person I might not be able to unleash the hero's flamboyance and power on stage. Someone else took issue with my color. "James Earl Jones is brown," someone said. "He is not a full-blooded African-American, as Jack Johnson was." They thought another actor should have the role— perhaps Yaphet Kotto, who later succeeded me, or Brock Peters, who took the play on the road. They looked much more like Jack Johnson than I did. (The converse happened when Sidney Poitier played Thurgood Marshall, who was lighter-skinned than Sidney. But do you cast for body type alone—or for the ability of the actor to achieve the role?) Also, I had the advantage in that nobody had seen Jack Johnson on television, so few theatregoers knew what he actually looked like.

* * *

There were strands in my own life that I could weave into the web of
this role I was about to play. My father was a boxer-actor; he fought
his way out of Memphis, Tennessee, during the Depression. Fighting
had become a metaphor for his life. I have never been a boxer,
perhaps because I had no taste for it. Papa, my grandfather John
Henry, had told me all about the great hero Jack Johnson. We lived
in Michigan then, where Joe Louis had lived as a boy. When I was
about seventeen, my friends got hold of some boxing gloves. We
started playing around with them after farm chores, and before I
knew it somebody had knocked me down. I did not take kindly to
that experience. It ended boxing as an endeavor for me.

Besides, deeply embedded in my whole psyche was "do not
strike"—Papa's punishment for hitting Randy; my refusal to fight
the St. Louis muggers. Admonitions and discipline from my
grandfather had long ago curbed any reflexes toward physical
violence I may have possessed. Even Army combat training could
not reawaken that.

Before we went into rehearsals for the play, I toured in Eugene
O'Neill's *Emperor Jones.* Jack Jefferson and Emperor Jones shared a
certain hubris, a certain power which probably fed my work on both
roles. In October 1967, we began six weeks of rehearsals for *The
Great White Hope.* We were scheduled to open at the Arena Stage in
Washington, D.C., on December 7 for a seven-week run, with the
production supported by a grant from the National Endowment for
the Arts. Ed Sherin, the director, cast Jane Alexander as Ellie, the
mistress.

Preparing for the role demanded intellectual exploration, and
physical exertion that I felt confident would be akin to basic training
in the Army. Actually, what I had to endure was much worse than
anything the Army ever required of me, even in Ranger training.
Every morning I got up early and ran three miles with my trainer, ex-
boxer Bill Terry. He put me through my paces: the morning run, and

then two hours of workouts at a gym, the whole gamut of the boxer in training—skipping rope, punching a body bag, working with weights, medicine balls, and split inner tubes for sweat bands. I lost twenty-five pounds, and built muscle definition and strength.

I read everything about Johnson I could lay my hands on, and watched every scrap of film footage I could find. Boxing style was different back in 1915, and as I studied the old movies of Johnson in the ring, I could see that he was catlike, defensive, outdancing and outclassing his adversaries. He was beautiful to watch, choreographing his approach to his opponent, trying to sneak in on his left foot, bending his upper body slightly back, away from the other boxer's reach. He and his opponent were gentlemen standing off, with only an occasional blow. The style was so reserved that when Johnson did spring into attack, he was frightening, like a killer cat.

I was flat-footed as well as slow-footed, so I worked hard at imitating the spring in Johnson's step. While there were no actual fight scenes in the play, I wanted to get inside the boxer's body as well as his psyche. Now, if Bill Terry was tough on me, my trainer in New York was a "sadist." His name was Ritchie Pitman, and he was unmerciful, although I came to appreciate it, as much as I hated the grueling regimen he put me through. Both were unrelenting, worse than the worst drill sergeant. With them I came to understand the fierce renunciation a world-class athlete endures, the harsh discipline of body and mind, the price you must pay to compete, with no success guaranteed. Robert Earl, a marathon runner, helped me with the phase of the boxer's regimen I found most interesting: the endless long distance running. It was a solitary act, and it kept my focus on the loneliness of the gladiator in the ring.

I needed to get inside Jefferson, skin, muscle, sinew, and bone. Then I had to try to crawl inside his head and penetrate his spirit. For his voice, I deliberately resurrected my Southern cadence, for he was a Southerner if there ever was one. The dialogue Howard wrote for Jack Jefferson was totally, poetically invented language, not like any I had ever heard, and not the way the real Jack Johnson talked at all. Any linguist trying to fix Howard Sackler's language to one particular region of the country would not be able to do so. Howard's Jefferson was less articulate than Jack Johnson in real life, so I chose to speak in a jagged, stunted rhythm, and to incorporate the kind of gestures I thought a boxer might use out of the ring, in conversation jabs and feints. I thought a boxer would punctuate his speech with his hands, even his fists. Makeup could give me gold teeth, of course, and I could provide the grin.

I read Jack Jefferson as a superman, endowed with a fierce pride, and a man who had during his lifetime earned even more reason to be proud. From the first instant, Ed Sherin and I connected in our vision of the man and the play. Immediately, I trusted Ed totally. He taught me to trust myself more deeply, and helped me climb into the ring of my own psyche to discover the power I needed on stage. Together, Ed and I explored the energies needed for each facet of the role.

Ed helped me use my own life experience to interpret Jefferson's. Jefferson's deep dependence on his mother probably shaped the intensity of his relationships with women. My mother's absence, the converse of that, has probably forged a similar intensity in me. We were both battlers, although in differing arenas. I had put much of my own rage to rest by then, but I wanted to extrapolate from Jefferson's experience what was universal about the experience of the black man in society. I interviewed a psychoanalyst who specialized in studies of black males and their problems, and read a book called *Black Rage* by William H. Grier and Price M. Cobbs. I tried to examine Jefferson's conflicts within a racist society, and the subtext of his conflicts with male authority figures and his tendency to trust white women more than black women. I wanted to capture both the quicksilver of Jefferson's moods, and the depth of his emotions.

All those seeds I nurtured in my imagination. They took root in that subterranean ground and grew out of our conjoined experience,

Jefferson's and mine, until I felt him spring through me to a life on stage. Ed, Howard, and I were nearly the same age, and Ed and I shared the same sign of the zodiac. Howard was more complex than Ed or I, but we were a troika as we worked together on *The Great White Hope.*

I was nearly thirty-seven years old when we opened at the Arena Stage in Washington on December 12, 1967. Producer Zelda Fichandler and director Ed Sherin had given me my big chance. I knew it, and I was grateful. Even though the roadwork and the exertion in the gym were hard on a thirty-seven-year-old body, it took a much longer apprenticeship in work and life to get me ready for this part. I had been scraping by on my acting income for fourteen years, playing every part I could find which would help me evolve as an actor.

I think we knew during rehearsals that we were involved in a significant theatre experience. But I was completely unprepared for the critical praise, the later fame, and the thunderous response of our audiences. There were rave reviews. "The acting is dominated by James Earl Jones, who is magnificent as Jefferson," Clive Barnes wrote in the *New York Times.* "With head shaved, burly, huge, Mr. Jones stalks through the play like a black avenging angel. Even when corrupted by misery, his presence has an almost moral force to it, and his voice rasps out an agony nearly too personally painful in its nakedness." Jerry Tallmer reported that the "Jones performance as Jack Johnson in 'Great White Hope' has been rated the most exciting by an American actor since Marlon Brando first walked on in 1947 as the Stanley Kowalski of 'A Streetcar Named Desire.'" One critic called me an overnight success. I was grateful for the affirmation, but it had been a long "overnight," fourteen years long.

Over time, I came to perceive our audiences at *The Great White Hope* as an organic force. They stepped into the performance with us, and fed us their energy. Ed warned me early on, however: if an actor seeks his energy from the audience, they will eventually turn on him. He felt that over the years I have relied too heavily on a cooperative audience to focus my energy. I will not argue with that, but I will not ever agree with it, either. I think an audience owes a certain obligation to events on the stage, but when they do not come through, the only thing that can save you is intense concentration on what you are doing. I agree with Ed that you have to build powers of concentration from the beginning so that you will not be vulnerable to distractions. Yet I think no actor can ever deny the voltage of the energy he can receive from those sitting out there in front of him in the dark of the theatre.

14.

THE GREAT WHITE HOPE GOES TO BROADWAY AND BARCELONA

The fight between life and death is to the finish, and death ultimately is the victor. . . . I do not deplore the passing of these crude old days. . . .

JACK JOHNSON, *IN THE RING—AND OUT*
(CHICAGO: NATIONAL SPORTS PUBLISHING CO., 1927)

Every actor—and every fighter—has his rituals before a performance. We opened *The Great White Hope* on Broadway at the Alvin Theatre on October 3, 1968. I liked to get to the theatre early, at least a couple of hours ahead of time. I would relax for a while, trying to shed my everyday skin. I would read my mail, and maybe glance over my lines. I would spend nearly an hour warming up physically, doing calisthenics and lifting weights. Each night I put in my two gold teeth, and oiled my whole body. I was pretty sleek, if I say so myself, six feet two inches tall, 200 pounds—never been in such good physical shape, before or since. Just before I went on, I would sit while Ed Sherin's secretary-assistant, who had become expert at the boxer's wrapping during our Washington run, wrapped my hands.

In Washington, when I was in training, I was still wearing my hair the way I wore it in *The Comedians,* but one day I decided to shave my head.

Ed had nudged me in that direction. "I'd like to see if it works." I hesitated, but eventually agreed; it seemed time to try the look, and I shaved myself bald. When I walked into rehearsal, my scalp shining, the actress who was playing my mother actually came over, introduced herself to me, and said: "We are very happy that you have joined the cast, but I must tell you that we did like James Earl Jones a lot." She simply did not recognize me, and just took it for granted that James Earl Jones had been fired and that I was his replacement. From that day on, I kept my head shaved.

Somebody once wrote then that I was a "highly respected but only moderately known young actor" before *The Great White Hope*. I had lived a fairly anonymous life up until then. I was stunned on opening night by the standing ovation, the bravos, the accolades. Before I went out to the party in the theatre lobby, and then over to Sardi's for the opening night party, I waited awhile in the now quiet, empty theatre. I stood again for a moment on the stage, specially built to jut slightly over the orchestra pit. The stage felt to me like a great hand stretching toward the audience, with the play as its offering.

When I stepped from the quiet stage out to the crowded lobby, I knew suddenly that my life had changed. Everybody rushed up to me, elbowing Julienne out of the way. I retrieved Julienne, and we walked over to Sardi's. One of the first people to greet me was Robert Shaw, whose controversial *Man in a Glass Booth* was running on Broadway. In his crusty way, he said, "I can't believe you did that to us, you son of a bitch!"

I follow the rule of not reading the reviews until the production is over, but the reviews were glorious. "Howard Sackler's play 'The Great White Hope' came into the Alvin Theater last night like a whirlwind, carrying with it, triumphantly, James Earl Jones," Clive Barnes wrote in the *New York Times*. "The play has an epic scope and range to it." He noted that our director, Ed Sherin, shared "fully in the triumph with Mr. Sackler and Mr. Jones," and praised the cast, especially Jane Alexander's "almost spiritual beauty. . . ." Barnes said that as he left the theatre, "Mr. Jones was receiving a standing ovation of the kind that makes Broadway history. If I had had the time I would have stayed to cheer, he deserved it. . . . If anyone deserves to become that occasional thing, a star overnight, then Mr. Jones deserves no less." Walter Kerr called it a "tidal wave performance."

I was suddenly inundated with requests for interviews, autographs, meetings. Julienne and I tried to go about our normal life in the apartment we had found in New York, but it was impossible. I kept wearing my old clothes when I was not working: jeans, a comfortable patched jacket I liked, a faded blue denim hat, my black work boots. People were calling me a star all of a sudden, and I didn't know what to make of it. I suppose I had worked so hard for so long without that being the goal that I never imagined being a star. I just wanted to be a good actor, perhaps at times a great actor. I don't think one is ever *always* a great actor. Greatness depends on many things. With the confluence of energies that occurred in *The Great White Hope*, and, many years later, in *Fences*, you can be great—but you do other productions where those confluences do not happen and, if you are lucky, you are just good.

Actors do not earn fortunes in Broadway plays. I believe I earned a thousand dollars a week for *The Great White Hope*—but how long would the play run? How long would I be out of work after the play closed?

Julienne and I had very little time alone, to the detriment of our marriage. We were so jolted by this sudden attention that we were diverted from working on the foundation of our new life together. But she understood my work, and cheered me on, reducing her own professional commitments more and more. She had worked hard as an actress and singer for years, and now wanted to enter another kind of life, choosing the role of housewife over her own career. We moved into a wonderful three-bedroom apartment on West End Avenue. I still don't understand how I let Julienne give up her career so easily—and I wonder how much that added to her disenchantment once our marriage became troubled.

Among blacks and whites in 1968, interracial relationships, while not popular, were actually more accepted then than they are now. We experienced no overt hostility because we were a married couple. Ironically, my stage mistress suffered more antagonism about our on-stage relationship than my real wife did in real life. Jane Alexander received numerous obscene letters about her role as my mistress in *The Great White Hope*. There were times after our performances that she feared she was being followed, and she had to be escorted home. Ugly letters accused her of being a traitor to her race. Jane is as strong off stage as she is on stage, so she spoke out courageously about the hate mail, which came to her in New York after the Broadway opening.

I loved her answer to one reporter who asked her about racial prejudice. "Most of my life I had never been exposed to prejudice," she told him. She grew up in New England, she said, and her parents never discussed race. "My father is a bone surgeon," she added, "and color is not very relevant to a man's bones. I have no unusual feeling as an actress about kissing Jimmy and getting into bed with him. If I were in love with him in life and he asked me, I'd marry him. Color means nothing. And then, too, Jimmy Jones is a great human being. He never makes anything of his color either."

There were sixty people in our cast in Washington, but Ed Sherin staged the play adroitly despite the size of the cast and the demands of the drama with its twenty-three scenes, later cut to nineteen. Zelda Fichandler, our producer in Washington and the founder of the Arena Stage there, believed that if the theatre was to reach black audiences, whom she called "America's new proletariat," we would have to integrate acting companies and find plays which spoke to black audiences as well as white. Her farsighted courage had given *The Great White Hope* a home in 1968, a difficult time, the dark year that would cost us both Martin Luther King and Robert Kennedy.

There were modern parallels to Jack Johnson's story—in 1967, current heavyweight champion Cassius Clay/Muhammad Ali had been sentenced to five years in prison and a ten-thousand-dollar penalty for refusing to be inducted into the Army on the grounds of religious principle. Clive Barnes wrote, "In these liberal times we can accept a black heavyweight champion, but can we accept a *Black Muslim* heavyweight champion? It is a question that seems to lurk like a silent ghost in the very corridors of Mr. Sackler's play."

Just as there is no one voice to speak for white people or Oriental people or Hispanic people, there is no one voice to speak for black people. There are many voices. Howard Sackler, a white man, spoke eloquently through his play about the experience of one black man, but the themes and questions evoked in the play reverberate far beyond that one life.

Ed Sherin was skillful at motivating the cast. I remember one night while we were still in Washington, he saw our energy flagging, summoned us to a meeting, and rallied us with a battle cry. He looked at each principal character, one by one, and demonstrated what we must do to consummate each role. I had a scene that wasn't working at all: Jack Johnson had tried to strangle himself once, which seemed out of character. I could not evoke that anguish in that way. We chose instead to have my character try to beat himself to death—self-flagellation.

"You have to go all the way, but don't hurt yourself," Ed admonished.

The Arena Stage in Washington is round, surrounded by the audience. We were in constant motion, so that nobody in the audience was denied the impact of any scene. You had to be a whirling dervish, without calling attention to the fact that you were whirling. Acting—in a pressure cooker. In theatre in the round, there is no way for actor and audience to escape each other.

I remember one night during this particular scene, a woman in the audience began to sob audibly. It became infectious. It was one of the most electric moments I can ever remember in the theatre. It happened to me when I saw Tony Perkins in *Look Homeward, Angel*. I sobbed openly.

When we brought *The Great White Hope* to Broadway to a traditional stage, we cut the number of scenes, the number of hours—and the impact. What you saw on Broadway was nothing equal to what you saw in Washington.

The play was physically, psychologically, and psychically exhausting, and after the first six months, I began to feel that in a week's time, we might get four of eight performances right. I wanted to get every performance right, and even though the director and producer observed that the audience will not always know if the performance is not totally realized, *I* knew. As a counterpoint to the sustained work of the play, I took on some other projects for fun. I have come to understand that to sustain creative work, you have to have re-creative work. Often, that means not retiring from the theatre, but simply doing something different—regenerating the creative stamina by simply pulling away from one energy and using others. They replenish each other. I still enjoy using one performing energy and, at the same time, using other performing energies— juxtaposing television, movies, even voice-overs.

That ploy served me well at Christmastime in 1968, when, in the midst of *The Great White Hope,* I narrated Charles Dickens's *A Christmas Carol,* starring Orson Bean as Scrooge. More than twenty-five thousand third- and fourth-graders came to see the free performances during that holiday season. These diversions helped to keep me fresh on Broadway.

Howard Sackler's *The Great White Hope* won the Pulitzer Prize, the Antoinette Perry Award, and the New York Drama Critics' Circle Award for the 1968–69 Broadway season. Jane Alexander was named best supporting actress. I was so overwhelmed to receive the Tony Award for best dramatic actor that I could hardly say a coherent thank you. I was also distressed that Ed Sherin, our brilliant and compassionate director, was not even nominated, and I said so.

Plans were well underway for the film version of the play, and Jane and I were signed to re-create our roles. Martin Ritt, a film director, was named to direct instead of Ed Sherin. I respected Marty Ritt, and I understood that Ed lacked film experience, but I felt his profound understanding of the play would overcome that. With a good cinematographer as his assistant, Ed could have done a fine movie. Hollywood just would not take a chance on him. Marty Ritt had a good record making films—*The Long, Hot Summer; The Sound and the Fury; Hud; The Spy Who Came in from the Cold.* He was thought to have a good record on films with social issues. Unfortunately, the producers of the movie looked at *The Great White Hope* as primarily a drama of social issues.

Yet the stage play itself is cinematic, and the poetic "ramblings" are wonderful. The screenplay eliminated every poetic aspect that the stage play had conjured, so that the stage characters who were mythic, gothic, larger than life, were reduced in the film to mere social entities. The black mistress became little more than a shrew; the conjure man became just another street protestor; that giant oak on stage, Captain Dan, the head of the clique of white American boxing officials, became another dirty trickster. In the play, when he walked on the stage, you knew Jack Jefferson had a real adversary. In the film script, it became a crime scenario. The film was about criminal behavior instead of the depths of human behavior. There were three boxing vignettes in the film, but they failed to arouse any passion.

"If you want to make the film more realistic," I asked, "why doesn't Jack do more fighting? Everything else in the equation was changed in the translation from theatre to movie screen, so why not the boxing?"

I began to wonder if there might be some unconscious motive to neuter the role, to diminish the tragic hero.

For a time I lived in a golden haze of love and glory—and then my life seemed to tarnish at the edges and finally in the center. My life in the theatre took its toll on my marriage. I always felt that I fell in love first with Julienne the actress rather than Julienne the person, which was probably a key to the difficulty of keeping the relationship together, especially when she gave up her career to concentrate on making a home for us. We very much wanted a baby, but we were unable to have a child. We loved each other, and we were good friends in the marriage and have remained so. We tried all the advice books and magazines recommended for making a marriage work. But we had such difficulties at times that we would separate for brief periods.

During one of those separations, I took a mistress in New York. It was 1969 and the play was still running then. When we started shooting the movie, I had to go to Los Angeles. During the early filming, the marriage was rocky. We lived in separate hotels. By the time the movie company moved to Barcelona to shoot the bulk of the movie, Julienne and I had acknowledged that our marriage was in serious trouble.

So I went off to Barcelona alone.

In Barcelona, there was the tension of the Franco regime, and Marty Ritt could not be comfortable in Spain, even though the Spanish people themselves were wonderful. It seemed as if they had democratized themselves on a spiritual and human level in spite of Franco and the fascist regime, and there was great prosperity as long as the labor movements stayed in line. Meantime there were people in Barcelona who were heavily anti-Franco and always had been. Their fathers had been. Barcelona is probably the most un-Spanish city in Spain. It could be northern Europe with the buildings and the tradition. It is heavily Basque in terms of the culture and the art museums, a highly developed culture.

I took photographs on the set. There were throngs of extras. Spanish soldiers were given ties, jackets, and straw hats, and marched in by the regiment for crowd scenes. On my birthday that January 1970, five thousand people sang "Happy Birthday" to me in Spanish in the Barcelona stadium.

I worked very hard: I became passionate about photography, flamenco dancing, and bullfighting. Although I experienced photography firsthand, flamenco dancing and bullfighting I watched at a safe distance.

I went to see authentic, gypsy flamenco dancers. Flamenco comes from gypsy culture, from North Africa and the Middle East. It is not Spanish. I love the music itself, apart from the dance. Flamenco music in Barcelona is "tear out your heart" music, not unlike blues, country and western, and soul. The rumor spread during my time in Barcelona that I had become a flamenco fanatic, a groupie, following flamenco dancers around. That was the fun of it all, that I had gone crazy for flamenco. And I had.

In Barcelona, I had a memorable affair. One of the people in the background of the film was a very innocent-looking blonde, with beautiful lips. She was Finnish, and she was smoking a pipe. I thought that was a great touch. I kept making eyes at her, and when I found out she spoke English, I invited her out to dinner. Leading actors should not date extras, but I could see that she was very special, and she was. She had come to Spain to study, had heard about the casting call, and, when she learned they needed Nordic types, she came and got a job with us.

On our first date, she said, "You want to be with me, don't you."

"Yes," I said, "very much." That began our affair, and it was a good relationship, although, confused as I was during that time, I did not think it would go anywhere. Julienne and I were separated, but we were still married.

There is an unforgettable still photograph of Jack Johnson lying on his back on the canvas, one arm raised, after Jessie Willard hit him in the twenty-sixth round of that 1915 fight in Havana, Cuba. Johnson claimed that the arm was lifted casually to shield his eyes from the sun while he took the count. That would seem incongruous for someone who was unconscious. Johnson used that picture to try to prove he was not knocked out.

Willard stood six feet five inches tall and weighed 260 pounds. They hired a real fighter, about seven feet tall, to play Willard in the movie. Part of the Jack Johnson mystery is that he claimed people told him they would kill him if he did not throw the fight in Cuba.

He knew he would be dead if he did not throw the fight. There were soldiers and snipers all around the ring. He did not know which soldiers were assigned to be the assassins. He just knew he would be dead if he won the fight.

Johnson was trying to pick a moment when he would not so much *let* Willard hit him, as be hit hard enough so that he could go down, and decide whether to stay down. His pride was so great that he did not want it to be obvious that he had thrown a fight. On the other hand, he had another pride working, the pride of a black man who confronted that kind of power structure. He also possessed the athlete's pride. This photograph, taken from a motion picture film, suggests that naked pride. The film actually shows the impact of the blow, and shows Jackson hitting the canvas—boom. His arm goes up, his hand covers his eyes.

He later insisted, "I was shading my eyes from the sun. Yes, I threw the fight because they said they would kill me, and I was lying there shading my eyes from the sun, I was so disdainful."

In the still photograph of that moment, there is no shade on his face. He took a blow hard enough to be knocked down. He went out and stayed out. But he had to conjure another legend, and this picture captures the moment just before he was going to be hit hard enough to stay down. The eyes tell the whole story.

Earlier his days of being champion, forced to stay abroad, Johnson kept saying, "Send me good fighters, or I won't draw." For a time he tried to augment his income with other work. He donned a matador's costume and went into the bullring. The legend is that once he put his sword aside, hit the bull on the head, and knocked him down. I question that—but that is how the legend goes.

The American boxing establishment wanted to get rid of Jack, and they would pay off good fighters not to go to Europe to fight him. They wanted to force him back to the United States so he would have to face the Mann Act charges. He and Charlie Chaplin got hooked on the same trumped-up allegations. Jack was suspected of being in the pay of the German government because he was outspoken in his pro-German feelings throughout Europe.

The boxing establishment would send Jack fighters, but not good fighters, and he tried to kill one of them out of his fury. To play one such inferior fighter, Marty Ritt hired a boxer who had suffered great damage when he was a fighter in real life. He was a sweet man, but so beaten down he seemed lobotomized.

One night I took him with me to see a prizefight in Barcelona. There were several fights that night. Finally, there was a match between a burly Spaniard and a tall Nigerian, elegant and stoic. My companion was increasingly unsettled and agitated as we watched that bout. I kept saying to him, "What's wrong?"

The Nigerian fighter never sat down between rounds. He stood each time, holding to the ropes. His trainer would come to him and give him water. He would never drink. Instead, he would open his mouth and his trainer would wipe a wet sponge over his tongue.

"What's that about?" I asked, but the boxer with me would not answer. He knew something was terribly wrong.

The Nigerian kept standing. He would not sit down. Round after round, he went back to the center of the ring. Finally, he got hit and sank to the mat. He never got up again.

The "dead" fighter must have known he was incapacitated, but he was a Nigerian in Spain: who knew about his "green card"? who knew about his contract? who knew about anything? He was forced to go back in and keep fighting. The doctors were not alerted because as long as he did not sit down he showed no signs of being in trouble. Standing, he appeared to be game, ready to get back in the battle.

The young actor/boxer on the film and I walked home after that tragic fight. He was so upset by the death of the boxer that he could not talk. We walked back wordlessly to the hotel, and I knew that the tragedy at the fight had resurrected pain in him. I also knew that I would not go back again to the prizefights in Barcelona.

* * *

On my days off I became addicted to the bullfights—the pageantry, the allegory. The Spanish were very concerned about clean kills—a matador getting a clean strike. The bullfight is full of ritual. The matador has the cape, and there is a kind of sword within the cape, but not a killing sword. He is almost defenseless, except for his wits. The bull is charging full steam, and the more the matador can thrust his groin into it, his masculinity, the more the crowd loves it.

With his codpiece protruding, he is saying, "My masculinity is better than yours, Toro." There is the macho choreography, and it is all in the hips, a balletic display of the male rooster ego. Suddenly, the matador decides it is time to kill. He reaches toward his second, and exchanges his staff for the real sword—sharp, shining, and lethal— and puts his cape away. He taunts the bull. The bull finally charges. He raises the sword and plunges it into the heart.

When this death dance is not expertly done, the crowd says the matador is a bad fighter. Brave bull, bad fighter. They want a clean kill. They do not want to be reminded that this is a slaughter.

In one fight, I noticed with fascination a "moment of truth," not the one Hemingway speaks of, but when the bull knows he is dying. Until then, it was really a big boy's game. The bull is in the ring charging away, chasing this silly red flag, strutting his stuff, until, from above his shoulder, suddenly a knife goes into his heart. He stops and his legs shudder. Swiftly he realizes it is not a game anymore. He staggers. He knows he is dying. With the crowd whistling disapproval, the bull begins to follow the matador around the ring, as if to ask, "Give me a hand. Is there anything you can do?" I would go to see the bullfights for that drama.

Later, I met actor/writer Jonathon Miller in Madrid. He was a bullfight aficionado. As a Catholic from birth, he was convinced— and I think Hemingway mentions this, too—that the bull was the devil, and the matador, Jesus; and the event was a battle between good and evil. All these experiences are about conquest, and a rich milieu for the work on *The Great White Hope* were feeding on a subliminal level.

We worked in Barcelona with an English-speaking crew and English-speaking actors, and on the set, lunches were catered to Western tastes. Only at night, if you had the energy and time and money to go out, would you have the chance to encounter Spanish culture. So nights and weekends gave me my exposure—flamenco almost every night, bullfights on the weekend. I discovered a dark Hamburgian world toward the end. In the last week of the filming, a lot of the crew began to invite us to their houses. They gave wonderful parties. Some of them played the classical guitar. Many of them were fringe people and closet homosexuals, forced by the repression of the Franco regime to act out parodies of "I am a Camera" or "Caberet." It was something they had felt they could not share with us in the beginning, but toward the end, they let us into their world.

There were accelerating problems on the movie set in Barcelona. Filming was not going well. It had started going badly once 20th Century–Fox settled on the script. One of the ironies is that it should have remained a simpler movie with a smaller budget, and they should have had the wisdom to retain Ed Sherin as director.

Marty Ritt, fine film director though he was, deferred too much to the stage performances entrenched in those of us who had been through the run of the stage play. Often, when we were wrestling with a scene for the film, he would ask us to tell him what we had done on stage. We would demonstrate, and he would try to incorporate that into the film. From the beginning, he said, "Give me your stage performances. I'll modulate them."

There are profound differences in acting for film and acting for theatre. On stage, your orientation has to be frontal, and you have to project to the last row in the house. On film, your orientation must be multidimensional, and your acting must be subtle, for you are engaging the audience person to person, one-on-one. The camera is at once a subtle and a transparent instrument, keyed to nuance and understatement. I think, in his respect for the play, Marty inadvertently preempted some of his skills and instincts as a director of motion pictures.

The movie did not do well, but I was nominated for an Oscar, although I thought my chances were slim. As I expected, it went to George C. Scott for *Patton*, and, as it turned out, he declined to accept. I was actually disappointed in my performance, and in the ultimate quality of the film. The lesson *may* simply be that it is almost impossible to transmute one form into another—a novel into a film, a stage drama into a motion picture. Maybe!

One lingering symbol for Johnson's fate lies in the imagery of the bullfight: in the beginning, he is the matador, full of his own virility and pride and power. At the end, he is the bull, attacked from all angles, fighting back with a kind of gallant hopelessness, waiting for the matadors to deliver the coup de grace.

One happy sidelight to my tenure as Jack Johnson was that I got to meet Muhammad Ali. He had come to see *The Great White Hope* on Broadway. Ali himself had appeared on the Broadway stage in a production called *Big Time Buck White*. He came backstage to my dressing room after a performance one night when the audience had left.

"James," he said, "go out in the auditorium."

Curious, I did what he asked. He stood up on the stage, and did one of the lines from our play.

"Here I is. Here I is," he said. "How was that?"

"Ali, that was great," I said.

"Not only great," he told me. "This is my story. You replace the issue of the white women with the issue of religion and the war, and this is my story." That began our friendship.

Once during the filming of *The Great White Hope* in Hollywood, Ali and I put on boxing gloves for a promotional stunt. Imagine standing there, glove to glove, with the great Muhammad Ali.

"Go on," he kept saying, dancing that famous dance of his. "Hit me. Hit me."

When I did not respond, he egged me on, that twinkle in his eye. "Hit me, brother, hit me."

Finally, I drew back and gave him my best. That handsome face hardly moved. Those eyes kept twinkling. Those feet kept dancing. I did not faze the champ.

He never laid a hand on me, but in the simple act of blocking my blow, he broke my thumb.

Ironically, Ali had had problems similar to Jack Johnson's, but had surmounted them. He told me a story that his father told him about Jack Johnson. It seems Johnson was once stopped for speeding in a Southern state. The policeman who pulled him over fined him fifty dollars. Johnson gave him two fifty-dollar bills.

"Why'd you give me two fifties?" the policeman asked.

"Because I'm comin' back," Johnson replied.

And he did, in Howard Sackler's brilliant drama, *The Great White Hope*.

With the filming of *The Great White Hope* in Barcelona completed, I returned home. It should have been a triumphant return, but I was troubled. I had a need to reground myself, to get back to the kind of acting and life I truly understood.

I joined John Berry again with Athol Fugard's *Boesman and Lena* off Broadway, with Ruby Dee and Zakes Mokae. I played the brutish Boesman, who brought me back to the elemental man. I hoped I could find the elemental man within myself.

I also had noticed within the whirlwind of *The Great White Hope* that one of the bitter fruits was that I was attracting insane people. I began to wonder what it was about me that attracted the insane. I wanted to explore this on a therapeutic level.

I began to examine a lot of deferred pain and emotion. When I read Dr. Arthur Janov's book *The Primal Scream*, I arranged to commit myself to his primal therapy institute in California in the winter of 1971. Julienne had already begun her therapy and training there, and I thought perhaps we could mend our marriage by remending ourselves, and find each other again through our individual therapies.

Janov urged his patients toward the primal scream, that uncontrollable natal scream that punctuates your reliving of the birth experience. When I began primal therapy, I built my own private, soundproof "scream room" in my garage. There, I unleashed emotions I had never faced before, and confronted long-submerged anger and pain.

Janov traces all neuroses and many psychosomatic disorders to birth and infancy. He leads his patients to relive their childhood pain. (In an article on Janov in *Newsweek* April 12, 1971, I sound as if I think Janov is a miraculous medicine man. I am quoted as saying that primal therapy cured me of a cigarette habit, sinus trouble, and a compulsive sexual urge, and, last but not least, cured my hemorrhoids. That seems like hyperbole now.)

Primal therapy did help me face some leftover business from my own childhood. Now, consciously, I know how lucky I was to be nurtured as I was by my grandparents. Now I am content that they, not my birth parents, were my guardians.

Ruth and Robert Earl were two very young people who could barely manage their own lives in the midst of one of the worst economic depressions in history. I finally accepted in therapy that no one in my family meant to do me harm. To be raised on a farm throughout the Depression and the war, through all those years into my adult life, gave me what balance and harmony I possess. In my therapy, we were all invited to accept the idea that any panic or fear we have has already been experienced in birth. We don't have any fears except those that have already been stimulated in us. Whether it is prejudice or paranoia, somewhere in childhood that little seed has been planted by direct experience at a time when we could not rationalize it.

You can deal more readily with present fear or panic when you realize you have been through it before. The infant confronts birth all by himself. He cannot conceptualize or take in what is happening to him during the trauma of birth. The fear of being buried alive may be directly connected to the birth trauma—the fear of being trapped, the fear of not being able to get out, or the fear of coming out at all. If death is fearful to you, you have to realize that you have gone through something very like death before.

Therapy helped me to express more freely my real self—not my black self or my American self or my male self—but my real self.

There was a certain concern that after the journey of therapy, I might not be the same person I was before. Of course, if the therapy has been effective, you shouldn't be the same person you were. The question was whether you could go back to doing the work you were doing. An actor often taps into the well of feelings, especially unresolved feelings. Sometimes acting—acting out—leads to resolution. You use that energy to feed your character's emotions.

The truth is that therapy helped me, as a human being and as a human being who is an actor, to reopen the well of my emotions, and to make a certain peace with the pain of my life, the pain inherent in life itself.

15.

OF MICE AND MEN

On the sand banks the rabbits sat as quietly as little
gray, sculptured stones. And then from the direction of
the state highway came the sound of footsteps on crisp
sycamore leaves. The rabbits hurried noiselessly for
cover. A stilted heron labored up into the air and
pounded down river. For a moment the place was lifeless,
and then two men emerged from the path and came into
the opening by the green pool.

JOHN STEINBECK, OF MICE AND MEN

JEJ has given John Steinbeck's social documentary of the
miserable lot of migrant workers in Depression-ridden
American of the 1930s, Of Mice and Men, the
emotional force of a Greek tragedy. The play has taken on
a new dimension. . . . His Lennie is a heart-stabbing
portrayal one rarely encounters on the Broadway stage.
This, also, is one of the finest performances of Jones's
career. . . . Pathos replaces social realism as the central
force of the drama. . . . Although a few lines were
rewritten, color, for me, seemed irrelevant. . . . From the
moment this incredible actor almost sways onto the stage
of the Brooks Atkinson Theatre, one feels, almost without
dialogue, both the force and the gentleness of this
mentally retarded figure, cast aside by the world. . . .

WILLIAM A. RAIDY, THE NEW JERSEY STAR-LEDGER,
DECEMBER 19, 1974

I think of all the characters I have played, my favorite is another elemental man, Lennie in John Steinbeck's *Of Mice and Men*. One of my richest experiences in the theatre has been my encounter with Lennie in two different productions. Both opened in university theatres—one at Purdue University in 1967, and one at Southern Methodist University in 1974, at the Bob Hope Theatre. There, Kevin Conway was brilliant as George, and my good friend Ed Sherin was a superb director.

We had worked together before, of course, so we did not have to start from ground zero to mold our working relationship. Our mutual confidence, respect, and trust energized the work from the outset. After the SMU tryout, we opened in the play on Broadway at the Brooks Atkinson Theatre in December 1974 and then at the Kennedy Center in Washington in 1975.

The play is about two migrant workers, Lennie, who is retarded, and his friend George, an American hero. George is the only person in Lennie's life who can reach him, especially when they talk together about the images of the farm they hope to own someday. George is devoted to the flawed and dependent Lennie, a victim, doomed from the outset of the play. I believe if there were a Greek god named Pathos, it would be Lennie.

He loves animals so intensely that he often kills them, literally loving them to death. He is totally unsophisticated, unselfconscious, and unaware of the "real" world. He is completely himself, a primal and elemental creature. He has no conceits about how he looks or how he speaks or what he thinks. In existential terms, Lennie just *is*.

One day Lennie meets a woman in the barn on the farm where he works. She, out of her own loneliness, allows him to fondle her long blond hair. When his touch frightens her, she screams. He does not mean to hurt her, but in trying to quiet her, he shakes her with such unintentional force that he breaks her neck and kills her.

George discovers what has happened, and he begins to search for Lennie, who is hiding in the brush, trusting that his friend will help him. Only George can protect Lennie from jail—or from sure torture and hanging by a posse already on its way. In the end, George knows that the only way to save him is to kill him. This tragedy is redeemed by George's extraordinary devotion to Lennie.

Steinbeck's short novel has been transmuted into several forms over the years. With Broderick Crawford as Lennie and Wallace Ford as George, the play, staged by George S. Kaufman, first opened on Broadway on November 23, 1937, running 207 performances and winning the New York Drama Critics' Circle Award as best play. Lon Chaney and Burgess Meredith starred as Lennie and George, respectively, in the movie made in 1940. The novel was adapted as a musical in 1958 and an opera in 1970. More recently, there was a television film with Randy Quaid as Lennie; John Malkovich played the role in the movie written by Horton Foote. Any story which modulates into so many different forms clearly strikes a universal chord.

In my student days, I played Crooks, the black farmhand, in *Of Mice and Men*, at the Walt Whitman Theatre at Brooklyn College. Robert Earl came out to see it, and said, "I love it." When I played Lennie at Purdue, Robert Earl played Crooks.

John Steinbeck was still living then, and, since Lennie is written as white, I asked him what he thought about a black Lennie. Steinbeck liked the idea, for he meant Lennie to be universal. We asked him for permission to change the word "nigger," which is spoken in Lennie's presence. Steinbeck laughed and said that since Lennie cannot appreciate the social and political context, he does not understand the derogatory meaning of the word. Thus, it would not harm him or offend him.

I came to that discovery myself as I played the role. For Lennie, other people's talk is devoid of organic context—just words. He cannot discern racial or sexual barriers, just as he cannot distinguish insult from praise. Only George can really communicate with him. They understand each other completely, in the realm of their friendship, especially when they are talking about their dreams of owning a farm.

Critic Didier Delaunoy reflected on the implications of a black Lennie, writing in the *Black American* that "The casting of Jones in the part brings in a whole new set of thoughts and motives. His relationship with George takes on a totally different meaning. The whole idea itself would have been an explosive one in 1937, when the play was written. Today, it still is an intriguing concept, one that draws on more than the mere relationship and friendship between Lennie and George."

I tried to create a hulking physical demeanor for Lennie. How would this gentle brute carry himself? In early photographs of myself as a boy, I see my shoulders slumping—as if I were carrying a burden. I decided Lennie's shoulders would droop with regret and sadness, when he had done something wrong or when his animals were taken away from him. I wore an old hat, and used it as a cradle for my small animals. When I had killed them, never meaning to, I used the hat as a temporary "grave," hiding them there when they were dead.

Preceding one production, I spent time at a center for the mentally disabled, a retardation center as they were called then. My experience in this center showed me Lennie's vulnerability, and his dependency. In the play, when Lennie tells George "If you don't want me, I can go off and live in a cave by myself," I wanted to believe Lennie could do just that: survive by his wits if he were to leave the pettiness and meanness of the "real" world and find a life alone in the wilderness. Yet even though Lennie cannot live with so-called normal people, he cannot live alone in the wilderness, and he would surely wither away and die if he were confined in an institution.

During the production at Purdue University, I got involved in an interesting psychological experiment. Director Joe Stockdale of the Purdue University Drama Department had gotten a professional theatre company underway. The head of the psychology department at the university was an avid theatregoer, fascinated with character studies of figures in plays. He was intrigued with Tennessee Williams's Blanche in *A Streetcar Named Desire*, for instance. He conjectured from her behavior, for instance, that the actress playing Blanche was temporarily schizophrenic. "When I sat watching the play," he said, "as a professional psychologist, I could easily allow myself to believe that that person I saw on stage was schizophrenic. I began to wonder to what extent her acting out a state of schizophrenia actually placed her *in* this state."

When I arrived at Purdue to play Lennie, the retardate, the doctor was ready to go into action. He sat through a couple of performances observing me intently. Then he said, "I think you have a temporary IQ of about seventy. I want to prove it."

He found a graduate student who was not aware of who I was and who had not seen the Purdue production of *Of Mice and Men*. He wanted this student to administer certain psychological tests to me, which he instructed me to take in the character of Lennie. After he found his student, the professor went shopping at the local Salvation Army thrift store to buy clothes for me so I could dress like Lennie. He wanted me to step totally into Lennie's character. Dressed in those Salvation Army clothes, I looked authentic enough so that the student obviously believed the story his professor concocted.

The doctor told him I had been discovered wandering around in a nearby cornfield, and asked him to test me. My job was to behave like Lennie. This was improvisational drama, not a story written by Steinbeck, and I even convinced myself that I was not very bright, and that I had only limited interests, curiosity, and knowledge. With the professor and his students observing through a one-way mirror, I took the tests as Lennie, not as James Earl Jones.

Most of the tests apparently confirmed the psychologist's theory.

By deliberately losing myself in Lennie's clothes and his character, I achieved test results in most areas such as those you would expect Lennie to achieve. But the one test I could not fake was the Rorschach test. I had to interpret those images as I saw them. When the student saw the discrepancy between the intelligence tests and the Rorschach test, he became visibly upset. He slipped out of the testing room and told the professor, "You should have him committed before he does something violent!"

Steinbeck wrote a character who had a very intense but narrow focus on physical reality, and, to that extent, on all reality. Tad Danielewski, one of my teachers in the early New York days, had directed me in a workshop production of *Of Mice and Men*. He dropped a bombshell about Lennie. Tad, with that European mind, went at the drama dialectically. "You would think Lennie is dumb. That is the cliché," Tad said to me. "It is not that Lennie can't think. Lennie thinks too much about one thing."

Some primal infancy of sensation forces his mind to focus on the softness of fur. It is not that he cannot think, that he cannot deal with other things, it's just that the whole lens of his mind is narrowed to one thing.

"Lennie is not dumb," Tad reiterated. "Lennie probably knows more about hair and fur than anybody in the history of mankind. This immense knowledge of this one minuscule area overwhelms his mind. There is no room for anything else." His real world was constricted and narrowly focused. My world, especially the world of my imagination, was somewhat more spacious. That disparity of vision, in the end, made it impossible for me to become Lennie in the realm of the Rorschach testing.

Consequently, the Purdue professor was both right and wrong. I could enter the character so fully that I could interpret his interior responses as well as his exterior words and behavior. But I could not get past the boundary of the imagination. A computer could probably take the focus of Lennie's real world and the content of his imagination and apply it to the Rorschach test. For me, that was impossible.

The actor must sometimes enter a state that is not his own. He transcends himself as he becomes a character on stage.

At SMU, Ed sent Kevin and me to a large institute for retardates north of Dallas. We spent a couple of days there with the good staff, who could show us around and teach us about their work with these special people. Many of the inmates were highly sexual. Their bodies, at least, had not failed them, despite the disabilities of their minds. There was no conventional way to communicate with many people we saw there. There was no way in, no way out. That said to me that Steinbeck knew Lennie's reality, that he is hopelessly locked away to everyone except George.

William and Jean Eckart designed impressionist sets and costumes for the Broadway production, evoking the Salinas River country of California, the isolation of the ranch, even the bleak aura of the Depression. Critics conjectured that our revival surpassed the original production, staged thirty-seven years earlier. I was pleased to hear that some critics observed that my portrayal of Lennie further solidified my reputation as an actor. ("With this performance Jones makes it abundantly clear that he is one of America's great stage artists," Emory Lewis wrote in *The Record* on December 19, 1974. "He captures the childlike openness of the character, and he discovers the beauty and delicacy of Steinbeck's poetry.") I have Lennie and John Steinbeck to thank for that opportunity. I also owed a great deal to Ed Sherin and Kevin Conway. Critics took due note of Ed's "magnificent" staging and Kevin's "brilliant" performance. Our chemistry empowered our performances, I believe, and when I discovered that my name stood alone on the marquee of the Brooks Atkinson Theatre on opening night, I asked to have Kevin's name inscribed up there, too.

I had known people with limitations of mind, someone who was like Lennie as described by one critic: "a gentle giant with the mind of a child." I had grown up in the country, with a visceral love for the freedom of the land and the refuge of nature. I believe that in a primal way, this love was the driving force in Lennie.

And Steinbeck gave George an instinct for simple caring. He cared as much for Lennie as he cared for himself. To care as much for someone else as you do for yourself—is to love.

George is a genuine tragic hero because he knows from the very beginning he must destroy Lennie. One fact that helps define George's heroism is the enormity of the responsibility he shoulders in his guardianship of Lennie. Because of the terrible history which already exists between them, George knows from the first moment of the play that he will someday have to kill Lennie himself. To George, Lennie is not "cuddly," he is lethal. The audience watching this story should be moved quickly past the rich humor that is evoked by Lennie's seeming innocence, to realize that because Lennie is not capable of will or any willful act, he is then not responsible and has nothing resembling a conscience to guide him.

The response of the Purdue graduate student to the discrepancies in my Lennie's test results—"commit him before he becomes violent"—is not too far off the mark.

16.

PAUL ROBESON, NAT TURNER, AND OTHER VOICES

You can cut off the concert halls, which you have done already, and I will still speak out . . . and if you silence my voice by making me a non-person there will be another voice and another voice. . . .

PAUL ROBESON, *HERE I STAND* (LONDON: DOBSON, 1958)

I am an actor. I believe the profession of being an actor should transcend the politics and the social order of the times. If he has his own clear priority as an artist, an actor can function despite the changing tides of politics in the world around him.

I have always believed that it is the right of an actor with a name people may recognize to use whatever notoriety he has to effect change. I have never been an activist. When I have spoken out, I have done so as a private citizen, as myself. But, inevitably, your art *is* your politics. The stage is your podium. The material you choose reflects the times we live in, and, at its best, illuminates them.

I think drama is about people in trouble. Often, when I find a play about people in trouble, it causes discomfort in the audience or off stage. Almost every single production in my whole career has somehow been touched with some kind of controversy.

When you are a black actor, you quickly become a realist. One of the realities I had to face early on is that there exists out there a deep sensitivity to the social issues implicit in stage and film productions. That complex sensitivity often erupts into controversy. I did not expect that it would explode—and more than once—into protests that could and did destroy several productions I had hoped to do, in film as well as theatre.

I have been caught in the cross fires of artistic and social disputes which have sometimes escalated to the point of abuse of freedom of artistic expression. I am a veteran of controversial productions, some making it to the stage or to television or movie screens, some aborted in infancy. Sometimes my adversaries were white, but as often, they were black.

Early in my career, in my first attempt to play Emperor Jones in Boston, I ran up against watchdog committees working through the

NAACP. The rationale for protest in 1964 was that society would be abused by hearing the "degrading" Southern Negro dialect and Eugene O'Neill's use of the word "nigger" in a script that was written in 1921.

In 1969, Ossie Davis spearheaded a campaign to block production of a film based on William Styron's *Confessions of Nat Turner*. Ossie and others contended that Styron, a Southern white man, could not possibly do justice to the life of a black man, especially a slave, and that, as a white writer, he had no right to create a novel based on Nat Turner. At no time did the protestors acknowledge that 20th Century–Fox hired a black writer, Lou Peterson, to render the screenplay, using all available sources besides Styron's book.

Styron himself has written about the Nat Turner backlash in the October 1992 issue of *American Heritage*. Heartened by the initial warm acceptance of his novel in 1967, he soon found himself engulfed in controversy. "It would have seemed inconceivable to me," he wrote, "that within a short time I would experience almost total alienation from black people, be stung by their rage, and finally cast as an archenemy of the race, having unwillingly created one of the first politically incorrect texts of our time." Styron and his novel were assailed in essays, some of them collected in a book called *William Styron's Nat Turner: Ten Black Writers Respond*. His novel was widely attacked and banned by many people who had not even read it.

Likewise, our film script was assailed by an ad hoc committee who had not read it—and who did not seem to know or care that the screenwriter was a black man. Sidney Lumet was signed to direct the film, and I was signed to play Nat Turner.

Suddenly, we were confronted by protestors who believed that no one could use Styron's book to render a movie they would accept, or, by extension, that black America would accept. Meantime, 20th Century-Fox was having financial problems. When the economic bottom fell out of Fox Studios and the film's production costs mounted to over six million dollars, the project was canceled. I suspect that Fox was looking for an excuse to drop it anyway. The protest group took credit for the fact that the film was aborted, and gained an illusion of power.

Opponents of the film specifically objected to Styron's conjectures about the sex available to Nat Turner. Surely, Styron had no evidence that some of the events he created truly happened. He was writing a novel, after all. But he offered a graphic and disturbing vision about what happens to a male child bound down by slavery. Protestors essentially said, "We don't want to see the image of a black man who masturbates while looking through the keyhole at a white woman. We don't want to see the image of a black man who, as a child, reached under the water and co-masturbated his fellow black slave, also a teenager." I cannot quarrel with their objections to the sexual details Styron had imagined for his novel. But I do quarrel with the tendency to deny the degradation that slavery wreaks upon a people. What is slavery if not degrading— and how else is a writer to depict that?

It became clear to me that protestors were not prepared to confront the degradation of slavery, as I am afraid black and white people today are not ready to confront it. It is too painful, not unlike the degradation of the Holocaust. Whenever television decides to create a project about the Holocaust, the word "trivialization" is always applied by the Jewish community. The black community feels the same about the subject of slavery.

All kinds of arguments have been used throughout my career to kill artistic projects. When playwrights and screenwriters have tried to address themselves to the richness of black American history, with its folk heroes and its political heroes—Malcolm X, Martin Luther King, Nat Turner—the projects seldom reach fruition because we do too good a job of killing them before Hollywood even gets a chance. There is a great mistrust that Hollywood will trivialize.

Consequently, some members of the black militant community and the black intellectual community have their guard up, and that defensiveness has contributed to the dearth of works done on black heroes.

It has taken decades for us to get to the day when Spike Lee and Denzel Washington can bring Malcolm X to the screen. Now I celebrate that it has happened, and happily watch Denzel, a younger black actor, play Malcolm X. I think objectively that perhaps we all needed this distance of time.

There should be freedom in this society of ours for every writer, every screenwriter, every sculptor to express her or his own vision. I think our mission as artists is to shine our own light, the light of our own vision on any subject.

I always want to fight for that right for the artist. To some extent, I have done so in my career, not always with much success. It is not my purpose as an actor to serve the temporary need of the time. I object to the attempt to make a subject palatable to a particular need of a social group or a particular time. I also object to the self-serving vision evoked by some ad hoc protest committees.

In 1978, I became entangled in a project fraught with politics, rough, off-stage politics, the composition and thrust of which stunned me. The subject was Paul Robeson, so controversial in himself that I should not have been surprised.

The poet Carl Sandburg wrote a poem for Paul Robeson to read as a tribute to Franklin Delano Roosevelt when he died in April of 1945. As far as I know, it has not been published, except in a newspaper. I think the first seven lines could have been written expressly about Paul Robeson himself:

> *The art of the man is still now,*
> *Yet his shadow lingers alive and speaking*
> *To the whole family of man round the earth.*

His teaching ran that all nations must be neighbors
That their only choice is whether they should be
good neighbors or bad.

Paul Robeson believed people on this planet should be good neighbors. Born in 1898, he was the son of a former slave who had made his way north to Princeton, New Jersey. Gifted as an actor, a singer, an athlete, and a scholar, Robeson was an all-American football player at Rutgers University in 1917 and 1918. He sang in the Rutgers glee club, graduated as valedictorian of his class in 1919, earned a law degree, and made his New York concert debut as a singer of spirituals in 1925. He had already appeared on stage in *All God's Chillun Got Wings* when he was cast in *Show Boat* in 1926. His other landmark stage roles included Porgy in *Porgy and Bess,* and Othello, and he made several movies, including the films of *Emperor Jones* and *Show Boat.*

Paul's passionate defense of human rights led him inexorably into conflict with many of his countrymen, especially after he affirmed what he believed to be the egalitarian treatment of blacks by the Soviet Union. The FBI kept watch on him. The State Department often made it difficult if not impossible for him to travel abroad. He was known around the world as a great singer and actor, and, increasingly, as the champion of oppressed people everywhere. Ultimately, his career and his reputation were subverted by the outcry against his politics.

He made his first trip to the Soviet Union in 1934–35, returning in 1936–37, 1949, 1958–59, 1960, and 1961. American newspapers writing about his 1949 trip observed that he was welcomed in Russia with more fanfare than any recent visitor from the United States had received. "I was, I am, always will be a friend of the Soviet people," Robeson said. At his concert in Moscow in 1949, he spoke openly of his friendship with Soviet Jews and sang as his only encore the Warsaw Ghetto resistance song, saying the words first in Russian

("And our marching steps will thunder: we survive!") and then singing them in Yiddish.

In 1952, he was the only American to receive the International Stalin Peace Prize. When Robeson returned to the Soviet Union to great adulation in August 1958, U.S. State Department observers believed that he was being exploited by the Soviet Union for propaganda advantage. Robeson's concert in the Lenin Sports Stadium drew eighteen thousand people, who heard him sing a Russian patriotic song, "My Broad Native Land," twice repeating the words of the refrain: "I know no other land where people breathe so free."

Robeson lived out his life a recluse, estranged from the American people, black and white, whom he had so wanted to serve. It is curious that although Robeson was persona non grata in Hollywood because of his political commitment and was blacklisted, on the day he died, television news was saturated with memorials to him. I think the nation awoke to the idea that a great hero had passed, and that they knew nothing about him.

A week after Paul died on January 23, 1976, I got a call from a television producer at NBC. He saw a great American hero being celebrated after his death. He asked if I would be interested in playing Paul Robeson in a television drama. "I would like to consider it," I told him.

Soon afterward, with no explanation, the project was dropped. Much later I heard reports that Universal, which would have produced the project for NBC, rejected the treatment written by Phillip Hayes Dean, a talented black writer. Apparently, when the production group began to understand how complex and controversial Paul's life was, they decided not to do it.

I assumed that if we did a drama based on Robeson, we would be able to use his voice. How could you tell Robeson's story without hearing him sing? And who could sing like Robeson? Later, I learned that there were legal stipulations that his voice not be used in any commercial venture on network television or in the movies. His voice could be used only for news exposure or for nonprofit events and noncommercial television. That reality would affect some crucial decisions I was later involved in.

After that aborted NBC proposal, I got a call from Don Gregory, who had produced *The Belle of Amherst*, a one-woman show about the life of Emily Dickinson. William Luce was the writer and Charles Nelson Reilly the director. Phillip Hayes Dean, meanwhile, had finished a Robeson script, which I liked to some degree, but not entirely. On June 22, 1977, I put my concerns in a letter and sent it to Don Gregory; Charles Nelson Reilly; my secretary and assistant, Susan Kellermann; and my agent, Lucy Kroll.

In part, I wrote of that first script that some passages suffered from "racial conceit." Every human being has racial consciousness, I argued, an awareness which should not preempt sharing and communication. But "racial conceit," I tried to explain, acts as a barrier to communication and defeats any attempts at enlightenment between people. It is merely a pointless venting of personal and subjective bitterness. These particular words in the script written by a black playwright did not serve the best purpose of the play.

I simply wanted to be sure that we tried our best to do justice to Paul Robeson. I argued for a script which would "Befit the heroic size of the man, the enormity of his intellect, and the dignity of the drama based on his life." I wanted to play the young Robeson "with all the brashness and arrogance inherent in youth," I said, but I refused to play him as a "tactless, reckless, self-defeating fool." Most of the problems which troubled me existed in the second act, when Paul's life was a morass of difficulties, and there was very little written about him once he became a leftist. How could we resurrect the life on stage in all its tragic complexity?

Don Gregory said he had sought access to the Robeson archives, but had been refused. Without permission to use the papers in the archive and the actual recorded voice, it was impossible to create a comprehensive documentary of Paul Robeson's life.

I recognized the difficulties. My acceptance of the role of Paul Robeson would be conditional on revisions in the script. But I felt that as a black human being, I had license to bring my own sense of dramatic, social, and political awareness to bear. I think I was the most valid actor to do that role in that time, although I am the first to acknowledge that I am not a singer. I felt a deep obligation to try to bring Paul's life to the stage.

I flew to New York to see *The Belle of Amherst,* and was very impressed. Don Gregory took on the Paul Robeson project, brought in William Luce to rework the script by Phillip Hayes Dean, and began to organize preview performances on the road.

We worked with a simple set representing the stage of Carnegie Hall on the night of the seventy-fifth-birthday tribute to Paul Robeson. (I had participated in that evening, along with Sidney Poitier, Harry Belafonte, Pete Seeger, Roscoe Lee Browne, Ossie Davis, Ruby Dee, Odetta, Coretta Scott King, and others.) The audience saw a piano, a lighted bust of Paul, a few chairs.

Because in fact Paul was not well enough to attend the Carnegie Hall celebration, the play opens with his expression of regret that he can't be present. Then in his privacy he looks back on his life from age seventeen to age seventy-five.

Charles Nelson Reilly, the director, is a genius at comedy; he always understood how to make the young Paul Robeson work. But once Paul became a committed human being, probably the most committed human being who ever existed—once the story moved into that drama of his life—Charles was at a loss. Perhaps it was simply unworkable.

We knew the first act was undergirded by good elements of theatre. There, we were dealing with the young Paul Robeson, the young man on the make, on the move, feeling his oats, feeling his

James Earl Jones, the young
actor, in an acting workshop in
the early 1950s.

James Earl Jones on stage as Brett
in *Deep Are the Roots* at the
University of Michigan, 1953.
F. W. Oradnik. Courtesy of the
University of Michigan.

James Earl Jones, third row, fourth from left, ROTC, University of Michigan, 1952.

Robert Earl Jones
with Eleanor
Roosevelt and
educator Mary
McLeod Bethune,
founder of National
Council of Negro
Women and director
of Division of Negro
Affairs of the National
Youth Administration.
Courtesy of Robert
Earl Jones.

James Earl in his first Broadway role,
as Edward the butler in *Sunrise at
Campobello*, 1958, with Ralph Bellamy
and Mary Fickett as Franklin Delano
and Eleanor Roosevelt. Billy Rose Theatre
Collection, The New York Public Library
for the Performing Arts, Astor, Lenox,
and Tilden Foundations.

Robert Earl Jones in his twenties.
Courtesy of Robert Earl Jones.

James Earl Jones in his twenties.
Courtesy of Robert Earl Jones.

James Earl Jones in 1961.
Estate of Carl Van Vechten.
Copyright by Joseph Soloman,
Executor.

James Earl and Robert Earl Jones in Central Park. Copyright © 1993
by Seymour Linden.

Joe Papp directing James Earl Jones as the Prince of Morocco in *The Merchant of Venice* in 1962. Photograph by George E. Joseph/New York Shakespeare Festival.

Third from left: James Earl Jones as Michael Williams in Shakespeare's *Henry V,* his first role in Joseph Papp's New York Shakespeare Festival, 1960. Photograph by George E. Joseph/New York Shakespeare Festival.

James Earl Jones as King Lear, New York Shakespeare Festival, 1973. Photograph by George E. Joseph/New York Shakespeare Festival.

James Earl Jones as Othello and Mitchell Ryan as Iago, New York Shakespeare Festival, 1964. Photograph by George E. Joseph/New York Shakespeare Festival.

James Earl Jones as
Lopakhin, Anton Chekhov's
The Cherry Orchard, New
York Shakespeare Festival,
1973. Photograph by
George E. Joseph/New York
Shakespeare Festival.

James Earl Jones as Othello and Julienne
Marie as Desdemona, New York
Shakespeare Festival, 1964. Photograph by
George E. Joseph/New York
Shakespeare Festival.

James Earl Jones as Claudius,
Colleen Dewhurst as Gertrude,
Hamlet, New York Shakespeare
Festival, 1972. Photograph by
George E. Joseph/New York
Shakespeare Festival.

James Earl Jones, Elizabeth Taylor, and
Richard Burton in Graham Greene's *The
Comedians,* 1967. © 1967 Turner

James Earl Jones as
Dr. Lou Rush in
"Dr. Kildare," NBC, 1966.
Courtesy of NBC-TV.

Lucy Kroll at the Lucy Kroll
Agency, New York, in the
early sixties. Courtesy Lucy
Kroll Collection.

James Earl Jones as Jack
Jefferson (character based on
heavyweight boxing champion
Jack Johnson) in the film version
of *The Great White Hope*, © 1970,
20th Century–Fox Film
Corporation. ALL
RIGHTS RESERVED.

James Earl Jones as Jack Jefferson in the Broadway version of *The Great White Hope,* 1968. Photograph by Lawrence Schiller.

Jack Johnson. UPI/Bettmann.
Courtesy of The Bettmann Archive.

James Earl Jones as Jack Jefferson and Jane Alexander as Eleanor "Ellie" Backman, *The Great White Hope* on Broadway, 1968. Photograph by Lawrence Schiller.

James Earl Jones making up for *The Great White Hope.* Billy Rose Theatre Collection, The New York Public Library for the Performing Arts, Astor, Lenox, and Tilden Foundations.

James Earl Jones in *The Great White Hope* on Broadway. Friedman-Abeles. Billy Rose Theatre Collection, The New York Public Library for the Performing Arts, Astor, Lenox, and Tilden Foundations.

Muhammad Ali and James Earl Jones, 1969. Photograph by Lawrence Schiller.

James Earl Jones as Village in Jean Genet's *The Blacks*, 1961. Copyright © 1993, Martha Swope.

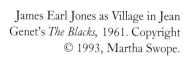

talent surge in him. The young Robeson was discovering his endowments of mind, spirit, and talent, and wanting to take on all that his endowments could touch. Up to the moment he hit the peak of his fame and wealth, Robeson was easier to follow.

Paul began to forsake his wealth and fame after his trip to Spain during the war against Franco. I believe that trip marks the crossroad in his life, with his career and with his family. That is when he became heavily politicized. From that moment on, Paul Robeson became very elusive, tremendously enigmatic. He lived out his life in controversy and struggle. It was a staggering challenge to a playwright to evoke that tragedy and at the same time to do justice to its complexity and its far-reaching significance.

As we struggled with our dramatic vision of Robeson, Charles wished for a quiet place to work. I had an eight-acre ranch then in Val Verde Park, California, a predominantly black community where I was trying to raise horses. Nearby, there was a little church.

"I'll talk to the reverend to see if he can give us a space to work in the church," I told Charles. "It's not a bad place to try to conceive a play about a man who sings and comes from a deeply religious background. His own father was a minister."

So we sequestered ourselves up there, and worked on the play. At one point, we invited the community to watch our last reading of what we had put together. Still, we had no second act. We had strung scenes together as best we could, and we read them to the audience gathered in that little church.

Don Gregory then suggested we read the play at UCLA before a large audience of invited guests. I did not look forward to that evening, and, symbolically, I got lost on the way to the theatre. I knew why I got lost. I drove round and round and round, unable to find that theatre, unwilling to stop for directions.

My producer and Lucy, my agent, held the curtain. "He is going to turn up," Lucy insisted, but she knew the way I felt and suspected what had happened. "He will come. He will be here."

And I got there, and got on that stage, and started reading. I read through the first act and got into the second act. Then I did something I hope I never do again. When a horse gets a load he cannot handle, he balks. I balked. I think I might have said, "What is this shit I'm reading?" If I did not say exactly that, I expressed my displeasure in an emphatically obvious way. The UCLA crowd probably knew more about Paul Robeson than I did, and I was not comfortable with the portrait we were evoking in that second act.

I asked for the houselights so I could see the faces of my audience. I had never before done a one-character play, and I felt that a visual connection with the audience might feed me energy to get through the struggle that night.

Afterward, Don sat me down and said, "What do we do now?"

"I don't know," I answered. "You want to start on the road in Louisville next week. I don't know how to do that. I don't know how to even memorize a script this incomplete and unfulfilled." But because of the commitments made, there seemed little else to do but to go on to Louisville and present the play there as it was.

That first night in Louisville, I came out of the theatre after the performance to find Paul Robeson, Jr., standing under the marquee.

"Hello, Paul," I said.

"Hello, Jimmy," he answered. Those were the only words we exchanged.

Paul Robeson, Jr., and I had met a few years earlier when I spoke at the 1975 Carnegie Hall tribute. Paul Jr. and I had always gotten along very well. Our fathers had been friends. He was the son of a noted and respected actor-singer-activist. I was the son of a noted and respected actor, who had also been an activist, and blacklisted, as Paul had been. We had our fathers in common.

But my effort to evoke his father's life on stage elicited his strenuous opposition, and it became obvious that night in Louisville, as Paul Jr. stood by himself under that marquee. From that moment on, Paul Jr. would appear under every theatre marquee on our road tour, with the exception of Cleveland, Ohio. In each city, he would arrive before our company got to town, meet with the press, and express his opposition to our production. He charged that the play falsified and diminished his father's life.

Paul Jr. was a bright and talented man, an engineer, a linguist, but overshadowed by his father's life in the world. He began to devote his energy to heading the Paul Robeson Archives. I wondered if Paul Jr. needed to bury his father as much as he needed to protect his legacy. He made it impossible to use any of the material in that rich collection.

He just did not want this show done. I began to believe that Paul Jr. did not want actors, singers, artists, writers—anyone—to address his father's story. He considered himself the sole custodian of that image, a position that warrants some respect.

Nevertheless, we went on with the show. And every opening night, in every town across the country, we would encounter Paul Jr., standing like a sentry. I suppose, as long as our play was in difficulty, he felt safer; his adversary was weak.

ROBESON SON DISLIKES PLAY ON FATHER, read the headline in the *Louisville Courier-Journal*, September 15, 1977. BACKSTAGE DRAMA IN BOSTON, read the headline in *The Boston Globe*, October 17. ROBESON PLAY CALLED INSULT, said the *Milwaukee Courier*, November 5. BUT ROBESON JR. REMAINS UNSATISFIED, said the *Washington Star*, December 7. So went the litany of Junior's discontent.

Usually, Paul Jr. would come in to watch the show. On stage, I wrestled with that defiant script. I wonder now what it cost Paul to sit through those performances.

When we reached St. Louis, en route to Philadelphia, I realized I simply could not go on working on the second act any longer as it was. It just was not getting anywhere. Charles would come backstage and say, "Jimmy, I don't know what's wrong. I can't assess the critics, but the play seems to work for the audience."

I had to tell Charles that the second act did not work for me, and that I did not think we could work together anymore. A couple of other possible directors came to see the production. Lucy made an overture to Don Evans to rewrite the material, although that didn't work out, either.

I had been Lloyd Richards's understudy in *The Egghead* years earlier, and I had often invited him to come give me counsel when I was performing. I had only met Paul Robeson three times through Robert Earl, but Lloyd truly understood him. He had an awareness of the man that would benefit our production. He joined us in Philadelphia as director and play doctor, and called in the original writer, Phillip Hayes Dean, to reconceive the second act. Of greater advantage than Lloyd's ability to work with me was his ability to work with Phillip. Lloyd had directed a teleplay of Phillip's, and I believed they could collaborate on *Paul Robeson.* They began immediately, while the production pulled out, heading for Boston.

Most writers don't want to change a word of a script, but Phillip did not care if things were changed, so long as it was an improvement and the legal responsibility to the Robeson estate was protected. He did not want to quote or misquote any of Paul's words that were not in public domain.

With its portrayal of Paul's youth, his ascending fame, his prodigious gifts, his humor and humanity, the first act always worked. But that somber second act was eluding us. It was riven with Paul's complicated political struggles and his "banishment" from the stages and concert halls. How to do justice to Paul's later life without oversimplifying it? How to convey the controversy and complexity without overwhelming—and losing—the audience? As we revised the second act, Phillip allowed us to amend and shove scenes around and experiment with the whole script until it began to work.

Somehow, as Charles had said, we seemed to be touching our audiences, for, in regular numbers, they came backstage after each performance, brimming with memories, stories, insights, details about Paul's life. One family came back with their daughter, who introduced herself as Paul's goddaughter.

"Even though I am his goddaughter," she told me, "the curious thing is that when he was banned by this government, my parents, who were his lifelong friends, forbade me to play his records in the house. They broke them all, every one, and threw them in the yard."

A friend of mine showed up one night with clippings from journals he had found about Paul's adventures in Russia in 1949. Paul had insisted on seeing a friend of his, the Russian writer Itzik Feffer, especially after he learned of the murder of their mutual friend, actor-director Solomon Mikhoels. Feffer himself had been arrested on Christmas Eve 1948, but Paul did not know that. Someone gave Feffer a suit of clothes, took him out of prison, brought Feffer to Paul's hotel room and left the two men alone to talk, but Feffer used sign language to warn Paul that the room was bugged. Through gestures and notes, Feffer told Paul the brutal details of Solomon Mikhoels's murder, and predicted that he himself would be executed. Tragically, Feffer's prophecy came true three years later.

Paul had been a champion of Jews all his life, and black people, and Irish people, and workers—all people everywhere whom he considered downtrodden. He was deeply shaken by this treatment of his friends Itzik Feffer and Solomon Mikhoels, but he would not give the United States government the satisfaction of hearing him admit any misgivings about the Soviet system. I think this was one facet of his father's experience that Paul Jr. was trying to protect.

Step by step, fragment by fragment, we moved closer to a drama we thought was workable. Lloyd would conceive a scene and ask Phillip to write it. For instance, there was the episode when Paul talked with a twelve-year-old German girl who played the piano. Because she was a dwarf, she was shy about meeting people. Therefore, she met Paul only reluctantly, even though he was a hero of hers. Lloyd would say to Phillip, "Write us dialogue that Paul would have with her and let her represent the whole Jewish nation." Phillip would go away, and return with a page, which he would toss to Lloyd to read. "That's it!" Lloyd would say. And Lloyd would rework it and I would rework it.

By the time that particular scene was written, it was October and we were opening in Boston. About three o'clock in the afternoon of opening night, Lloyd handed me the revised scene. "Can you do it tonight?" he asked me.

"It's so good I've *got* to try it," I told him. In the scene, the dwarf, who is just three feet tall, feels embarrassed to meet Paul because of her deformity. As Paul, I leaned over, as if she were actually standing with me on stage, to tell her a fable about a giraffe and a rabbit, the tall and the short, who face different obstacles and surmount them to find their unique places in the world. Then I shared with the audience my vision of her death at the hands of the Nazis.

I was so focused on the drama on stage that I did not at first comprehend the drama escalating off stage. I did not grasp the magnitude of Paul Jr.'s protest. At first he had been a lone figure under a theatre marquee, but soon it became apparent that a complex organization was rallying around him, intent on destroying our production.

He and fifty-five black artists, scholars, politicians, and other celebrities organized the National Ad Hoc Committee to End the Crimes Against Paul Robeson to protest and block our production. I was stunned to read the statement they signed and published in *Variety,* calling our play, among other things, "a pernicious perversion of the essence of Paul Robeson." Coretta Scott King signed this "Statement of Conscience" damning our play. So did Ossie Davis, Alvin Ailey, Julian Bond, Mayor Coleman Young, James Baldwin, Gwendolyn Brooks, Maya Angelou, Nikki Giovanni, and Vinnette Carroll. James Baldwin and a few others on the list of fifty-six acknowledged that they had not even seen the production, but were protesting out of principle. Many of them claimed that they had read the play, but most of those, I discovered, had read only the original script, which we had all long ago rejected.

Besieged by pickets, protestors, and this powerful Ad Hoc Committee, I was now challenged to turn my attention from the play itself to the volatile drama surrounding the play.

17.

THE ROBESON
RUCKUS AND
AD HOC ART

I can do no better than to do my own work and develop myself to [the] best of my ability. . . . If I do become a first-rate actor, it will do more toward giving people a slant on the so-called Negro problem than any amount of propaganda and argument.

PAUL ROBESON, *NEW YORK HERALD-TRIBUNE*, JULY 6, 1924

[In 1924, Paul Robeson] argued that the negative reaction to the play *[Eugene O'Neill's* All God's Chillun Got Wings*]* was one of *"the most serious drawbacks to the development of a true Negro dramatic literature. We are too self-conscious, too afraid of showing all phases of our life—especially those phases which are of greatest dramatic value. The great mass of our group discourage [*sic*] any member who has the courage to fight these petty prejudices."* He acknowledged *"being damned all over the place for playing in* All God's Chillun,*"* and also acknowledged feeling annoyed at the criticism: *"Those who object most strenuously know mostly nothing of the play. . . ."*

MARTIN BAUML DUBERMAN, *PAUL ROBESON*
(NEW YORK: BALLANTINE, 1989)

As I look back, I believe that we were still so close to Paul Robeson's death that for all of us, but especially for Paul Jr., it was too soon to unravel all the meanings of his life. I think Paul Jr.'s pain erupted from the reality that his father had lived in conflict with his time.

Most of us live in conflict with the time in which we are born, but we do not deal with it as clearly and bravely as Paul Robeson did. I think he was totally unselfish, totally committed to changing the world into a better place for all people. Few people in any age are so dedicated.

I had a twofold motive for playing Paul Robeson. One was as simple as my reason for needing to play Jack Jefferson in *The Great White Hope:* there was a mountain to climb. Second, I wanted to do it for all the young—and the not so young—people who had not been fortunate enough to know Paul Robeson even as little as I had. It was 1977. We lived without real heroes, without examples and alternatives. People, especially black people, searched desperately for alternatives. They craved heroes. Here was an epic hero.

But there was so much of Paul Robeson to see and to know that there suddenly seemed to be as many Robesons as there were voices arguing about our play. I never imagined our version of his story would please everyone, but I did fight for a strong script and a clear vision.

When we revived interest in Robeson with our play, some people perceived it as a spiritual experience, a reincarnation of hope and pride. Other people perceived it as a criminal experience, and accused us of defaming this great man. Paul Jr. charged that we had subordinated his father's political radicalism to his humanism. We had portrayed him as "only a humanist." Paul Jr. believed, he said, that this was like writing about Nat Turner and omitting the rebellion, or about John Brown and leaving out Harpers Ferry. I knew by then that nothing we could do would please Junior. If we had said Paul had a sense of humor, Paul Jr. would have said he *didn't* have a sense of humor. I believe he would have said anything to invalidate the play.

For every charge there was a countercharge. Some called the play a product of the establishment, spawned by John Foster Dulles—an effort to undermine and trivialize this great hero. Others viewed the play as the product of those seeking to mythologize a black man who was a traitor to his country. Some people argued that the nation owed it to Robeson, to black people, and to all citizens to examine this great life. Others contended that the nation should not resurrect such a "dangerous" man. While some believed that Robeson belonged to his family and outsiders had no business transgressing the wishes of his son, even his own grandson, David Paul Robeson, stated that Paul "belonged to the world."

There were some members of the black community, unaccustomed to the way plays evolve en route to a "fixed" form on the stage, who only read early passages of the first draft of the play. Others saw the metamorphosis of the play as some sort of sinister manipulation, as if by editing the play, we were trying to "edit" Paul's life. Even such a routine process as writing, rewriting, trying out a version of a play, rewriting some more, seemed ominously circumspect to those critics.

As the controversy grew over the effort by a black actor, a black director, and a black writer to produce a theatre piece about a great black figure, there were white onlookers who wondered at this conflict with the black intellectual/political establishment, and our seeming self-destructiveness. How could we as black people sabotage ourselves by this unseemly and often illogical "civil" war?

Paul Jr. stood in the center of this maelstrom. Once again, he got to town ahead of us. In Boston on October 11, 1977, he released the familiar statement. Our play fictionalized his father, he said. It distorted, misrepresented, and trivialized, making his father's basic character unrecognizable. It whittled "the giant stature of Paul Robeson to such an extent that he is made to resemble the false image that has been created by the White Establishment." The play was "an insult" to his father's memory. One could understand how people supported Paul Jr. Here was the dutiful son defending the honor of his father. People who did not know the full story would say, "Well, of course, if this production defames his father, young Robeson would be the first to know it and would certainly have a right to destroy it. What son wouldn't?" Often, people did not look beyond that.

I heard the story that Lillian Hellman and Paul Jr. once argued about who and what Paul really was. Exasperated, Lillian said, "Oh, Paul Jr., just shut up. I fucked him before you were born." That was not the father the son wanted to convey.

On the eve of our October performance in Boston, a committee organized itself and printed a public statement: they intended to "protect the diverse political background and honorable stature of the late great Paul Robeson. . . ." They were "shocked" by my participation in this play "over the adamant objections of the Robeson family." Furthermore, they objected to the fact that the Colonial Theatre, where our play was to open, fostered employment practices "unfair and extremely exclusive of Blacks [sic] and Third World people, and totally structured to foster and preserve the White status quo." They warned that in the "not too distant future" they planned to "seek legal redress" over that issue. For the time being, they called for a "night long candlelight vigil" in front of the theatre to protest our production and try to "stop that play" which "fictionalized and distorted" their hero.

As I walked toward the stage that first night in Boston, a stranger approached me. He was not a member of our company.

"Can I help you?" I asked him.

"I'm your man," he told me, patting the bulge under his coat. He sketched an incredible scene. A volatile crowd outside the theatre was growing in size and energy. Mounted police had been summoned. This man, packing a .357 magnum under his coat, was assigned to protect me.

Eerily, I remembered similar protests and criticism levied against Paul Robeson himself by blacks when he acted in Eugene O'Neill's *All God's Chillun Got Wings* at the Provincetown Playhouse in 1924. The producer decided to shuttle traffic, except for pedestrians, away from the theatre. He also got a bodyguard for Paul, an Irishman who was about half Paul's size in height, with a gun half as big as he was. I frankly accepted "the man" when I learned the candlelight procession had been exploited to riot proportions outside the theatre by a fake-dreadlocked crazy.

The ruckus followed us to Milwaukee and Chicago, and then, in December, to Washington. Tension mounted. People who had never known Paul or seen the play expressed strong opinions in the matter. On December 6, the "Washington, D.C., Committee to End the Crimes Against Paul Robeson" issued a "Statement of Conscious [*sic*] to Citizens of Washington, D.C." condemning our production. The statement was signed by illustrious members of the national black community.

Despite this, we had great audiences in Washington, largely because of—or in spite of—the clatter about the play. We had been working hard, and improving. By the time we got to Washington, all the dreams Charles Nelson Reilly and Don Gregory and Phillip and Lloyd and I had poured into the play crystallized. The experience was at its best in Washington, where a large, eager black contingent came to see us and discover the man as best they could.

The city holds a large, cosmopolitan black population, and our play drew them to the theatre. Black women in particular discovered in Paul Robeson a black male hero they could admire, even in a play now so infamous as ours. We played to full houses. People flocked backstage.

They told us that the play gave them a hero and a man. They saw Robeson's political choices in an understandable context. They saw a man who had found a way for most of his life to use the abundance of his endowments. Then they saw him punished for his beliefs by being denied the one gift which held him together—his ability to sing.

I was happy when people came to me backstage to say they connected with Paul Robeson in our production. Women who had problems with their children came to me as if they felt that somehow, having played the man, I carried some of his mystique back to my dressing room with me. They approached me as if I had some of Paul's wisdom.

"My son has strayed." "My daughter has this problem. Can you help?" They were not seeking money; they were seeking spiritual advice. The play had that kind of effect on people. But they sometimes did not separate the role and me, and that was disturbing. I saw how desperately they needed valid heroes. People often may believe that heroes can give clarity to their lives. There is an urgent need for that, especially among black people—and especially among black women, who like women of most societies, have looked for men to lead the way, often to their great disappointment.

Even some of Paul Jr.'s supporters turned up. Ossie Davis came to see the play for himself, finally, and so did Coretta Scott King, who, like Ossie, had signed the protest against us before she saw it for herself. Mrs. King came backstage afterward, and told me that she admired my work in the play. The critics began to absolve me and the director, but to excoriate the writer and the script.

You have heard me say that I cannot sing, and if you heard me sing the snatches of song I dared to try in that production, you know for yourself that I cannot sing! Several coaches and singing experts tried to help me, teaching me to open my throat and take advantage of the timbre. In Philadelphia, my old hero Todd Duncan recommended a young protégé to coach me. But I never pretended to be a singer. I was grateful to have the presence on stage of pianist Burt Wallace, playing Paul's own accompanist, Lawrence Brown. I knew better than anyone that I could never do justice to Paul's supreme gift.

One of Paul's old friends and colleagues, Lloyd L. Brown, was one of our most outspoken critics. I must say I had to agree with him totally on one point, which he expressed in a letter to *The Village Voice:* "It may be news in some quarters, but not all of us black folks can sing and dance. It hurt me to my soul to hear James Earl Jones as Paul Robeson. . . . The cultural racism involved in that kind of miscasting is obvious when we realize that no white producer would present that excellent, nonsinging actor, Hal Holbrook, as Enrico Caruso, singing 'Celeste Aida.'"

Lloyd Richards pointed out that it was absurd to compare me as a singer to Paul. But, Lloyd reminded me, "You will evoke Paul through your acting, not your singing."

Washington, D.C., did not give us our only positive reception to the play. Audiences in Cleveland, Ohio, had come, I think, for a different reason. They, having been sensitized by Kent State events, adopted a political position of not protesting the play, but of celebrating Robeson. They just wanted somebody to tell a story about this man.

I could see then how powerless most black people feel in this nation. Sometimes they will climb on any bandwagon if it gives them a chance to express their concerns. Since Robeson, since Martin Luther King, since Malcolm X, there has been so little guidance to help people channel their energies.

Heroes are not always saints. There were facets of Paul's robust life that we could not touch on. He was immensely attractive to women, especially in that glorious circle of young belles in London society. He had affairs, probably including some that he did not instigate, for women offered themselves to him. He was the toast of the British aristocracy.

We did not want to portray Paul as bitter, for that would be only for the man himself to confess. Bitterness is an intensely negative emotion, and I did not want to invest the character with that, not even with bitterness about the blacklist. I read the transcript of Paul's testimony before the House Un-American Activities Committee, and was struck by his sharp and gallant sense of humor and wit. I wanted to keep that in focus. He was usually able to ride the most dangerous waves with humor and grace, as well as passion.

One of the most painful encounters for Robeson came when he was denied his passport to travel to London for his last version of *Othello*, with Sam Wanamaker and Mary Ure. Paul's passion was fierce and immense, almost, Robert Earl observed, irrational, but one can understand that. Robert Earl and I listened to Paul speak publicly about the conflict.

"Oh, no," my father said. "Paul missed his target by overshooting. He blew it."

Even so, he finally received the passport, but he remained openly outspoken about the blacklist.

When it was time for us to leave Washington, we knew the bandwagon would precede us. Sure enough, when we got to New York, the National Ad Hoc Committee pulled out all the stops. They ran a full two-page advertisement in *Variety*, January 11, 1978. PAUL ROBESON: A SACRILEGE ON BROADWAY announced the *Black American* in a special eleven-page supplement on January 26. We were big-time news by now.

Appropriately, our Broadway run coincided with the great blizzard of 1978, a ferocity of snow and wind that paralyzed New York and almost every other city and town from the Midwest to the Northeast. We got a frigid reception from the Ad Hoc Committee and mixed reviews from the critics. The script was "loose, somewhat rambling," one reviewer wrote, although "well-intentioned." Glenne Currie wrote in *Theatre World* that the play was not really a play, but "a portrait," and that while the first act worked well "despite a certain amount of sentimentality," the longer second act was "almost all bald political statement—anger, frustration and polemics." T. E. Kalem wrote in *Time*, "Unfortunately, the format of this one-man show resembles a 25th-reunion class yearbook, a précis of achievements." Jack Kroll in *Newsweek* thought that the script provided "only the barest sketch of [Paul's] courage, his accomplishment and his prophetic force." But there was praise from the critics for the acting and the purpose of the play.

The Ad Hoc Committee, however, in their escalation, now ceased to absolve me as the misguided actor and instead started a very subtle campaign to discredit me personally. They did so by unearthing some comments I had made earlier which they had not then seen as important enough to address. I did not help matters when I was quoted in the press—correctly sometimes, incorrectly others. A *Washington Post* interview quoted me as saying "I listen to three opinions—my producers, my director and the writer. . . . I'm not a missionary, I'm a mercenary with a capital *M.*" By "capital *M,*" I meant to imply that I don't take battle directives from anyone, but choose my own battles in whatever war. The "Paul Robeson People's Commission" put that quote in the middle of the fliers they distributed to theatre audiences.

Journalist Carl Stokes, who had been the first black mayor of Cleveland, Ohio, had known Robeson well. He was the first journalist to investigate the controversy thoroughly and objectively. I welcomed his inquiry, even though I had no idea where it would lead. He was certainly not the cavalry rushing in to rescue me. He looked into the issue on WNBC-TV's "Urban Journal" in February 1978, because, as he said, so many of his friends signed the protest, and because he knew Paul Robeson, whom he considered a mentor, as well as one of the greatest black Americans of all time.

He said he found it ironic that the first stage production of Paul's life was attacked not by the government establishment or the white media, but by prominent members of the national black community. I did indeed tell Stokes when he interviewed me for "Urban Journal" that I thought it approached criminality for people to try to tell other people what they should or should not see. I thought these efforts to boycott our play constituted censorship, and I said so.

"I'm not just a bystander," I told Stokes. "I am not just a stupid, misguided artist. I am involved in this production. I am committed to this production. And I think what the Ad Hoc Committee is doing is wrong." Of course, my remarks, especially my suggestion of criminality, heightened the furor, and threw me into the center of the storm. That was the focus of the battle cry.

Later, an intellectual said, "Jones accuses the Ad Hoc Committee of criminality, but does he consider Clive Barnes a criminal when he gives Jones a negative review?" This gentleman seemed to equate censors and critics. I do not.

Carl Stokes documented the reality that a number of the fifty-six prominent black Americans who had signed the "statement of conscience" condemning *Paul Robeson* had not seen the play before they signed the protest, and never did see it afterward. He reported that Alvin Ailey signed because his friend Ossie Davis asked him to. Nikki Giovanni indicated that she signed because she owed a favor to the friend who asked her to sign. Other people on the list told Stokes that their names had been used without their knowledge or permission. Still others on the list, of course, had seen the play, had known Paul well, and objected to the production. That kind of opinion I could accept, although I still believe that the method used to express that opinion certainly was reckless and verged on censorship.

Stokes himself pronounced the play fair, honest, and accurate, and he had been Paul's protégé. He observed that our production was only the first about Paul, and that other plays could and should be written, perhaps by some of the people who signed the protest attacking us. He voiced his concern about a "pronounced and self-destructive divisiveness in the black establishment."

Stokes interviewed people on both sides of our battle. Paul Jr.

charged that the Robeson we created on stage was not real, and that we must have thought that "the real Paul Robeson" wouldn't sell as well as the "fake Paul Robeson" we allegedly created.

I responded that this was the sixth time I had been attacked by a watchdog committee protesting my work. "I resent it," I told Stokes during our interview, "but the only real counterattack I have is not to yield. I will always do roles that I think are important."

Paul Jr.'s reasonings were kaleidoscopic, constantly shifting, adjusting, evolving—and always fascinating. When Stokes asked Paul Jr. if any play could present an acceptable image of his father, Paul Jr. answered emphatically: "No play could do that, particularly a one-man play. So it would be absurd for me to criticize a play, or an actor, for that matter, for a portrayal that doesn't do what you said, in a man as complicated as my father."

Carl Stokes concluded his commentary this way: "This is a play Americans need to see, not because an actor rises to superlative heights in his portrayal of a character, which Jones does, but because this play re-introduces Paul Robeson to the American public and causes white and black Americans to confront the atrocious treatment they accorded this remarkable man."

We had opened in New York on January 19, and by the time of Carl Stokes's investigation, it was clear to all of us that our days were numbered. Even families seemed split over what we were trying to accomplish in *Paul Robeson*. Ossie Davis avidly supported the protest, but his wife, Ruby Dee, wrote kindly of us in the *New York Amsterdam News* on February 11, 1978:

A play about Paul Robeson at the Lunt-Fontanne theatre comes then as if in answer to "What is a great man?" Perhaps we are beginning to feel the need of such a presence again in this time fast becoming void of greatness. James Earl Jones is Paul Robeson for us for a little while, giving us a powerful picture of a powerful man who walked among us and sang and tried to fight some battles and to win some victories and by so doing to shore up our collective dignity as human beings. . . . With the skilled assistance of the director Lloyd Richards, the difficult task of portraying a man very much alive in memory is well met. Phillip Hayes Dean as author of *Paul Robeson* has opened a door for us to begin to look and measure and rediscover a beautiful man in a hard time and we are grateful to him for ourselves and for all who missed Robeson in life.

In my own family, this struggle brought my father and me as close as we have ever been, friend to friend, actor to actor. That winter of 1978 was fiercely cold. In the aftermath of the worst blizzard in decades, I took a hotel room within walking distance of the theatre, for public transportation broke down under the weight of the snow and ice. My father and I spent a lot of time together then talking. While Paul Jr. joined the picket lines protesting the play outside the theatre, Robert Earl took his own place under the marquee. On the coldest winter nights, he could be seen there, sometimes in his tuxedo, encouraging the crowd to come step into the theatre and see our show. My father would often stay out in the bitter cold, like a palace guard. I think he loved the whole thing.

He was not really taking sides. He knew Paul. He knew Paul Jr.

He would say, "My son is in there doing a play about my old friend, and my old friend's son is out here clamoring that what my son is doing in there defames his father." He would stand out front, not trying to justify me, but trying to explain that *he* knew Paul Robeson, and Robeson *did* laugh and *did* have fun, that Paul was a healthy human being whose great passion for life enfolded everything he committed himself to. Robert Earl understood how it feels to be censored, for he had sat before a Senate committee and suffered the blacklist. He was deeply conscious of the precious right to free expression.

There were preposterous charges toward the end. Just as the CIA had monitored Paul, someone reported that we were on the CIA payroll. There was paranoia and counterparanoia. There were even innuendoes that our production was bankrolled by the CIA to let blacks blow off steam, as artists and as citizens. They were referring to a tactic left over from the old Agit Prop theatre days, when the CIA did do such bankrolling.

From the time that I spoke out on Carl Stokes's television segment, I was the target for much of the protest which had been directed at Phillip. The volume was turned up so loud on the picket line outside the theatre that it became difficult to perform the play. The audience and I could hear those voices protesting outside.

Paul Robeson closed at the Lunt-Fontanne Theatre on February 26, 1978. Like everything else about the production, our closing was shrouded in confusion. *Hello, Dolly!* held a prior booking in that house, so we were forced to vacate by February 26. Our producer had implemented a two-for-one policy on ticket sales, and had not yet found a suitable New York theatre. No doubt the controversy tugging at our coattails complicated matters. Many of the protestors saw a victory in our closing.

As the final curtain fell that wintry night of February 26, 1978, I stepped beyond the footlights to do something I had never done before, nor have I since—I made a curtain speech:

> Ladies and gentlemen, I've never before stepped beyond the footlights to address myself to the conditions of a production. I've felt my best defense of a play is to go on stage every performance and play the play within the limits of my talent and according to the dictates of my conscience as a citizen and as an artist. But my feelings are constantly awake to those conditions and issues that arise outside the production, and now that the play is over I want to air some of those feelings with you. If you have a bus to catch, please do so.
>
> The two-week closing notice that appeared two weeks ago was technically in error. As *Hello, Dolly!* had prior booking in this theatre as of tomorrow, we have to vacate it, and as of yet have found no house on Broadway large enough to continue the "two seats for the price of one" policy that the producer feels necessary to continue.

He has been looking at other options: back on the road, Los Angeles, and London. At the moment London seems the best bet.

Beyond that there are plans to record the show as is for public television. I am personally open to any medium that can address itself to the life of the great man Paul Robeson, and I invite all artists, writers, directors, actors, painters, sculptors, and composers to do the same; to address themselves to the life of Paul Robeson and all other great people of our time, black and white, male and female, because our freedom to do so is at stake.

We cannot enjoy our freedoms without exercising them and defending them. The freedom to protest is also a precious one. With that freedom goes a grave responsibility *not* to abuse the cultural apparatus that makes that protest viable.

And that is really what I want to talk about now.

I have not made a personal investigation of all the cultural apparatus—the use of prestigious names to give credence to boycotts and protests which too few responsible journalists have sought to investigate. While I give credit to those who have, I would chide those who exercise a hands-off policy, as if the culture of the society is not important, or as if it is all right to let different factions of the society kill each other off in a din of confusion when much light could be brought to bear onto that confusion by daring to look under Pandora's lid.

In my twenty-one-year career as an actor I have been caught in the cross fires of many artistic-social disputes, watching them escalate to the point of abuse to freedom of artistic interpretation and therefore, as any "veteran" of those conflicts, I have some first-hand observations I feel I must share with you.

Early in my career, in my first attempt to do *Emperor Jones* (in Boston), I ran up against watchdog committees, then functioning through the NAACP. The rationale behind that protest (almost two decades ago) was that the society would be abused by hearing a degrading Southern Negro dialect, as conceived by Eugene O'Neill.

Then there was a TV production of "The Neighbors" that Gene Hackman, Beverly Todd, Kathy McGuire, and I did that was taken off the air, again by agitators through the NAACP, because my character (a jazz musician who loved Harlem and didn't give a damn about integrating neighborhoods) held a point of view that was not helpful in the NAACP thrust to bring about open housing throughout the nation.

Then there was "Nat Turner," where there was a campaign spearheaded by a friend of mine, Ossie Davis, against the film production because the film company had bought the book *Confessions of Nat Turner* written by a Southern white person, William Styron. At no time did the protesters acknowledge that 20th Century-Fox engaged a black writer, Lou Peterson, to render a screenplay, using all available sources besides Styron's book. When Sidney Lumet, the director, and I agreed to do Lou's first draft, there was no recognition of our possible good sense. When the economic bottom fell out of Fox Studios and the production cost for the film had already mounted to over six million dollars, the production was canceled. But the protest group took the credit and gained in its illusion of power.

Then there was *The Cay*. A protest was mounted (based on a reading of the book, not a viewing of the finished work). The argument was, "Why should this character speak with a degrading Caribbean accent and give his life energy and finally his life to the salvation of an eleven-year-old white boy?"

And now there is *Paul Robeson*. —Starting with an impasse between the production and Paul Robeson, Jr. over the use of the Archive. — Continuing with a campaign mounted in Louisville, Kentucky, against the play, a blanketing of the press with the points of view of the protest. —Escalating to a full-scale picket in Boston by very vocal and erratic bandwagoneers. (My first and last bodyguard was laid on then by the theatre manager). But in spite of this, with the help of Lloyd Richards, we got our first set of unanimously good reviews and continued to the Midwest and finally to D.C., Baltimore and New York.

The National Ad Hoc Committee to Stop Crimes mounted a protest. When that protest was discredited by some resourceful journalists, that picket and their leaflets were withdrawn and replaced by the Paul Robeson People's Commission (against James

Earl Jones), where a misquote through a Dorothy Gillian interview was used to try to discredit me along with my *record,* specifically in relationship to "Nat Turner."

When the closing notice for Lunt-Fontanne was posted, the protest withdrew altogether—claiming another victory!

I've been asked by several people if I wanted them to mount counter-pickets and counter-protests. I said no. I don't work for gangs, and I won't work through gangs. I'll do my own fighting. As Paul in the play says, "I don't like people getting behind me, and I want both my arms free." My personal protest will be to continue, through the nature of the plays and characters I choose, to assert my freedom and responsibility as an actor.

But I feel I must address myself to the cultural apparatus (to use the words of Prof. C. Wright Mills) that fails to take responsibility and continues to escalate to a position of power and control that amounts to censorship, and threatens not to "stop crimes against men like Paul Robeson" but to continue the crime of silence against Paul Robeson. Too many names keep popping up for me to ignore, not all black and not all left, but fossilized in an intellectual position and a rhetoric and a theatric more suited to the '50s than to the '70s and '80s.

As I ask no one to do anything for me, I beg artists and public alike to do something for themselves, first for our freedom (fight for more rather than less) to express and interpret. What is the function of a playwright if not to give to an audience his special insight about the essence of a great hero? Deny that right to fulfill that function, and there is no point in being an artist.

It is important because there is a confusion as to what is "degrading to the public" and "what is disturbing to the public." Every play, at some point, should be disturbing.

I don't stand here on the stage to make people go out of the theatre feeling *good* over *nothing.* I'd much rather let them go out of the theatre *disturbed* over *something.*

And so I'll see you in a couple of years, as soon as I've found a play through which I can disturb you—Good night.

* * *

The drama was not over, off stage or on. My good friend Joe Papp sat in the audience that last night at the Lunt-Fontanne with Sidney Poitier and Harry Belafonte. Joe decided to invest more than a hundred thousand dollars to open the show under the umbrella of the New York Shakespeare Festival at the Booth Theatre in New York. Joe praised our production, and asserted his belief that keeping the play alive would ensure that thousands of people who knew little or nothing of Paul Robeson could be inspired by his life. We would alternate with the play he had already running at the Booth, *For Colored Girls Who Have Considered Suicide/When the Rainbow is Enuf.* The author of that play, Ntozake Shange, spoke out for us. Poetic people should have poetic license, she said as she criticized protesters who disrupted the creative process.

Joe gave *Paul Robeson* a new home, new life. The bandwagon packed up and rolled out of town. They claimed a symbolic victory in the closing of the play, and did not bother to picket when we opened at the Booth Theatre. Yet the debate wore on. Norman Mailer wrote about the ongoing saga of *Paul Robeson.* James Baldwin, who had read only an unfinished draft of the script and who confessed that he had not seen the play, defended the Robeson Ad Hoc Committee in *The Village Voice* in late March. Only Jimmy could write, "It has been obliquely suggested that, since I have not seen the play, I can have no judgments concerning it, or that my judgment is doomed to be unfair. This is nonsense. Plays are read and judged—*seen,* in the mind's eye—long before they are produced: Indeed, this is *how* they are produced."

Paul Robeson closed at the Booth in March, but we did complete a PBS film of the show and we went on to London. Pickets waited for us there. The controversy had crossed the Atlantic, and was even more vocal. Pickets bore signs reading "Sidney Poitier and Harry Belafonte Don't Like this Production." That is not what Harry or Sidney said, but the name-dropping had its effect.

May 12, 1978, marked the grand finale of this long ad hoc spectacle. All of us associated with the production were immensely heartened when the Dramatists Guild issued a statement that day protesting that group censorship of a play violates the principles of the First Amendment and threatens freedom of expression.

"The Executive Council of The Dramatists Guild deplores any attempts on any grounds, be they political, artistic, philosophical or moral, to influence critics and audiences against a play," the guild statement said. "We are particularly concerned when this action is taken prior to the play's actual presentation. . . . If the practice of group censorship takes root in the American theater, freedom of expression will be gravely imperiled." Thirty-three members of the Dramatists Guild Council signed the statement, including Edward Albee, Paddy Chayefsky, Betty Comden, Marc Connelly, Jules Feiffer, Herb Gardner, Frank D. Gilroy, John Guare, Lillian Hellman, Garson Kanin, Sidney Kingsley, Jerome Lawrence, Alan Jay Lerner, Terrence McNally, Arthur Miller, Mary Rodgers, Richard Rodgers, Dore Schary, Stephen Sondheim, Peter Stone, Jule Styne, and Jerome Weidman.

But the last word came from the opposition. That Friday night, May 12, James Baldwin chaired a forum at Hunter College: "Paul Robeson—The Play, the Protest, the Legacy and the Lessons." The panel members—Jimmy Baldwin, Ossie Davis, the writer Clayton Riley, English professor Dr. Jewell Handy Greshman, and Paul Robeson, Jr. More than a thousand people packed the college auditorium. I was not invited to attend.

But I did not intend to miss this forum, and I told my father I meant to go. "Let me go with you," he said immediately. He knew this was going to be a hornet's nest of angry, frustrated people. So I walked into the auditorium that night with Robert Earl at my side.

I sometimes think many of the people agitating against the play were somehow trying to work out the guilt of having failed the living Paul Robeson. They needed to make amends, and our play became the vehicle for their expiation.

As I remember, Jimmy Baldwin flew in from Paris or Turkey or somewhere for the forum, as was his habit in crucial moments when he decided there was a need for a spokesman. He would fly back to the United States to join the fray. Treating this forum like a photo opportunity, he just wanted to express his need to protect one of the greatest heroes that black America will ever know.

The memories of that night still hurt. I sat there with my father while they all had their say. Jimmy Baldwin had his say about the play he had not seen. Ossie had his say, his comments deepening my distrust for him. Many people had good lies to tell, often about me. Whenever that would happen, my father would pat my knee. He kept me from standing up and shouting out to challenge them.

"This is a hotbed," he would say. "Just keep your seat and hold your tongue. This is something you know too little about." He was referring to the whole gathering. He had learned his own hard lessons in the thirties and the fifties about the frustrated activist, the feelings of impotence. We got through the meeting.

Some women sitting just in front of us were having a good time throughout the session, often at my expense. When the lights came on after the forum, they turned and saw me. They said, "Oh, we didn't know you were sitting there." It did not really matter.

I remember that forum as a painful final exercise in futility.

I keep among my papers a poem written by David Robeson, Paul's grandson, Paul Jr.'s son. It is dated January 26, 1976, the day Paul Sr. died. For me it is a treasure, and a comfort. I think of it, too, as a prophecy. It goes in part:

> *He is not mine ...*
> *He passes by me,*
> *But he does not pass from me ...*
> *He does not belong to me.*
> *I may keep memories of him*
>   *but not his essence,*
> *For that will pour forth tomorrow.*

Today, sponsored by Malcolm X's daughter, Attilah Shabazz, actor Avery Brooks adds his own ability as a singer to the play and performs it all over the country, without any form of protest.

In spite of the turmoil, I enjoyed acting in that play, and I appreciated my father's strong hand of friendship and support during the off-stage ordeal. When Don Gregory asked me to take the performance on the road, at first I said, "I'd love to, and I also need a job." But in the end, I decided not to go. I felt I would have problems working with Phillip, for I still wanted some refinements in the script, and he had been so exhausted by the ordeal that he resisted changing a word. The play was imperfect, and could still evolve, still gather strength. But I saw that was not going to happen.

I withdrew, and at that point Don Gregory said, "Why don't we do *Othello?*"

18.

GRENDEL

At certain times I have no race, I am me.

ZORA NEALE HURSTON

Brute existents, you know, are a dime a dozen.

JOHN GARDNER, GRENDEL
(NEW YORK: ALFRED A. KNOPF, 1971)

In John Gardner's novel *Grendel*, we see mythological figures acting out a universal drama, the ultimate witch-hunt. There is a cave. Inside the cave, Grendel the monster lies in hibernation with his family. There is also a dragon. Outside the cave are the Norse people, barely evolved above cavemen themselves, enduring harsh and precarious lives. And there is Beowulf, who was to become the matador to Grendel's bull.

As the story begins, Grendel goes out to forage. He does not know the difference between one animal and another—between elk and man. The mythology begins to build up about him. The young Grendel simply sees himself as the being he is. He does not know what to make of it at first, but when he goes into the village, the people go into hysterics. It begins to excite him.

"Did I cause that?" he begins to wonder. He eventually accepts the mythology and begins to act it out. Then he meets Beowulf, whose immortality is dependent on Grendel's mortality. The Norse people cannot find a hero until they create a monster. John Gardner writes about it this way in *Grendel:*

> The dragon tipped up his great tusked head, stretched his neck, sighed fire. "Ah, Grendel!" he said. He seemed that instant almost to rise to pity. "You improve them, my boy! Can't you see that yourself? You stimulate them! You make them think and scheme. You drive them to poetry, science, religion, all that makes them what they are for as long as they last. You are, so to speak, the brute existent by which they learn to define themselves. The exile, captivity, death they shrink from—the blunt facts of their mortality, their abandonment—that's what you make them recognize, embrace! You *are* mankind, or man's condition: inseparable as the mountain-

climber and the mountain. If you withdraw, you'll instantly be replaced. Brute existents, you know, are a dime a dozen. . . .

"Brute existents," powerful mythologies can be embodied in one image. The heroes—and monsters—of a time are rooted in its mythology. I believe the roots of both *racism* (the prejudice of the majority—the group who has power) and *racialism* (the prejudice of the minority groups without power, who begin to act out defensively) are planted deep in the psychotic side of mythology. Racism is an offensive act, racialism a defensive act. Both are sick, in myth as well as a reality.

In recent times, the Los Angeles riots have revived the issues of race, racism, and racialism in ways I had hoped we would not ever have to consider again. Rodney King became Grendel the minute he stepped out of his vehicle and allegedly shook his ass at sheriff's deputy Melanie Singer, the minute that Sergeant Koons took matters into his own hands. The defense in the state trial got all the officers off once it convinced the jury that Rodney King evolved to a superhuman threat, making monster sounds, exhibiting monster strength. The boys who beat Reginald Denny acted out the mythic drama of racialism, getting back at the monster they conceived as "whitey." In their "responsive" brutality, Reginald Denny's attackers probably thought they were attacking Beowulf.

It becomes clear that the problems of race transcend social and political issues. Race is a problem of mythological proportion, even though it is a fairly new insanity, less than five hundred years old— and it is universal, as demonstrated today in this country, in Germany, in Eastern Europe, in Africa and South Africa, and elsewhere—everywhere.

Once you begin to explain or excuse all events on racial grounds, you begin to indulge in the perilous mythology of race. It is dangerous to say "The white man is the cause of my problems" or "The black man is the cause of my problems." Substitute any color— the danger is implicit.

My concepts of race, racialism, and racism go all the way back to my mama, Maggie, and her ways of interpreting the world, and her fierce indoctrinations. Since my childhood, I have tried to keep from sinking into the mythological fears of racism: that is something I have always tried to resist, and that resistance necessarily infuses my work as well as my life. I cannot walk back over the landscape of my life without encountering outcroppings of racism.

When we were children, Mama and Papa ensured that we would scamper indoors before dark by evoking the specter of the boogeyman. "The boogeyman is out there in the dark, in the woods. The boogeyman will get you if you don't come in." Sometimes it was the muleheaded man or the woman with snakes in her belly who threatened us in the dark. This childhood intimidation is not unlike the mythology that begins to evolve on a whole cultural level.

I remember once walking down the road from school in Michigan and being pelted with clods of debris thrown by fellow students in a passing forestry truck. I always examined such incidents. Was I pelted because I am black? Was it only a random prank? Once in our school yard a black person dear to me was forced to put his face into the snow where older white boys had just urinated. Was it simply an initiation into their circle, as they claimed—or was it racial humiliation? I could not bring myself to automatically assume that we were racial targets. I had to allow for other possibilities.

When my house in the country burned, the sheriff assured me it was not racially motivated, yet a curious legend was woven out of the incident. In the charred ruins lay the remnants of what looked like a terrorist's arsenal. In reality, the guns were harmless reproductions, or "counterfeits," but because many people bought into the mythology of the dangerous, revolutionary black person, rumors swirled that I was such a terrorist. I suffered further rumor-mythology—a charge I could trace to the door of a respected local preacher—that because I am a black man, and because black men are supposed to be endowed with great sexual prowess, I was running a harem at my house. I never knew whether it was in private or from his pulpit that he spoke of the iniquities of James Earl Jones, black actor, on (his term) "Harem Hill Road."

I see myself as vulnerable in a way that I try to put in perspective, not only giving the other fellow the benefit of the doubt, but sparing myself rampant paranoia.

Once in the sixties, I was cautioned that another black actor was masquerading as me. Apparently, with beards, we looked somewhat alike. He was introducing himself as James Earl Jones, using me as a way to seduce women: the sex-power-race mythology. Whether that mythology is exploited by a black person or a white person is irrelevant. It is still mythology, and dangerous.

Whenever racial tensions get ugly, the man on the street, often the white man, ends up saying, "Why don't you niggers go back to where you came from?" The answer to that is, "Why don't you Europeans go back to Europe?" Only the Native American Indians are at home on this continent. The rest of us came, by desperate choice or force, as strangers to a new land. In the land of the Native American, two strangers, two newcomers, one black, one white, stand toe-to-toe in the battle over a land that historically did not belong to them.

Once the Native American population was decimated or subordinated, Caucasian Europeans constituted the majority. The majority has the power. Consequently, the majority is dominant. That is a condition to be acknowledged, not rejected. As long as democratic principles are being exercised, the fact that one culture is dominant should not be a problem.

The minority culture tends to know the majority culture better than the majority understands the minority. This is so because the survival of the minority depends upon a much broader awareness. I have always felt that while black students must understand black culture for enrichment, they can never hide in it at the expense of understanding the larger society. That can be too risky, too limiting. All of us have to learn to negotiate the majority culture. For instance, no matter what your race, it is important to learn to speak standard English and to understand all the lore written in that language. I cannot imagine a black American entering an African society where the dominant language is Swahili, presuming he can afford not to know that language in all its classical accuracy.

Sometimes I paraphrase an old man who used to say, "Ah, yes, the Comanches. I have lived amongst them nigh on to twenty years. I know them well."

I say, "Ah, yes, the white men. I have lived amongst them for nigh on to sixty years. I know them well."

When I have to state my racial identity on some legal document, I could as well sign "Negroid-Caucasoid-Mongoloid." I possess all those genes, and I have to account for all of them in my identity. All of them define who I am. To the extent that genetic energy is spiritual, my spirit is forged from all those ancestors—the African, the Irish, the Cherokee-Choctaw.

I once said that if I had not become an actor, I probably would have become some sort of revolutionary. I probably would have been militant if I had not been able to find release through artistic expression.

I think the entertainment industry is making an effort to confront racial issues today, but certainly not enough. There is the whole issue of equity in casting, not only for the African-American, but for Asian Americans and Hispanic Americans and others. I have serious concerns about the regressive treatment of certain issues—interracial marriage, for instance. Some plays and films have attempted to put that issue into perspective. But because race is a myth, dramatic conflict based only on race is conflict based on myth and should not comprise the primary drama in films or plays involving people of differing races and cultures. Spike Lee, in a new generation, is doing very well in his films, admirably developing his own style; it is hard to criticize someone who is doing well. I see his *Jungle Fever*, for instance, and say to myself, "I thought we had already dealt with those issues." Then I see that each generation must discover certain realities for itself. Yet I still feel Spike is sometimes reaching back regressively, fueling the old dilemmas without clarifying them.

The primary drama in the black man's life in this country has not been his conflict with the white man. There is racism, for sure, but there is life beyond racism. There are things more important.

Back in the sixties, the common challenge of black militants to black moderates such as myself was, "When you wake up in the morning and you look in the mirror, what do you see?"

"I see a human being," I would say.

"No, no, no," they would say. "You better see a black human being"—because that is what the white man would see.

What they were saying is that I must see myself in the context of how others see me. I say no to that. That is buying into racial insanity. They tell me that I have to see myself as a black man first or I fail to face the reality as it is in this country. But when I wake up in the morning, I see myself not as a black human being, nor as a male human being. I see myself as I am—as a human being, and that is also the identity with which I retire at night.

There is nothing wrong in being seen as a black person so long as that perception stops with color. But the harm comes when certain stereotypes are automatically applied—"a black person, therefore an impoverished person, therefore a disadvantaged person, therefore an inferior person." These prejudgments—prejudices—carry danger.

I know there are values in retaining the cultures of distinct ethnic identities, but I deeply believe that as Hispanic kids, Asian kids, and black kids are encouraged to indulge in their minority cultures, they have to deal with the majority culture. Whether they want to call it the white man's ways or not, they have to confront the reality of the majority culture. Because they have been forced to live on reservations (ghettos), Native Americans (and African-Americans) are getting into some heavy-duty isolationist movements. They are skirting reality by doing so. For instance, it can be self-defeating to try to keep non–Native American or non–African-American parents from adopting Native American or African-American orphans. That becomes a game of political agendas, and a child in need of nurturing guardians is not political.

I look at the plight of Native Americans, their progress forestalled by the reservations. They are Americans; they cannot keep holding to the reservation out of defensiveness any more than blacks can hold to the ghetto out of defensiveness, as if to say, "This is our place and our *only* place." The need for "our place" is misplaced. The early Malcolm X had the idea of carving out a section of the United States to make a black nation. I genuinely believe that was the stupidest idea that wise man ever proposed.

I think all ethnic minorities have to be encouraged to step into the majority culture, to take it on, consume it, and produce in it, to work with it and get past cultural habits that may keep individuals from moving ahead. I believe this can be done without yielding pride in ethnic origin, or betraying ethnic identity.

It is time for us to resolve to move ahead. If a black child or an Oriental child or a Hispanic child says, "Does that mean I have got to be better than anybody else," I have to answer, "Yes, it may—and it has always been that way." That may never change. In the movie *Soul Man,* there is a white student who is posing as a black man in order to get a scholarship. As his professor, I accept him as black, and I say to him, "If you have to be, if it means that you have to be twice as good as these little white shits, then get busy and *be* twice as good as they are."

I don't think we can be slack about that. To indulge in resentment dulls the mental framework. In the ghetto it is too easy for a child to be encouraged to approach life the dangerous way, the criminal way. For instance, if you let a child accept the drug scene and step into the drug trade as consumer or purveyor, you do him irreparable harm. White or Asian drug dealers would not be accepted or tolerated in the white or Asian community. Black drug dealers should not be tolerated in theirs simply because they are black. Likewise, you cannot encourage a black child to grow up saying, "I don't want to be whitey, I don't want to talk like whitey, I don't want to get an education like whitey." There are too few alternatives, and if you reject education in particular, you are left with ways of survival which are not very healthy. Too many blacks get trapped in the syndrome of petty gangsterism, and part of it is because they are encouraged out of a good old healthy sense of racial identity to reject the mainstream. That is very treacherous. I've always found it curious that other ethnic groups have been more able to use crime only as a temporary step in their quest for the American dream, whereas African-Americans too often get caught in the loop of crime perpetuating crime.

Again, we are strangers in a strange land, so to speak, much as Othello was. He had to enter that land and live within it, not repudiating his identity, but honoring it at the same time that he confronted the challenge of the new land. You have to summon up enormous grace to live so that the frustrations of racial barriers do not defeat you. You have to command that grace in order to survive in spirit. Taking pride in what you are has got to include a healthy acknowledgment of what the society surrounding you is.

I look back at my own family and see people who always managed to keep pushing ahead without losing any of what they were. I am not saying that every single member of the family has been upwardly mobile or that each one is an assimilationist trying to be just like "whitey," but most of them have taken full advantage of the opportunities open to people at large. We cannot reject education or ways of speaking or the positive aspects of the dominant culture simply because they seem to be the white man's education or the white man's language.

Ideally, every ethnic group contributes vitally to the national culture, but for the minority to shut itself out is a tragic choice. We face enough obstacles without erecting self-made ghetto walls.

*   *   *

The first honorary degree I ever received came from Fairfield University in Connecticut. Gordon Parks, the photographer, also received a degree that day, and he delivered the commencement speech. He addressed young black people, telling them that if they felt hostility between white people and black people, the worst thing they could do was separate themselves from society.

Gordon urged the students to get themselves into the white man's reality as much as possible, to stay under his wing, right beside his elbow. He was saying that you don't separate yourself from the white man, especially if you think he is your enemy. You stay in lockstep with him. It was an interesting challenge. You cannot isolate yourself from the world and function in it. You cannot hide behind the walls. You just have to face that reality.

I believe that culture is based on language. If that is the case, we as black American people have a tenuous cultural identity. We tend to be identified as a group merely by a certain configuration of facial features or darker pigmentation of the skin. But we are not simply one single culture. Black people come from many rich cultures and languages—cultures and languages whose roots were severed by the institution of slavery.

I have never found solace in herds of any sort. I have always been a loner. This has nothing to do with my color. It has to do with my temperament. I have found the deepest bonds of my life to be interior connections of temperament. I have learned that color alone is not sufficient reason for conflict or for connection. Color does not inevitably bond, just as it must not inevitably separate. There is nothing inherently, automatically bonding about skin color. Skin is only tissue, pigment, surface. Skin is not identity.

Nelson Mandela, in his court defense thirty years ago, argued passionately that if you allow a degradation to continue for more than one generation, it becomes genetic. It is the damned "sins of the fathers" all over again. Degradation built into the society, the economy, the national psyche, quickly has its mirror image in degradation built into the individual psyche. I contend that any human being who for any reason is subjected to degradation must confront it and do his or her individual best to transcend it.

We all know the myriad roots and reasons for prejudice, and, obviously, we must work together, all of us, for social justice and equal opportunity. Otherwise, ultimately, not one of us is free or equal or safe. But it is not enough to cast the blame elsewhere and live lives of quiet or violent desperation. That does not solve anything. Each of us of every race must say for ourselves, "This has got to stop. I am going to stop this, in my life."

I could not ever allow myself to say in the earlier years, "I will never make it in the theatre because I am black." I had to say, "I may never make it because I lack talent or drive or commitment, but I will never *not* make it simply because I wear black skin."

In my own family, my father grew up without his father. I grew up without my father. My father passed on the legacy of the absent father. My mission has been to break that chain in my own life, to stop it with my son Flynn and me. I will always be there for my son. It is as simple as that. That is all it takes, just to stop it. I have that power and that choice.

Likewise, my father Robert Earl chose to escape the oppression of the South in the 1930s. Inch by inch, he worked his way, as prizefighter and as actor, through the obstacle course society threw in front of him. Inch by inch, he helped to open doors in theatre and in movies which had always slammed tight against the efforts of black men and women who wanted to enter there to make use of their craft on the visible stages and movie screens of this country. Inch by inch, as Robert Earl fought for these rights, he exposed himself politically. But those inches my father chose to walk, joined to the inches won by so many others, undergird the strides taken by Sidney Poitier, Ruby Dee, Cicely Tyson, Morgan Freeman, Oprah Winfrey, Danny Glover, and Denzel Washington, and by a whole new generation.

It was a hard path my father chose, but out of his choice sprang greater opportunity of choice for me and for other actors. What little choice my father had, he exercised. What choice I possess, I have tried to exercise.

And these are universal human choices, not confined to any one race.

19.

TELEVISION FROM TARZAN TO PARIS TO GABRIEL'S FIRE

Gabriel Bird (James Earl Jones) is an ex-Chicago cop who has spent the last 20 years in prison for shooting his partner to death during a raid gone awry. . . . Just out of prison, Gabe orders a hot dog—with the works—from a street vendor. He takes a bite, then roars with delight, literally savoring his first taste of freedom.

TV GUIDE, September 15, 1990

In the early days of my television career, I seemed to be typecast as a doctor, a detective, or a tribal chief. I did my doctoring on "As the World Turns" in 1965, the first black actor to play a recurring role on a soap opera. Curiously, it turned into an interchangeable role, with Brock Peters sometimes playing the same doctor, with the same name. I did a guest appearance as a doctor on "Dr. Kildare" in 1966, as a detective on "The Defenders" series in 1964, and as a tribal chief on "Tarzan." There I did double duty—as Chief Bella in 1967 and Chief Nerlan in 1968. In one of my more memorable scenes, the Supremes appeared clad demurely in habits, playing African nuns. I appeared more flagrantly attired in the stereotypical loincloth and feathers assigned to the African tribal chief. For reasons now obliterated from my memory, the script called for the nun-Supremes and the tribal chief to sing "Michael, Row the Boat Ashore." And we did, habits, feathers, loincloth, and all. I sang with the Supremes, and it was recorded.

I was promoted to preacher in a WNET Playhouse production of *Trumpets of the Lord* in 1968, and gave a number of performances drawn from stage productions—excerpts from *The Great White Hope* on the "Ed Sullivan Show," for instance (Ed Sullivan introduced me as Jack Jones), and scenes from *Of Mice and Men* on the "Today" show.

In 1969, David Susskind invited me to a meeting to discuss the possibility of starring in a television series. David, I think, had a lot of intellectual pretensions (he himself claimed he was the most intellectually endowed man in the world), but he was a sharp businessman. He was doing a television series called "N.Y.P.D.," which was to be one of the first times—even before Robert Culp and Bill Cosby did "I Spy"—that a "salt-and-pepper team" was assembled and cast. It was one of the first "cop" series to put a white man and a black man on equal footing, two New York City policeman working side by side.

There were several meetings. Finally, there was one crucial one at which I met with the casting people and then got to meet with David Susskind himself. As our meeting terminated, he turned to me and said, "Jones, pound for pound, you're the man we want."

I said, "Well, thank you," and I left.

Shortly after that, just a few days or so, I went to an opening night party, and I saw Robert Hooks. At one point, Robert very casually said to me, "Well, it's starting, it's starting. I got my first job in TV—on the new series 'N.Y.P.D.'"

"Really?" I gasped.

I didn't tell him about my meeting with Susskind. I became aware there and then that until a producer has signed the papers, he might just want to hold you until he decides if he needs you. David Susskind's words were merely his way of giving me what they call some sort of expression of interest. But I took it pound for pound.

Then I began to wonder if Susskind had been teasing me. Was he telling me I was too heavy, too fat for the role? Well, I was fairly thin then, and it was a part I wanted. I felt I was ready for television. Later, I went on to do a guest shot on "N.Y.P.D." I had had my head shaved for *The Great White Hope* at the time that I was offered the role of Candy Latson, an ex-convict who ran a halfway house, Phoenix House in New York. It was two episodes—the story of his life and of how the N.Y.P.D. interacted with him and Phoenix House. I had met Candy and interviewed him as I prepared for the role. He was very dark, very smooth, very sophisticated—something I was not—but I played him with my usual stage simplicity, something he was not.

Lucy put me up for the leading role in the television series "Quincy," which Jack Klugman made a great success, but I was much more attracted to the format of Peter Falk's "Columbo," which came on only once or twice a month. At the time I had a problem with doing a weekly hour-long series. Lucy also suggested me for a new series called "The Streets of San Francisco," a show about an older and a younger cop. "The Streets of San Francisco" was my first real chance at a series. The producers were quite serious about casting me, for I had just come off my first notoriety with *The Great White Hope*. "If I'm to play the older cop, why couldn't my partner be Oriental?" I asked, oblivious to the general Hollywood "concept" of so-called salt-and-pepper casting. They could not conceive of both characters being from minority groups.

I was still concerned about the time commitment. "I don't think I have the kind of energy to sustain a series," I said. I didn't think then that was what I wanted. So I passed on both "Quincy" and "The Streets of San Francisco." Julienne and I were divorced. I didn't have a child. There was nothing that made it imperative that I have a steady job in television. But I find it heartening that producers that far back were that willing to go with a black star. But because of those two choices I made, you had the greater pleasure of watching Jack Klugman on "Quincy" and Karl Malden on "The Streets of San Francisco."

I once entered into discussions to play Martin Luther King, Jr., in a television film biography. I met with the director and writers several times. It was quite clear that they had a certain respect for the quality of my acting on the stage. The director thought that I could play the role.

"But," he said, "physically and vocally, you are nothing like King. I am willing to overlook that, although of course Coretta King has the final say about casting. I'd like you to read, and we'll set up an audition."

It might be irrelevant, but I think that my name was a factor. "*James Earl* Jones" had to remind Coretta of the name of Martin's assassin, James Earl Ray. Other people have confused us; ironically, I have even been introduced as James Earl Ray, even by Jesse Jackson. It might have been my imagination, but every time I met Coretta, I thought I could see a haze come over her eyes. But more likely it was because I didn't resemble Martin in any way that she chose Paul Winfield to play King.

One of my most interesting journeys into television occurred in 1973 when I was host for a television variety show called "Black Omnibus," interviewing black men and women in show business, sports, medicine, the arts, politics—any area where interesting people were doing interesting work. My dream was to make journeys not unlike Charles Kuralt's "On the Road," going to different parts of the country where the black story is rich. Economics did not allow that to happen. We tried to design the show to reach a general audience, but we put the spotlight on black people.

I had to learn to relax during the interviews, for the stuttering made me less comfortable just "rapping" without a prepared script. We hoped the show would be an introduction to black history, and to interesting contemporary black notables. Young Richard Pryor was one of my guests, in a roster that included singing groups, politicians, ministers, and such luminaries as Eubie Blake, Lou Rawls, Althea Gibson, Odetta, and Dr. Alvin Poussaint.

In 1974, after a PBS recording of the successful stage production of *King Lear,* I got a chance to portray another old man, Timothy in the "Bell System Family Theater" television drama *The Cay,* based on Theodore Taylor's novel. This is the story of an aging black Caribbean seaman who befriends and ultimately gives his life to save a young white boy. The show got a befuddling response—awards and praise for its humanity on the one hand, censorship and criticism for its "racism" on the other. Racism and racialism actively existed in some black protestors who campaigned to keep the story out of schools because they were incensed that a black man would give his life for a white boy.

I played Alex Haley in *Roots II: The Next Generations,* and learned from that the indelible impact of the stamp of television exposure. I still meet people who saw me in "Roots" and insist, even after his death, that I am Alex Haley. "No, I played Alex," I tell them. "My name is James Earl Jones." They argue with me, and ask for Alex's autograph, not mine. "Come on," they'll say. "Write your *real* name."

* * *

By 1979, I thought I finally was ready for a television series. In the past, I had resisted a weekly series on the grounds that it ties you up for nine months of the year and saps too much energy. Then I looked at it another way: a series can give you a few months of freedom—and it is the only chance an actor has to become wealthy these days.

In 1979, Steven Bochco created "Paris" with me in mind. We had been friends for years; his mother Mimi Bochco was my agent Lucy's oldest and dearest friend. Steven has said that when he talked to his boss Grant Tinker at MTM about the series, Tinker told him, "If you can deliver Jones, you've got a commitment for a series." Paris was a police captain who taught criminology at a local university. I wanted him to be a shrewd detective who solved his cases by deduction and who held to an unswerving sense of justice. I hoped that he would come to be known as a *great* detective, period—not a great *black* detective, just as Charlie Chan was known as a smart detective, not a smart Chinese detective.

Steven envisioned "Paris" as a vehicle centered around one dominant character. He later went on to become the master of the television ensemble cast series—with "Hill Street Blues" and "L.A. Law." "Paris," however, lasted only thirteen weeks. Steven thinks the series failed because I was a black man exerting authority over whites. On the contrary, I think we failed because we blew it—unsatisfactory stories and an unworkable one-character concept. "Paris" and "The Lazarus Syndrome," starring Louis Gossett, also introduced that year, were the first network series with black stars concentrating on serious, straight drama. It became fashionable to say both failed because the general audience was not comfortable with blacks in serious roles. We should admit poor quality when *that* is the problem.

I enjoyed the work on "Paris" while it lasted. I liked the stimulation of meeting a weekly deadline, and I did not mind the weekly grind, or the drive to pull a show together in a few days. I liked the steady work, and being able to stay at home. But most of all, I liked all of my fellow actors, especially a beautiful, bright, sassy, sexy actress named Cecilia Hart.

When I did *The Great White Hope* in Washington, D.C., Ceci was a student at a Washington junior college for women, where she was enrolled in the theatre arts program. Occasionally, the head of the drama department allowed certain drama classes into Washington to see plays, especially those at the Arena Stage, where we were playing. It was thought it would be illuminating for the students to see *The Great White Hope*—because the play had gotten "second-coming reviews," as Ceci puts it. Then the dean heard that the play had to do with a love affair between a black man and a white woman. Without any explanation, the field trip was canceled. So fate thwarted my first encounter with Cecilia Hart. We didn't meet until ten years later. By then, I had had my first success as an actor, and so had Ceci. Yet we did not meet in New York, where she had been a smash hit on Broadway in Tom Stoppard's *Dirty Linen.*

What actually brought us together is that when Steven Bochco was casting *Paris,* he did what he often does and looked about among his friends and colleagues. He had gone to Carnegie Mellon with Ceci's then-husband, Bruce Weitz. Steven told Ceci he was working on a pilot for a series with me, and offered her a part, without an audition—and warned her that it was a small role, with very little money.

"Are you interested?" Steven asked Ceci.

To hear Ceci tell it, her response was, "What? Are you nuts? To work with James Earl Jones? When will I ever have another chance like this? I'm in."

Of course, her agents threw a fit, for they hoped to find a big role for her in a sitcom, on the heels of her success on Broadway.

"We don't care if Bochco's show stars Jesus Christ," they told her. "You are taking a small part with no money, and you will take yourself out of the running for other roles."

There must be a benign spirit watching over me: over her agents' considerable protests, the contrary Ceci Hart made the decision to join the cast of "Paris."

We were friends from the beginning. We met at a party at Steven Bochco's house. I took my current fiancée, and Ceci came with her husband, who was also an actor, and who went on to a long run in "Hill Street Blues." I have never liked Hollywood parties, and I came late to this one and left early.

We got to work in the summer of 1979. I respected the fact that Ceci was married, but thoroughly enjoyed her company on the set. We had many friends in common in New York. She made me laugh. She was stimulating. And she did not seem to take me seriously at all, which meant I could relax and be myself with her. We would sit in my trailer between scenes and read the *New York Times* and all the other New York newspapers, gossip, and talk about everything on earth. We had a wonderful time—and there was no doubt that we were attracted to each other, although I would look at her, so young and beautiful—and married—and doubt that she could ever be attracted to me, a middle-aged, slightly overweight black man.

All too soon, "Paris" was canceled. The ratings were not high enough to keep us going. I headed back to New York, and Ceci stayed in California. During the work on the series, I had broken my engagement. I said to my betrothed, "If I can be as attracted to someone I am working with as I am to Ceci, even knowing I can't consummate it, then I don't think I am ready to marry. Later, when Ceci was legally separated from her husband, we started seeing each other in New York. We would go to dinner or to the theatre, and we would talk a lot and laugh a lot.

I knew I wanted to get married again, and even more, I knew that I wanted children. I was so passionate about becoming a father that I doubted I could have ever married anyone who couldn't have children. When Ceci moved to New York permanently, I was elated. She was going to be a free woman, and I was going to court her and, I hoped, persuade her to marry me.

By 1981, we were spending most of our time together. I was doing *Othello* on Broadway. I loved Ceci so much that I was determined to get married, whether we could have children or not. I resolved to talk her into it and I succeeded. We were married in a simple ceremony at the United Nations Chapel in 1982. Lucy hosted our wedding reception at her Manhattan apartment, where our friends and families helped us celebrate. On our wedding night, we conceived our son Flynn.

I have done some of my best film work in movies made for television. I have had the chance to do new plays on such programs as "American Playwrights Theatre" on the Arts and Entertainment Network. Mario Van Peebles and I did Marsha Norman's *Third and Oak: The Pool Hall*, a collaboration I enjoyed not only because of the play and because Mario is a talented actor, but because his father, Melvin Van Peebles, directed my father in a film years ago. Mario later directed me in an episode of my television series "Gabriel's Fire."

In 1990, eager to settle down at home in Los Angeles with my family, I undertook my first weekly dramatic series since "Paris." With my son Flynn enrolled in school in Los Angeles, the family was no longer free to travel with me on locations around the country and the world, as they had been. I had been looking for a television series for several years. My agents and co-producers had been casting about for just the right format and material. In 1989, they brought me a drama and a sitcom, and I liked them both. To my surprise, Lorimar Productions and ABC chose the drama, "Gabriel's Fire," an unorthodox story set in Chicago, written by Coleman Luck and Jacqueline Zambrano, the writers and producers of "The Equalizer." I was to play Gabriel Bird, a Chicago policeman imprisoned for twenty years for killing his partner.

We went to Chicago in the winter to film the pilot. My co-stars were remarkable—Madge Sinclair, my longtime friend, and my colleague on stage and in film; Laila Robins, a graceful young actress just out of the Yale Drama School; and two fine young actors named Brian Grant and Dylan Walsh.

Gabriel Bird fascinated me. He was a character with many facets and great potential for development. He was an elemental man, like Steinbeck's Lennie and some of Fugard's characters, stripped to the essence, without a load of trappings, sophistication, conceits.

Suddenly, after twenty years of being locked away, he is ejected from the prison world into the real world, a world which has changed drastically since his incarceration began. While he has heard and read about this world and witnessed its transformations on television, he must now confront it in all its true unpredictability.

Gabriel Bird steps into this new world with a certain purity of vision: he looks at things for what they are, not for what he expects them to be. And for the first time in twenty years, he has to make choices; no longer subject to the rigid order of the prison system, he has to establish order within his own new "freedom." Running through the drama was an inescapable theme—the syndrome of incarceration, from the time of slavery up until today. There were rich psychological, sociological, and historical reverberations to explore. I have visited prisons many times, going up to Greenhaven in New York to celebrate Christmas with the inmates; helicoptering into Sing-Sing for IBM's celebration of the completion of its computer course; going to Stateville Penitentiary in Joliet, Illinois, to film parts of "Gabriel's Fire." Each time I have entered a prison, I have left a society that has a majority of white faces and a minority of non-white faces—and entered a society that has a majority of non-white faces and a minority of white.

The only thing left of freedom in prison is your mind and your imagination. If those are lost, you die. You just have to die, in that compulsory solitude. On the first day of work on the pilot of "Gabriel's Fire," I was locked in a prison cell at Stateville Prison. The producers had made a deal with prison officials to use a cell that was actually occupied by a prisoner. It was furnished as Gabriel Bird's cell would have been, with a fan, books on the shelves, and in a world where TV's and radios blared incessantly, no television.

I did not ask this prisoner about his crime, although I think he had been convicted of murder. As part of our deal, he said, "I'll let you have my cell if you take a picture of you and me." We complied hesitantly, knowing that a picture of a convict with someone from the outside could become a barter item among prisoners.

The night after we left the prison, someone was killed in a fight over the fan. One small fan, used to provide a little relief from the summer heat, became so important between two men in prison that one of them killed the other for it.

A number of films have been made at Stateville. During one project, a prisoner actually escaped by stowing away in one of the trucks belonging to the film crew. People lost their jobs over that incident. Security clearance became a much more sensitive, rigorous ritual. On our last night of filming at Stateville, our cast and crew were carefully screened. The producers and I departed, but some of our teamsters stayed behind, still loading the trucks with all the lighting equipment. There was the usual prison lock-up. At lights-out one of the convicts hid under his bed as a joke. Of course, the guards thought he had escaped, and they immediately detained the teamsters. Every truck had to be searched. Finally, well after midnight, somebody heard the "missing" prisoner snoring under his bed. Only then did they let our crew go.

For the filming on location, our producers wanted real sounds and sights. We were shown an abandoned building which had been a circular prison. A guard told us that the building was abandoned because with that circular design, the prisoners saw only other prisoners. Whenever people were confined here, they ended up cursing and spitting and pissing on each other. Wherever they looked there were only more prisoners, mirrors of themselves.

In the building currently in use, prison officials assigned us a wing—called a gallery—of about 150 occupied cells. Each member of our company was under the direct charge of a guard. Mine was a handsome young woman who stayed at my elbow at all times. In one of the early scenes, my character comes out of his cell and gets bumped by a young convict.

"Watch where you're going, old man," the convict says to Bird.

Gabriel reflexively grabs this kid and slams him up against the iron bars of a cell door. As we rehearsed several times, I slammed my fellow actor, knowing, of course, that his back was protected with padding so I could really push him hard against the iron bars.

"This is a good actor," I said to myself. "He is really giving me the eye contact. He knows how to adjust with his body to make the slam look really painful." I thought they must have gotten one of the best stuntmen in Hollywood.

We kept shooting and reshooting the scene. Slam. Slam. Each time we did it, I got better at it. I got more confident. I would slam him a little harder, a little harder still. His eyes got bigger and bigger. Finally, they did the close-ups. Now our eyes were really getting into it. His eyes were big, mine were narrow.

At last the director said, "That's it. Let's go to the next set." And the actor walked off.

"Who was that kid?" I asked an assistant director.

"A convict," he said. They had found a convict and trained him to do the scene. Had I known I was abusing an actual convict, I don't think I could have done the scene. If I had known those eyes were a killer's eyes, I would not have slammed so hard, so often.

This convict was part of a unique prison education program run by a woman who teaches convicts to act. They love and revere her— and protect her from any harm. She has discovered that the reason so many prisoners gravitate to her program is because many of them are rapists and killers who never learned to express themselves appropriately. Acting enables them to express themselves. She calls her program "Con Artistes."

There were about a dozen men in the program—black, Hispanic, white—who began to be "superstars" during our sojourn. They were allowed to walk around without guards, and in some cases, if the scene called for it, they ate with us. Other convicts used as extras in the prison yard got into the spirit. To be in our show conferred a certain status. The convicts involved began to ask for pictures and autographs—anything to keep up the relationship. It was their way of stalling our departure.

One day when we were filming at the Cook County Courthouse in Chicago, I witnessed a scene more cynical than anything I had seen in prison. A group of young male prisoners were being marched through a hallway in transit between the court and the jail. An older guard with a cane watched them pass.

"Link arms, now! You link up your arms!" he said to them. "We're all lovers here. Come on, two by two. You are all lovers, now—or gonna be."

I promised all the convicts I met as we worked on the series, "I will not tell your story. I will not take on that responsibility." We would not tell the story of "the" convict, we would tell the story of "a" convict. Similarly, we were not trying to tell the story of black life, but the story of all these lives, black and white.

A successful television series is most often built around a family of characters, not one top banana. We had such a family on "Gabriel's Fire," and I regret that the dictates of the marketplace prevented our having more time to let that family develop its identity and its audience, and to permit the writers to get their act together. The show was simple, gritty, grainy, understated, innovative. And it was scheduled opposite two of television's top-ranked programs, "The Cosby Show" and "The Simpsons." Our ratings were low, and only by reconfiguring the show could we keep ABC's commitment to it. The plot line, setting, and cast were transformed, and, with my good friend and colleague Richard Crenna co-starring, we came back in 1991 as "Pros and Cons." Unfortunately, we fared no better, having now totally confused our following, we lasted only part of the season. That made me wonder seriously if the network should have given up so quickly on "Gabriel's Fire."

20.

OTHELLO
ON BROADWAY

*. . . Still this is a much finer Moor of Venice than Jones
has given us previously, and is the best American Othello
I am aware of, Paul Robeson's not excluded.*

*Yet if Jones, at the last, skimps a little, Plummer is
overgenerous with his Iago. The play, after all, is not the
tragedy of Iago . . . under the direction of Peter Coe,
whom I sense to be too weak to contain Plummer, we get
an Iago who even has the last, albeit unspoken, word in
the play. . . .*

JOHN SIMON, NEW YORK, SEPTEMBER 7, 1981

"Why don't we do *Othello?*" Don Gregory set out to make that happen at the Shakespeare Festival in Stratford, Connecticut, in 1981, with Peter Coe as director and Christopher Plummer as Iago. Peter had directed me in 1963 in *Next Time I'll Sing to You.* I had seen him direct Chris in *Macbeth* in Stratford, Canada years before. Yet when we got into rehearsals, Peter proved to be a different man from the director I had admired so much. Something had happened to him. He is dead now, and one should not speak ill of the dead, but he and I had real artistic differences.

We came to our first impasse over Peter's wish originally to cast Ian McKellen as Iago and portray Iago as a latent homosexual. I told Peter that I admired Ian's work, but I did not want to play Othello to an Iago that was not clearly heterosexual. Peter was incensed, but I felt the issue was central to the understanding of the play. Don Gregory resigned over this controversy, and the production almost ended there, but co-producers Fran and Barry Weissler stepped in to mediate. Peter momentarily considered casting Roy Dotrice as Iago.

"You are determined to choose a British Iago," I told him. We proceeded with casting, but Peter and I worked with increasing wariness of each other. I noticed from the beginning that he could not deal with the concept of the third pillar in the structure of the play—Desdemona. Peter had trouble casting the role.

I thought Shannon John, the first one, was emotionally well equipped to play Desdemona. She was a lovely young Texas girl, but, as we Southerners often do on stage when we delve into the emotions of a role, she reverted to her original accent. To my surprise, people said, "We can't understand her when she is talking with a Texas accent." My agent, Lucy Kroll, a former actress herself, called my attention to the problem, too. I was so involved on stage, totally confident in this Desdemona so rich with the emotions of the role, that I was sold on her performance.

Sometime during rehearsal, I learned that Shannon did not have a car, and I started driving her home. We began to talk, and during those private conversations, she revealed to me more and more of herself—her early marriage; her futile attempts to live with her husband; the alcoholism and suicide attempts in her family history. Sure enough, our growing personal relationship, even without having an affair, altered the chemistry of our performance. She had disclosed so much of herself to me that I began to feel very protective of her. (If I had not been betrothed by now to Ceci, I probably would have taken Shannon not only under my wing, but under my sheets!)

Even though the relationship was not a sexual one, it had become irrevocably more personal. I was allowing my compassion for her to make me self-conscious on the stage. She saw it right away. "You are not looking me in the eye the way you were last night," she said after one performance.

Shannon came to the role with great emotional range and depth. It would be hard for me to accept another actress, no matter how well she spoke. The pillar concept had begun to work for us, although tenuously. It was hard to look at Shannon's face, usually lit with tears, without deep feelings. It was difficult for me to change when Roy Dotrice's daughter Karen joined the cast as Desdemona number two. Karen had a wonderful voice, but lacked the emotional equipment for the role, just the opposite of Shannon.

Christopher Plummer, who was finally cast as Iago, was also starring in *Henry V.* He worked doubly hard, often to the point of fatigue.

Peter and I continued to disagree. I thought some of the secondary characters were weak. Despite Peter's protest, I won the battle to recast Cassio. I wanted a strong, virile Cassio, a match for Iago and Othello. Cassio is a man accused of seducing Desdemona. For me it was crucial to play opposite an actor who could command her affections. Kelsey Grammer, later achieved fame in "Cheers," took over Cassio and did an extraordinary job, especially with the help of the choreography of the stage combat master. Kelsey gave us a dashing young hero who could plausibly win Desdemona's love. It was wonderful to see Kelsey flower, both as an actor and the character. I think he gave probably the best performance in the play, because the evolution of his character was the clearest and least mucked over.

I have always felt that the right woman can direct *Othello* with more sensitivity than almost any man. My experience with Peter Coe confirmed that conviction. You have to be in good hands to get to the heart of this play, and as hard as we tried, we failed to get there in this production.

I had followed Christopher Plummer's career since he was in his twenties, even then an accomplished Shakespearean actor. I admire his great talent and his deep commitment to his characters. Often, a lead actor will walk on stage to audience applause, in the same way that the audience applauds a great set on first sight. But audiences seldom did that with the early Plummer because, from his first instant on stage, he wove such a spell that they were too absorbed to applaud. That silence was a greater tribute in itself. I never saw Chris get applause when he entered, even in some of his greatest work.

Back in 1964, Joe Papp had envisioned a militant, defensive Othello. Gladys Vaughan had evoked the sun god. In 1971, John Berry had proposed a more cynical, subtle Othello. Over a lifetime, I have created my own complex approach to the character, and I recognize that Iago is equally complex.

Most actors play Iago as farce, which is what Chris did under Peter's direction. And Chris won great acclaim for playing Iago doing so. Yet Peter and Chris dealt with *Othello* at the expense of the great tragedy of the main characters, Iago included. Once Iago elicits a cynical response, and lets them off the hook, the audience does not want to take any of the tragedy seriously. It happened similarly at times when we were doing *Fences*. People identify with a character. They are taken in by the conflict, the drama. Then, suddenly, the knife turns, the character takes them by surprise, and they feel betrayed. They say, "I liked that guy. Why is he doing this to me?" From that point on, they have to save themselves, and there is the danger that nothing an actor can say that is intended to be serious that will be accepted as serious.

If you give an audience an excuse not to confront pain, they will make use of it. They may have thought they came to the theatre for that, but once the lights go down, they will not risk involvement unless they feel certain they are in good hands.

And unless you deal with Iago's tragedy, you cannot really do justice to the tragedy of Othello. You get the bulldog and the bear. Iago can be thought of as Lucifer, once the most beautiful angel in heaven, God's favorite, who becomes the fallen angel. Iago is a highly endowed person, but embittered by his life, most probably because he lacks station. His circumstances relegate him to a subordinate role. He is not a gnome, a stooped Napoleonic figure. He is not Richard III.

A good director will not let the actor playing Iago dive into the farce but will guide him into the tragedy. Yet no actor wants to go into that very troubled territory alone without skilled hands to guide him. Iago's cynicism should not infect the audience simply as amusement. It should alarm them. They should not laugh and say, "Aha! I know exactly what he means." They should say instead, "I have never seen anything like this in my life."

An Iago playing for farce will inevitably yield an Othello who is a dupe. Once I walked across Manhattan with Sidney Poitier, who told me he had been asked to do *Othello* years ago. "I want you to know, James Earl, why I am not doing it," Sidney said. "I cannot go on stage and give audiences a black man who is a dupe." Simple as that. I understood what he meant: without a good director, that is often what you get.

Zoe Caldwell once came to see us perform in Stratford. We all respected her judgment, and our producers Barry and Fran sought her advice. In the Stratford performance, against Peter's wishes, the choreographer had implemented one brilliant stroke. He resolved the problem of vengeance on Iago: after all the other deaths, Iago is castrated. Symbolically, he falls on the bed. Chris, to gain back his stage power, then improvised an unusual closing gesture. As the lights went down, and the pin light focused on the bed, he raised his head and smiled.

When Zoe saw this, she said, "Chris, that is outrageous! Three dead bodies on the stage, and you make the audience laugh?"

At least someone had the courage to say what Peter never could.

I was not happy in the Stratford production, but it was so successful in its own perverse way that we were getting ready to take it to Broadway. After I had tried everything I knew to try with Peter, I had breakfast with the producers one day.

"I have a problem," I told them, "but if I can work it out in spite of the director, we might be able to make this an even stronger production on Broadway." They took this to mean that I was courageous, a good soldier, and we went ahead full steam.

But I was still troubled, and I told Ceci so. At that same time I met with Jennifer Dunning, an interviewer from the *New York Times*. While I did not confide in her about the backstage problems with the production, she did get me to open up about my feelings in general, and our talk somehow crystallized matters for me. I suddenly knew I had to be a more responsible actor, not a better soldier. I told Peter Coe I could no longer work with him.

Peter threatened to blackball me.

"Who do you think you are?" he asked. "I'll make sure you never work on Broadway again." (Much later, when some Broadway producers told me that they had heard I was hard to get along with, I knew Peter had to be at the root of the rumor.) He accused me of being upset that Iago got more laughs than I did. We were dealing with a tragedy. We were not talking about laughs. Earlier, I had asked Lloyd Richards to come up and see the production and give me some advice. Lloyd told me, "If you want to get laughs, Othello would have no trouble getting laughs. You can drop your pants, any number of silly things to get a laugh if that is the contest." And, of course, it was not.

"You must be out of your mind," I said to Peter. "I've got something to tell you. There are many problems. In the scene between Emilia and Desdemona, for instance, you have Emilia insensitive to the foreboding Desdemona feels. If Emilia can't be sensitive to Desdemona's anxiety, no one can. Therefore, the audience will not be. You have misdirected Emilia and Desdemona and Iago. You are trying to misdirect me. So let us just stop now."

The argument continued, and at one point, I said, "That is all I have to say. You heard me."

"I hurt you?" Peter asked.

"No. You heard me."

And that was it.

Rehearsals were held up for a while. The producers tried to proceed by having the stage manager and the director's assistant work with us. There was much discussion back and forth.

Ceci visited me during that time at a little place where I was staying in Stratford out on Long Island Sound. My cottage was hidden away, approachable only through an alley that led to the Sound. One day, out of the corner of her eye, Ceci glimpsed Peter Coe and his wife walking outside. He had to have known that this was my house.

"That looks like Peter Coe," Ceci said.

I said, "Let's let him be."

He was trying to find a way to make contact, I think. He never knocked on the door. He must have been hoping I would see him and say, "Come in. Let's talk."

I didn't.

* * *

From Stratford, we went on a nine-city tour before Broadway. Peter's assistant had taken over and he did his best. He kept us sane, but he did not have the experience the production needed, or the authority, especially with Chris Plummer, who could and did direct himself. The assistant listened to us, though, and tried to help us resolve some obvious problems. One of them was that Peter wanted me to whack Desdemona, knock her to the floor in one of the confrontation scenes. I don't think Othello was a man who would do that. He could have killed her, and he *knows* he could have killed her. I carried a scroll in my hand, rolled up so that it would not hurt Desdemona as I hit her, but the gesture was brutal. When she fell, the full, heavy skirts of her gown billowed out and she seemed to sink down into the floor.

The audience howled every time, laughing at the very moment they should have been absorbing her pain. At a moment of impending doom, calling for shock and violence, we gave the audience an image which evoked only laughter.

"So let's change that," I said to Peter's assistant, and he tried to help us work it out. There was a similar response when Iago's sidekick Roderigo dies. Once, I suggested to Chris: "If we allow the audience to laugh at Roderigo's death, think about what follows. He is a jerk, true, and he is a victim of Iago's manipulation, yes. But Roderigo is human. Let's not let the audience laugh at his death, because if they do, they will laugh at every death after that. And there are several—including mine." And Chris said, using a phrase coined by an early critic and scholar of Shakespeare's plays, "Oh, Jimmy, but you know, isn't this play after all a bloody farce?"

On our tour there were, sure enough, gales of laughter at the deaths in the play. Much later, on tour in Florida, there were many older people in the audiences, experienced theatregoers who knew Shakespeare and who listened. The laughing stopped. They proved to me that the play, even as we were doing it, had a validity beyond farce. A play does not evoke laughter unless you provoke it.

* * *

Oddly, every time there ever was a conjunction of the energies of
Peter Coe and James Earl Jones, there was a disaster that
Nostradamus would have been proud to have predicted. If we had
been planets, we would have been in opposite spheres, and in danger
of collision. Whenever one of us entered the other's sphere, there was
sometimes friction between us, and always disaster beyond us. It
seemed to extend beyond the theatre: When we did *Next Time I'll
Sing for You*, we were about to go into previews. I had taken a lunch
break that day when I heard the terrible news that John F. Kennedy
had been murdered. Peter, with some grace, dismissed the company
to mourn.

Years later, when I flew to New York to complete the
arrangements to begin working with Peter on this *Othello*, even as I
was signing the contract I heard the news that Ronald Reagan had
been the victim of an attempted assassination. I guess Peter and I
should have known by then that we had best avoid each other.

We never resolved our artistic differences. When we opened our
Washington run of *Othello*, still headed for Broadway, the producers
once again invited Zoe Caldwell to see the performance, thinking she
might be the best replacement for Peter. Zoe, by Band-Aid and
persuasion and exerting strong control, almost salvaged the
production.

Zoe did not buy the laughter of ridicule. Chris was a brilliant Iago
and won great critical acclaim. Peter had given him license. It was too
late for Chris to change his interpretation. We were getting ready to
cast our third Desdemona. I was in a deep depression, and Zoe had a
hard time getting the best out of me.

Dianne Wiest joined us as our third Desdemona. She started
working with Zoe in Chicago, and joined us on stage in Florida.
Dianne and I had worked together in *Hedda Gabler*, and I welcomed
her to the cast. But she had walked into a very uncomfortable
situation.

"I arrived too late," she told me. "All the love in this play has been used up between Othello and Iago. There is none left for me."

I found it uncanny that she understood then, as Gladys Vaughan did years before, that there has to be room in the play for Desdemona to exist as an equal. If Dianne had been with us from the very beginning, she could have fought for her space and found it. But by the time we got to New York, where she got some disappointing reviews, she came to me and said, "Jimmy, aside from everything else, I am tired of dying every night for nothing." It was depressing her. Beyond what I was feeling, Dianne was feeling worse. Soon she relinquished the role.

There had been only two actresses I wanted for the part of Desdemona from the very beginning—Dianne or Ceci. Here again I have to puncture the myth that I marry my Desdemonas: I fell in love with Ceci long before she played my Desdemona, and whereas we were married *after* *Othello* opened on Broadway, it was before she joined the cast. Zoe had considered casting Ceci earlier, but had cautioned us about the criticism we would get for casting her while she was my "girlfriend." But I should let Ceci tell you that story in her own words:

> I will never forget the meeting I had with Zoe Caldwell in Washington. This stunning, dynamic, passionate theatre icon sat me down and said, "My dear, I am going to give you an invaluable piece of advice. Once upon a time, a very long time ago, I was performing in a play opposite a major star. He got absolutely great reviews and I was savaged. Do you know, it completely spoiled our relationship. Now, I am quite sure that you as an actress are capable of playing Desdemona. But if you are embarking on a life quest with your man, then you shouldn't ride his coattails to greater glory. And, my dear, God forbid you shouldn't come off well critically. Say I'm superstitious but I would feel much better about casting Dianne in this role now than you."
>
> Well, I absolutely agreed. I did not want to be in the position of being Jimmy's girlfriend coming in to star as his Desdemona.

Later, when Dianne chose to leave the play, Jimmy and I were already married. I had no qualms now about joining the cast. Zoe had finished her direction by then, so I was directed by our dear stage manager, and I had seen the play so many times that I knew the part even better than I wanted to.

And—what the hell—no one was going to review me; the production had already been lavishly reviewed. This major revival was sold out. One could not ask for heavier weights on stage than Chris and Jimmy in a classic production of a Shakespearean play. Thank God, I had done enough Shakespeare so that I was comfortable with the classical, technical aspects of the work. But who needed this? It was a favor to Fran and Barry Weissler, the producers, so they'd be sure to qualify for a Tony Award.

For the modern actress, the modern woman, Desdemona is a very difficult role to play, or at least it was for me. I found it hard to carry that kind of numbskull innocence right to the very moment two and a half hours later when Othello wraps his hands around her throat before she even asks what is wrong. When I went into the role, I said, "Forget it. I've just spent seven months watching three very talented actresses fail at this part. I only want to be the single prettiest Desdemona imaginable, so that whether the audience believes me or not, they will simply be delighted whenever I walk on stage." I wanted a change of costume and a change of hair every time I came on stage, whether it made sense or not. I wanted to be the daughter of a senator. I wanted to look magnificent.

The brilliant Patrick Morton created beautiful wigs, and I was fitted with unbelievably sumptuous costumes. And I took a huge (albeit shallow) satisfaction at the collective gasp I heard every night on my entrance. Each time I entered a scene, I stepped out in glittering new wardrobe, and the audience seemed to get the effect. So much for the "When will I ever work with James Earl Jones?" and so much for the classics.

Ceci brought not only beauty but regal presence and strength to her role. She quickly established her own place in the triangle. She was a master of the adroit gesture. There were moments in the play when Chris was used to getting laughs at what Ceci perceived to be Desdemona's expense. Ceci now deflected them with a graceful, well-placed movement or countergesture—no laugh.

What we gave our audiences in 1982 was essentially the cynical comedy of Iago and the attempted tragedy of Othello. The audiences who attended Paul Robeson's *Othello* in 1943 were confronting then the turbulence of a world war. They were hoping and praying that there were heroes who could save the world. Our audiences in 1981 and 1982 had suffered Watergate, and Vietnam, and the death of our real heroes. Disenchanted, they had concluded that there are no heroes. They could look at Othello and say, this is archaic. In a time of national cynicism, our play worked, but sadly enough, it worked like theatre of the absurd works. Audiences found it perversely exciting. It received a Tony Award for the best revival of the year. It ran for about nine months, and could have run for another year.

But Chris and I were tired. I was weary of playing this Othello, even with this beautiful Desdemona.

I was nearly fifty-two, and deeply in love with Ceci. She and I had worried at one time that we might not be able to have children. Now we carried a secret with us on stage. She was pregnant. At long last I was going to be a father. "The fountain from which my current runs—!"

I was resting in the country on my day off when Ceci called. She had the results of the amniocentesis, and she called to tell me some additional wonderful news.

"All chromosomes present and accounted for. But we have to have real second thoughts about our little girl's name. It's back to the drawing board, love. We have a boy."

I was speechless. I wept.

"It gives me wonder great as my content," Othello had said to Desdemona, "To see you here before me. O my soul's joy."

* * *

The reality of Ceci's pregnancy empowered my performance, despite my burnout in the play. This Othello's Desdemona was carrying my child. That fed me at a deep psychological level and resonated in Othello's lines, for he, too, longed to issue progeny:

> *But there, where I have garner'd up my heart;*
> *Where either I must live, or bear no life, —*
> *The fountain from the which my current runs,*
> *Or else dries up; to be discarded thence!"*

One night Desdemona moved to the bed for the final scene of the play. I entered to speak Othello's lines:

> *It is the cause, it is the cause, my soul . . .*

Suddenly, I realized that a man had come out of the audience down to the stage. He stood leaning on the lip of the proscenium. He didn't do anything, but here was an intruder in the sanctuary of the actor's terrain. Not only was this a violation of stage space—but more urgently for me, this was a man who could be threatening my wife and child. I could see Ceci's concern. I could think only of protecting her.

Imperious, as Othello, and furious, as myself, I strode over and ordered this menacing stranger to leave. From that time on, we could not wait for *Othello* to be over.

Recently, I came across a note I wrote to Ceci during her pregnancy: "My dearest keeper of the seed," I called her, then wrote of some mundane business, and closed, "I'm losing my mind to our child. I pray he's gifted and special."

He is. Flynn Earl Jones was born on December 13, 1982.

21.

THE MAGIC HOUR

Fiction relies more on the imagination of the reader, while movies often seem to be imagination made solid. This potential for solidity in movies, their ability to make you feel the tangible weight of objects, the immediate consequences of actions, has something to do with why some stories present themselves as movies and some don't. We do some of our understanding straight from the gut, and if we can be made to feel the damp and cold of the mine shaft, feel the weight of the pick, breathe the dust-thick air, we're going to have more of a handle on a coal miner and his feelings than we could get just from reading and thinking. Thinking in pictures is a way to inhabit the bodies of characters as well as their minds.

JOHN SAYLES, *THINKING IN PICTURES:THE MAKING OF THE MOVIE MATEWAN* (BOSTON: HOUGHTON MIFFLIN, 1987)

I saw my first movie in the town of Coldwater, Mississippi. There were no cinema houses, no television sets, nothing to prepare me for that experience. I was three or four and the oddest thing was that it was dark, yet there was a small crowd of strangers watching the same thing. The film projected onto a plain white linen bed sheet stretched between two stores. One store sold soda pop and the other sold popcorn. This tradition of "free" outdoor summer movies continued through my youth until I was about fourteen, when I saw my first cinema in a warm and darkened theater.

Given the state of film preservation, I could probably view some of those images today. One phenomenal fact of film is its permanence. You can take a reel of film out of its can years after the actors generated it, and if it is a good movie, it still evokes through imagery, flesh and blood feelings, preserved emotions. Years after a good movie is produced, new generations of viewers can experience its images and energies.

I served my actor's apprenticeship in the theatre, which requires a different kind of energy and focus from film acting. I am still learning to act in films. Because the eye of the camera zooms closer than the eyes of the audience in live theatre, film requires more subtlety and nuance. Stage acting: a man on a soapbox on a street corner, speaking to the crowd around him. Film acting: a man walking down the street, talking to himself.

I have always found the camera intimidating, especially in close-up shots. The camera got in my way when it loomed between me and another actor in a scene. True, the camera was a perfect witness. It was there to record the truth. But I found it disconcerting, that act of recording and absorbing energy while not giving any of it back.

When I made *Soul Man* in 1986, I confessed to the director Steve

Miner, that I was not comfortable with close-up shots. I had never admitted that to a director before. Steve was surprised. His solution to my problem was to work with excessive close-ups. Gradually, on that film, I learned to relax, to work with the camera, to feel more at home. When your training is in theatre, you have to be retrained to be in stride with the dynamics of motion pictures. The best retraining happens when I work with other actors who understand film technique.

I often choose film roles in order to work with particular actors. I worked on Horton Foote's *Convicts*, regardless of how small the role was, so that I could have the chance to act with Robert Duvall. The experience was memorable for me. It gave me insights into how another actor builds character. Duvall is always looking for gestures and actions which fit the reality of the moment, finding in his character telling gestures or attitudes which are not in the script, but which he adds so deftly and naturally that they become clearly part of the character. In *Convicts*, he plays Sol Gautier, an ancient, tough, often demented prison-plantation owner who uses convict labor to work his sugarcane plantation at the turn of the century. As he strides about his land, he connects himself to it by gesture. There is an old alarm bell beneath an oak tree behind the house, and, spontaneously in one scene, Duvall as Sol pauses and rings the bell. It is not in the script. He just rings the bell, and it echoes the past, some other time in his life, some long-buried panic or crisis or celebration.

In another scene, a convict has been shot trying to escape. He is wounded and shackled, waiting for the sheriff to come. Duvall approaches the convict, and, unscripted, picks up the shackles. He pulls them, tests them. In his paranoia, he wants to be sure the chain is strong enough to hold the convict. Even after the convict is taken away, he bends down to test the chain, to be sure it is still a good chain, fit for future escapees. This is an eccentric old man behaving in eccentric ways, but those sharp, subtle choices intensify his performance. He seems to know his character down to the bones. As

critic Jerry Tallmer wrote of Duvall's performance in *Convicts*, we see
in him "the whiplash of all mortality."

Denial, in 1963, was the first movie in which anybody ever
entertained the thought of casting me. It was an odd little story about
a college-age black kid who was denying his racial reality. Ghetto
kids today would say he acted like he was white, that he had
assimilated so much mainstream culture that he was denying his
blackness. It was much more complex than that. He was in
psychological denial. He did not know he was black. He was
imprinted by the reality of his white friends and assumed he was like
them. Finally, he was forced to face his identity, and that
confrontation brought on a psychotic episode. The movie never
happened, and I am not sure why. I think there was no money. But I
felt, after the meetings to discuss it, that I was ready to try movies.

I got my first chance in Stanley Kubrick's *Dr. Strangelove: or, How
I Learned to Stop Worrying and Love the Bomb* in 1963, playing
Lieutenant Lothar "Jimmy" Zogg. I was the bombardier, and the
only one who questioned the patriotic mission we were on. I liked the
fact that the black man was the one who asked the hard questions. To
my great disappointment, those lines wound up cut out of the script
before we even shot them. This was my first film, though, and I did
not have the clout to challenge Kubrick. I was upset enough,
however, to need to talk to him about it. He never gave me a
satisfactory answer.

My next movie role came in Peter Glenville's production of
Graham Greene's *The Comedians* in 1967. Elizabeth Taylor and
Richard Burton, at the peak of their married romance, starred in that
film. It was not until 1968, after the Washington stage production of
The Great White Hope, that I got a significant role in a movie. It was
End of the Road, an adaptation of a novel by John Barth. I took the
part just after a three-month-long vacation in Canada where I had
simply vegetated. I wanted to get back into gear for the Broadway

run of *The Great White Hope;* the movie seemed just the right challenge and change of pace.

It was shot in Great Barrington, Massachusetts, in and around a textile mill that served both as production offices and studio. *End of the Road* was an independent production without any of the trappings of the movie studios of Hollywood or New York. The protagonist, played by Stacy Keach, is Jacob Horner, a student who lapses into a catatonic state because of his anguish over the shortcomings of the world. My character, Dr. D, comes upon Jacob after the student leaves his graduation exercise and, literally, while taking his first step into his adult career, gets frozen in a state of catatonia. I hospitalize him in an unorthodox mental institution where I enact a multiplicity of "roles" as part of the "love and hug" therapy I impose on him and other patients. Sometimes I play a fool, sometimes a counselor, sometimes a militant, or an Uncle Tom, or a savage. I was intrigued, too, that Doctor D manipulated his blackness when he chose to, to suit his needs and objectives. As I said in an interview in *Life* that November of 1969, the whole issue of color became a fourth wall to bounce off in the film.

At the end of the film Doctor D has to perform an abortion. I wanted that to be accurate in every gesture. Writer-director Aram Avakian and I had long talks beforehand with his wife, Dorothy Tristan, the actress who played the patient, so that we could plan the emotional as well as physical sequence of the scene. Then we called in a physician to check the technical details, and he pronounced it so realistic that he suggested only minor changes.

Not all facets of the film were so carefully planned, however, and as I look back, I believe that there was too much freedom and informality. Consequently, the film lost coherence, and the characterizations were often haphazard. Stacy and I as stage actors leaned too heavily on theatrical techniques, and I feel we failed to evoke the reality of catatonia. Even so, *Life* called *End of the Road* the "film shocker of the year" in 1969. The film had the potential to be serious and important, as well as chillingly entertaining. Many critics, piqued by *Life*'s premature praise, blasted us. The overall assessment was that we were way ahead of our time.

My next film project after *The Great White Hope* was actually made for television, but it generated enough interest so that it was released first for the big screen. It was *The Man*, a screenplay by Rod Serling based on a novel by Irving Wallace. I played the first black man to become president of the United States.

The film was made as an "ABC Movie of the Week," and was being readied for airing on television when Robert Redford's *The Candidate* came out to much success. The people in charge of *The Man*, Barry Diller in particular, thought the time was right for political films, and decided to release it in cinema houses. This view was resented by everyone involved in *The Man* because we had made a television movie, and we thought it unfair to present it otherwise. A movie production schedule would have given us more time, staff, and budget for higher production values. Indeed, *The Man* was never successful as a motion picture. However, when it is seen on television, it is a surprisingly eloquent film.

John Berry directed me in one of my best movie experiences ever in *Claudine*, the first feature film produced by Third World Cinema, a company owned and operated by minority filmmakers who sought to train blacks and other minorities for jobs in the communications industry, and to produce good films which spoke to a wide general audience, but with special appeal to minority groups. Critic Judith Crist and others praised this film about blacks. Crist wrote that it was "more importantly, about people and alien to no one." Actress Diana Sands helped to found Third World, and would have starred in *Claudine*, but her fatal illness tragically intervened.

I had gotten a call earlier on about playing the role of Roop, the male lead. I said I was still committed to my run of *King Lear* in the Park, and I didn't see how it was possible. One day, after production on the film had started, I got a call from Diana Sands. "Why aren't you in this movie?" she asked me. "John Berry wanted you in it and I want you in it. Why don't you reconsider?"

Somehow, the timing worked out so I could finish my stage production and then have a week to rehearse with Diana. I called the director and accepted Diana's offer. The next day I got a call from Bernie Hamilton. Unbeknownst to me, he had been cast as Roop before this call from Diana came in. He said, "Jimmy, how can we let them do this to us?"

"What do you mean?"

"They just fired me without even discussing it with me. How can we let them do this to us?"

I had no answer. I went to work into daytime rehearsals for about a week, but Diana was not the same Diana Sands I had known earlier in our careers. She was as vivacious and effervescent as always, but something was taut about her physically. I couldn't figure it out.

We rehearsed and prepared for her first day of shooting. Suddenly, I got a call not to show up for work. The shooting had been suspended. That is when I learned Diana was dying of cancer. She realized on her first day of filming she could not go on. She was in great pain. She asked to be replaced by Diahann Carroll. I got the feeling then that Diana all along was setting up another pair, Diahann and me. So it was that Diahann Carroll played the starring role of one of the first modern single mothers on the big screen, and I played her boyfriend Roop, a cocky, laid-back, rowdy garbageman.

It was interesting to change orbits from the formality of Shakespeare to the jive street talk of Roop. I worked confidently and comfortably with John Berry. Diahann was exceptional. We had some delicious kissing scenes, but you never could get very close to Diahann. She has had to be a fighter to sustain her place. She has had to be as strong as she is attractive, and she knows how to protect herself so she can do her work.

One day, a teenaged actor playing one of her brood was horsing around on the set, delaying the work and messing up a prop scene. Diahann grabbed him and said, "Look, you are messing with my money," meaning, "You are going to mess up my time and my performance."

He got her point, and cleaned up his act.

Claudine gave me a Golden Globe Award, an NAACP Image Award—and more satisfaction than any of my earlier films. I was beginning to understand a little more about the enigma of this medium, but always by contrasting it to the stage.

On the stage, the actor's job is to fill the whole space with sound, movement, emotion, animal presence, and energy. The simpler the character, the better on stage. On film, just the opposite is true. The acting must be subtle and suggestive. Film is far more subliminal than theatre, depending on imagery more than on words.

I love the magic of film—the interplay of truth and illusion. Those film magicians, the lighting technicians, have coined the phrase "the magic hour" for that hour between sunset and dusk when there is no artificial way of replicating the natural light, so luminous with vibrations of color. Sometimes a day's shooting is geared toward that capstone scene filmed in the inimitable light of the magic hour.

My favorites among the movies I have made are *Soul Man, Claudine, The Man, Matewan,* and *Field of Dreams,* the simple films that tell a simple story with an ensemble cast. I was also the voice of Darth Vader in the *Star Wars* trilogy. Before that was widely known, I used to tell people that the film's producers first called up Orson Welles, and he was busy, so they called up Victor Jory, and he was busy, so they called me. For a long time I denied that I was Darth Vader's voice because it was fun to deny it. Some black people, Raymond St. Jacques in particular, were upset by a perception that the only black entity in outer space is the evil Darth Vader.

The role set off a chain reaction of voices in my career. With Darth Vader, that mythical character, my voice came to be used more and more frequently as a voice of authority. It brought me a lot of commercial and voice-over work. The voice-over work led to more and more opportunities for narrations and on-camera commercials, with their own milieu and craft so different from movies and theatre.

We knew from the first that *Field of Dreams* was a special film. You could feel it in the energy on the set. I love working with Kevin Costner, and I value his friendship. He has a truly special cinematic vision. It was thrilling to work with Burt Lancaster. I was very fortunate that the novelist J. D. Salinger put his foot down about the script for *Field of Dreams*. I play a journalist who was based, in the novel, on Salinger. He is fiercely protective of his privacy and his image. He let the novelist get away with it, but threatened to sue if the film made use of his name or evoked his image. Out of respect for his privacy, the character was transformed from a white man to a black man, and named Terrence Mann.

It is interesting that many people left the film convinced that they knew the novels of Terrence Mann. With Rose Kennedy's permission, photographs of Robert Kennedy were used, "doctored" to include my image. The same was done with photos of Martin Luther King and Malcolm X. The photographs filtered subliminally into the minds of many viewers, eliciting the conviction that the journalist really existed. This transformation from Salinger to Mann was lucky for me, giving me a role I treasure and a film I am very proud of.

I have made some mediocre movies in order to earn the money my family and I need to live on, and, sometimes, in order to earn the money to subsidize my theatre habit. You don't make much money even on Broadway. Often in the past, I would work in theatre until my accountant would call and warn, "James Earl, you are about to go broke again." Then I knew I had to take on a movie assignment to shore up the treasury so I could work in theatre again. Early in my career, I swore I would never do a script which was not profoundly and beautifully written. Well—that was an idealistic dream. Particularly now, with a family to support, I sometimes take on projects because I need to work, not because I embrace the script. One of my conspicuous failures in film was *Allan Quartermain and the Lost City of Gold.* Even failures yield compensations, however. In that case, I got to make my first trip to Zimbabwe, an experience I cherish. Literally losing my head in *Conan the Barbarian* took me to Spain. And in Mexico filming *Swashbuckler* in 1976, I almost lost my leg. This epic pirate movie starred Robert Shaw, and among others, Genevieve Bujold, Beau Bridges, and Anjelica Huston. I am sure we all joined the cast to work with Robert Shaw. I played his sidekick, a swashbuckling pirate named Nick Debrett. In one scene, doing my own stunt, I had to cling to a hurtling stagecoach. The director had told us to let go and jump off if anything went wrong with the action. Sure enough, something went awry, but I froze and was unable to bail out, and my leg was caught in a wheel of the stagecoach. I had to be flown to Los Angeles for emergency treatment for the injury.

There is a fine line between art and propaganda, and sometimes you catch flak from people on either side of that invisible line. I made a baseball film, *The Bingo Long Traveling All-Stars and Motor Kings,* with an exuberant cast—including Richard Pryor and Billy Dee Williams. Many of my family traveled south to watch part of the filming in Georgia, and this upbeat movie captured a lot of fans. But the critics were hard on us because they expected a black cast to exude black rage. They wanted the tragedy of black baseball players in the black baseball leagues, not the comedy we gave them. They wanted political relevance and content and protest. They couldn't accept that this was not a black film, but simply a film about black people.

At the other extreme I chose to do John Sayles's excellent film *Matewan.* I played Few Clothes, an aging coal miner who found the courage to challenge the system. We shot the film on location in West

Virginia, and I saw my part in it as a tribute to Robert Earl, a salute to him as an old unionist who put his neck on the line. I wove my father into my characterization, to the point that I even look strikingly like him in the film. Few Clothes, however, was speaking out of personal courage and conviction more than political motivation when he sought to defy the mine bosses for fair treatment for the workers in the mines. Like my father, Few Clothes, while not instinctively political, was an instinctive unionist, simply because he believed in work. Because he was a working man, his heart was with working men everywhere. The real Few Clothes was totally committed, and was indicted in the bloody Mings County trials.

Matewan is named for the West Virginia town where the story took place in 1920, when mine company thugs evicted the families of striking miners from their homes. In the real life strife that followed, ten people were killed, including the town's mayor. When a United Mine Workers of America member and Matewan police chief Sid Hatfield (of the Hatfields and the McCoys) were gunned down on the courthouse steps, there was a massive uprising in West Virginia, triggering a battle between ten thousand coal miners and federal troops and planes deployed by President Warren G. Harding. John Sayles explored in his realistic film the multiple viewpoints which fire any controversy, but he was clearly in sympathy with the miners' struggle to unionize.

I took the role in *Matewan* because my agent and I thought the project was interesting and important, and because I wanted to work with John Sayles. I did not expect to make any money in this movie, for I knew it was a low-budget film. Besides that, John L. Lewis was one of my heroes when I was a boy. I knew all about the United Mine Workers, because I used to listen to John L. Lewis on the radio. When I first began as an actor, I even thought about making myself up as a white man and playing Lewis some day.

I have lately taken on cameo roles in films such as *The Hunt for Red October, Patriot Games, Sneakers,* and *Sommersby.* In some cases, simply because this gives me the opportunity to work with an upcoming new crop of actors—Kevin Costner, Alec Baldwin, Courtney Vance, Richard Gere, Harrison Ford, Jodie Foster. In other cases, it gives me the chance to work with people I have admired for so long, such as Sean Connery, Sidney Poitier, and Robert Redford.

I suppose that the film which has given me most visibility in recent years is Eddie Murphy's *Coming to America*, with Madge Sinclair, my television co-star, and Arsenio Hall. Wherever I travel, from Italy to the Caribbean, I meet young people who recognize me as "The King," Eddie Murphy's father. One young person who knows me as the voice of Darth Vader and the father of Eddie Murphy was recently overheard to say, "That James Earl Jones—his career is really about to take off."

22.

FENCES

*Alright . . . Mr. Death. See now . . . I'm gonna tell you
what I'm gonna do. I'm gonna take and build me a fence
around this yard. See? I'm gonna build me a fence
around what belongs to me. . . .*

TROY MAXSON, IN AUGUST WILSON'S *FENCES*

An actor is blessed if once in a lifetime lightning strikes him with a thunderbolt of a role. He is extraordinarily blessed if he gets struck twice, and that has happened to me, with *The Great White Hope* in 1968 and then again with *Fences* in 1987. August Wilson's play was first written in a longer version than the later one and presented at the Eugene O'Neill Center in Waterford, Connecticut, in a stage reading in 1983. Mary Alice, that wonderful actress who was my co-star in *Fences* on Broadway, took part in that initial reading. She told me that when she first read the script, she said, "These are interesting characters." But she said she did not appreciate the full power of the play until she read it on stage with other actors. Then she suddenly realized that it pulsated with a harmony of sounds and voices, and all these characters were something very special indeed.

Lloyd Richards asked me to read August Wilson's new play, set in the fifties. I have been told that August once said that sometime during the process of writing *Fences*, he began to hear me in the role of Troy. It was a role I took to immediately. I read the script, and saw right away the poetry of the writing, even though the work was still in progress, and rough-hewn in places. I reread the play, and before I read it enough times to evaluate the dramatic structure, I knew I wanted to play Troy Maxson. Here was one of those rare roles which, like Jack Jefferson in *The Great White Hope*, I knew on sight would exact a total commitment, all I could give to the stage night after night of my energy, of my imagination, of my talent.

In the winter of 1985, Mary Alice and I went into rehearsal with Lloyd, who was now dean of the Yale School of Drama and director of the Yale Repertory Theatre. Lloyd had cultivated a large, responsive black audience in the New Haven community, and they locked onto this play. When we opened in May of 1985. August

Wilson was enjoying his first big success on Broadway with *Ma Rainey's Black Bottom*. In addition to Mary Alice, our cast included Ray Aranha as my friend Jim Bono, Charles Brown and Russell Costen as my older son and my brother, and Courtney B. Vance, then a Yale drama student, as my son Cory.

August was rightfully praised for his ear for black vernacular and his "genius for finding the poetry hidden in the rhythms of everyday speech." He set the play in 1957 in industrial Pittsburgh, August's own city. *Fences* tells the story of fifty-three-year-old Troy Maxson, a garbage collector; his second wife Rose; their family and their friends. As a young man, Troy was a talented baseball player, never allowed by the color barrier to make it beyond the old Negro professional leagues. Twice-married, he is an ex-con who served time in a penitentiary for killing a man in a fight. Troy is angry about his failures, especially his failure to achieve his dream of a sports career. When his son Cory is offered a college football scholarship, Troy forbids him to take it. Not surprisingly, his reasoning on race, success, and failure is complicated.

The central conflict here hinges on this tension between father and son, although there are many layers of conflict, many symbolic "fences." Troy and Rose have their heartbreaks. There is also tension between Troy and his son by the previous marriage, Lyons. Then there is Troy's brother Gabriel, irreparably injured in the war. And there is Alberta, Troy's other woman.

At the time of its first stage reading *Fences* ran about three and a half hours; but then August pared it by an hour for the Yale production. Despite its great success at Yale, the play still had problems. Every play keeps evolving as it moves closer to Broadway, or to its final form. One of the most exciting things about the theatre is this metamorphosis of a written script into a living drama. Undoubtedly, August Wilson is a great dramatist: he is essentially a poet, and he is a brilliant editor. But his work is hampered, I think, by his inability or unwillingness to resolve the drama. I hope it is something he can learn, especially if he renders his plays into film. Lloyd and I felt the need of changes in the script, but August could not always achieve what he knew the two of us wanted.

We as actors have to dig in deep to substitute feelings for dialogue that should be in the script. There is a scene in *Fences* in which Troy has to explain to his wife Rose about his involvement with another woman. He does not say, "Forgive me." He says, "Understand why I went to the other woman." He finds himself able to do that only in baseball terminology. Troy explains it this way:

> But . . . you born with two strikes on you before you come to the plate. You got to guard it closely . . . always looking for the curveball on the inside corner. You can't afford to let none get past you. You can't afford a call strike. If you going down . . . you going down swinging. Everything lined up against you. What you gonna do. I fooled them, Rose. I bunted. When I found you and Cory and a halfway decent job . . . I was safe. Couldn't nothing touch me . . . I was on first looking for one of them boys to knock me in. To get me home. . . . Then when I saw that gal . . . she firmed up my backbone. And I got to thinking that if I tried . . . I just might be able to steal second. Do you understand that after eighteen years I wanted to steal second.

Lloyd and I thought August shouldn't leave it at that, but should make it very clear, if only by suggestion, what, in Troy's inarticulateness, the baseball metaphors meant to him. To leave the speech alone, by itself, was misleading, incomplete. It begged the audience to laugh it away, which some nights they did.

What is missing is the link between what Troy would have said were he an educated man, and what he is capable of saying as an illiterate man. We all know that he is trying to say something about his own value, his own worth. He is saying that he became aware of his own value only in the company of the other woman. He does not mean that he finds fault in his present wife, whom he loves very much. He just feels free to let a flowering happen with the other woman—far away from being beaten down by the duties of his daily life.

Consistently, we found that audiences began to interpret this speech to mean that Troy was simply conning his wife. Yet what he is really saying is, "With you I got to first base and with her I felt I could get to second base—and maybe get home." The original text read, "I wanted to steal second." I added the word "home" because that had a meaning to me. The audience usually laughed because that implied scoring with a second woman, not the inner psychological reality that is deeply troubling Troy. I felt we had to adjust the script in these areas if we were to clarify and enhance the undercurrents of *Fences.*

We opened at Yale Rep on April 30, 1985. Despite the great success of the Yale production, no one in the Broadway producing community wanted to touch the play. It was a drama about a black family, written by a black man, directed by a black man. That did not appear to some to be a salable commodity for Broadway. A lot of prospective producers came to see the play, and a few considered taking it on. Eventually, all of them passed.

Lucy and others kept fighting for us when we moved the production to the Goodman Theatre in Chicago. Carol Channing saw the play and encouraged a young producer named Carole Shorenstein Hays to come to see *Fences* there. Carole immediately booked us to play at the Curran Theatre in San Francisco, and then on Broadway. Other prospective producers who saw the play tended to say, "Well, it's about a black family. We don't know if that will work in the commercial theatre." Carole, to the contrary, told me that when she saw the play, she saw her own family up there on the stage.

"I realized," she said, "that no matter what your station, no matter whether you are wealthy, educated, poor, illiterate—all families wrestling with anxieties and hostilities tend to work them out the same way. All families have the power structure of parent and child. All families have rivalry." Carole comes from a wealthy Jewish family in San Francisco, but she said, "Background is irrelevant when it comes to families in crisis. The interior energy is the same in every family, no matter what the exterior circumstances, when push comes to shove."

Lucy set up a meeting with her once we finished the Chicago production, and I laid out to her all the problems I had had with the script to date. The production had been a great success in New Haven and Chicago. But reviewers saw the play as flawed, especially in the second act. This was my own sense of the play's weakness— that there was something unresolved in the second act in the scene when father and son physically confront each other. Their conflict is the crux of the play; the script's flaw rested in its void of resolution.

I could not argue the point very well without sounding as if I wanted Troy to die on stage. "What if we revive the gun?" I asked, referring to an early draft of the play which actually suggested that the father confront the son with a gun. Lloyd opposed that idea for social reasons.

"The main character, the father, ends up unresolved," I said. "You see him outcast because of his liaison with the other woman, and his commitment to raising the child—his child—she dies giving birth to. Then, suddenly, as the final scene opens, you learn that Troy is dead. He dies off stage. The audience has not seen Troy's death, much less seen him come to terms with himself. There has been no dramatic resolution of Troy Maxson's life. No one else in the play seems to resolve him. The mother tries to do it by *telling* the story of his life, but that does not resolve the conflict dramatically. I think the only person who can resolve it is Cory, the son. Somehow the resolution has to happen with the son."

Carole listened. I told her I had a problem with the laughter we were getting in certain places. I confided to her that at Yale and in Chicago, I would usually go home from the theatre at night depressed. I knew it was because I carried unresolved emotion home with me. I would go home to see my own young son lying there asleep. I would look at him and say, "Does this have to happen—this desperate, wordless physical confrontation between a father and a son, so choked with words they can't speak that they risk killing each other? Does this conflict between father and son have to be that brutal and deadly?"

Caught between the reality of my experience with Robert Earl and the potential of my experience with Flynn Earl, I had to have resolution of the issues between Troy and Cory. Without resolution, you had a man who does not learn anything. When you present a character who does not learn anything, there is always the even graver danger that the audience will not learn anything.

I hoped August would rewrite to achieve that catharsis. Yale gave him an ivory tower, an isolation and an insulation. Lloyd, as dean of the Yale Drama School, was determined that his new playwrights would be buffered from the pressures of commercial theatre as long as possible. He wanted to harbor them as long as he could because he felt the best creative work is done through fulfilling your own vision without yielding to the pressures of commercial theatre. August is a very private man, and I respect that. When Athol Fugard worked on new plays at Yale, he would always be available to hang out with us, to have a drink. The cast always had access to him. That was his choice. August's temperament does not seem to invite discussion.

I relied on Lloyd as the director to convey concerns to the playwright, and frankly, I preferred it that way. I didn't know how to talk to writers, particularly this one. Carole said that she would make sure we got the best production that a producer could give. Soon afterward, we had a meeting that included Carole, August, Lloyd, and myself. I thought we were going to lay our cards on the table, yet every time I said, "I have a problem with this scene, this point," August and Lloyd countered with reasons for not making changes.

I thought Carole was being stonewalled. I felt stonewalled myself, and became more and more frustrated. I left that failed meeting knowing that nothing was resolved. As frustrated as I felt, I perceived that Carole had it worse than I did. She was white, Jewish, rich, and young, and I saw something personal in the subtly negative way she was dealt with.

Early in the play, Troy is explaining to Bono how he met Rose, who is sitting on his lap: "I told her, 'Baby, I don't wanna marry, I just wanna be your man.'" And Rose says, "I told him if he wasn't the marrying kind, then move out the way so the marrying kind can find me."

They joke about how they met, and at one point Troy says, "Well, you know, so I married her 'cause I didn't want no coal black woman no way."

In the black community ever since slavery, tones of blackness have played a large role in the intricate social and political workings of intraracial conflict. There are phrases such as "The blacker the berry, the sweeter the juice" to express an appreciation of the pure blackness of a woman's skin. On the other hand, some black men choose "high yellow" women, women who look white. It is uncomfortable to play on those themes now, but the play was set in the fifties, and August had written that negative line about being "coal black."

"I've worked too hard to bring black women into my theatre," Lloyd said. "I don't want that line to offend them." So we struck it. I raised a similar issue about another moment early in *Fences*.

"Troy is not a racialist," I said, "but he says things which suggest he is a racialist. At the very beginning of the play, I say this line— 'the white man ain't gonna let you get nowhere no way.' I don't know why I should want to make the white males in the audience feel uncomfortable. Since we've already excised the lines which might offend black women, by that same logic, we should delete this line as well."

"I just want the chips to fall as they may," August answered. By now I feared that we all had different agendas.

"But Troy is not really political," I argued. "First of all, he is illiterate. He is inarticulate. He speaks only three languages—farm language, prison language, and baseball language. So what is this constant harping on the white man? It reduces him. It would seem more valid that he would say 'the man,' meaning the power structure. He lives in Pittsburgh. He is not directly confronting that polarized situation in the South. He should be larger than that. Such lines limit his dimension too much for me, especially at the beginning of the play when I want to achieve as much scope as possible with the character. I want to ensnare the audience, not repel them."

I persisted in my vision of the need for resolution. Since the father dies off stage, unresolved, something had to be resolved through the son.

I tried again for change. In the last scene, Cory has virtually nothing to say. Rose does all the talking. It is wonderful for Rose to have a final scene in which she comes into her own, but that happens at the expense of any catharsis, any resolution of the central conflict in the play. Carole promised me as we moved to San Francisco that we would resolve these issues, but she was too young to take on Lloyd, who had much more experience and who was caught between his producer and his playwright. We had good audiences in San Francisco, but critics there were not totally kind. Yet, for all of our problems, I had great faith in *Fences*. I knew it was worth a fight to make it work.

"I don't rewrite," August reportedly said. "That's it. What you've got is it." Now Lloyd was caught between his playwright and his actor. The day after we opened in San Francisco, Lloyd decided to fly back to Yale to resume his duties as dean of the Yale Drama School. Carole called him back and said, "We have work to do." She began to apply her muscle as a producer from that moment on.

When it came to the scenes Troy played in, I battled for what I believed in. I respect the writer's domain, but the actor lives out there in the words in a dimension the writer does not have to enter night after night. I think writer and actor can collaborate on honing a script

Paul Robeson as Othello with Peggy Ashcroft as Desdemona, London, 1930. UPI/Bettmann. Courtesy of The Bettmann Archive.

James Earl Jones as Paul Robeson, 1977. Bert Andrews. Reprinted by permission of the Estate of Bert Andrews.

James Earl Jones as Lennie in John Steinbeck's *Of Mice and Men* on Broadway, 1975. Copyright © 1993, Martha Swope.

James Earl Jones as Othello and Jill Clayburgh as Desdemona, Los Angeles, 1971. The Mark Taper Forum.

James Earl Jones as
Paul Robeson, 1977.
Bert Andrews.
Reprinted by
permission of the
Estate of Bert
Andrews.

Billy Dee Williams, James Earl
Jones, and Richard Pryor in *The
Bingo Long Traveling All-Stars
and Motor Kings,* 1976.
Universal. Copyright © by
Universal City Studios, Inc.
Courtesy of MCA Publishing
Rights, a division of MCA, Inc.

James Earl Jones as Leon
Carter in *The Bingo Long
Traveling All-Stars and Motor
Kings,* 1976. Universal.
Copyright © by Universal
City Studios, Inc. Courtesy
of MCA Publishing Rights,
a division of MCA, Inc.

James Earl Jones as Nelson
Mandela. Photograph
copyright Brownie Harris.

James Earl Jones, the voice of
Darth Vader, *Star Wars,* 1977.
Courtesy of Lucasfilm, Ltd.

Danny Glover and James Earl
Jones in Athol Fugard's *Master
Harold . . . and the Boys,* 1982.
Copyright © 1993,
Martha Swope.

James Earl Jones receiving honorary doctorate
of fine arts, Princeton University, 1980.
Courtesy of Princeton University.

James Earl Jones as Othello on
Broadway, 1981. Copyright ©
1993, Martha Swope.

James Earl Jones, his father Robert Earl
Jones, and his half brother Matthew Earl
Jones. Bert Andrews. Reprinted by
permission of the Estate of Bert Andrews.

James Earl Jones as Othello and Cecilia Hart as Desdemona, 1982. Copyright © 1993, Martha Swope.

James Caan, James Earl Jones, and Francis Ford Coppola, *Gardens of Stone*, 1987. Photograph courtesy of Tri Star Pictures, Inc., copyright © 1988.

James Earl and Cecilia "Ceci" Hart Jones at their wedding on the Ides of March, 1982, at the United Nations Chapel, on James Earl's afternoon off from *Othello*. Copyright © 1993, Martha Swope.

James Earl Jones as Troy Maxson in August Wilson's *Fences*, 1987. Photograph: copyright © 1987, Ron Scherl.

The playwright, the director, the producer, and the cast of *Fences*, 1987. Front row, left to right: Frankie Faison, Karima Miller, Courtney B. Vance; second row: Charles Brown, James Earl Jones, Mary Alice, and Ray Aranha; third row: Lloyd Richards, Carole Shorenstein Hays, and August Wilson. Photograph: copyright © 1987, Ron Scherl.

Courtney B. Vance and James Earl Jones as son and father in *Fences*. Photograph: copyright © 1987, Ron Scherl.

James Earl Jones in late 1980s. Scavullo. Photograph courtesy of Scavullo.

James Earl Jones as Terence Mann and Kevin Costner as Ray Kinsella in *Field of Dreams,* 1989. Universal City Studios, Inc. Copyright © 1989 Universal City Studios, Inc. Courtesy of MCA Publishing Rights, a division of MCA, Inc.

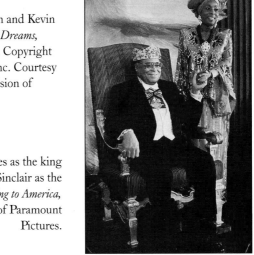

James Earl Jones as the king and Madge Sinclair as the queen in *Coming to America,* 1988. Courtesy of Paramount Pictures.

James Earl Jones as Gabriel
Bird in "Gabriel's Fire," 1990.
Courtesy of Lorimar TV.

Robert Earl Jones in his late
seventies. Courtesy of Joanna
Miles, photographer, and Robert
Earl Jones.

James Earl Jones in *Sommersby,*
1993. © 1993, Regency
Enterprises, V.O.F. and
Le Studio Canal+.

James Earl Jones and Robert
Redford in *Sneakers,* 1992.
Universal. Copyright © 1993
Universal City Studios, Inc.
Courtesy of MCA Publishing
Rights, a division of MCA, Inc.

Cecilia Hart Jones as Desdemona. Copyright ©
1987 Al Hirschfeld. Drawing reproduced by
special arrangement with Hirschfeld's exclusive
representative, The Margo Feiden Galleries,
Ltd., New York.

Flynn Earl Jones. Copyright © 1988 Al
Hirschfeld. Drawing reproduced by special
arrangement with Hirschfeld's exclusive
representative, The Margo Feiden Galleries,
Ltd., New York.

Robert Earl Jones. Copyright Al Hirschfeld.
Drawing reproduced by special arrangement
with Hirschfeld's exclusive representative, The
Margo Feiden Galleries, Ltd., New York.

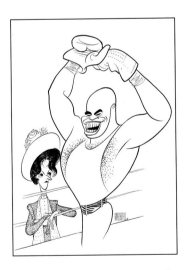

Jane Alexander and James Earl Jones in *The
Great White Hope*. Copyright Al Hirschfeld.
Drawing reproduced by special arrangement
with Hirschfeld's exclusive representative,
The Margo Feiden Galleries, Ltd., New York.

James Earl and Flynn Earl Jones, 1991.
Copyright © 1993, Danny Feld.

James Earl Jones at the White House
receiving the National Medal of the Arts
from President George Bush, as Mrs. Bush
looks on, July 22, 1992. Courtesy Susan
Biddle/The George Bush Library.

James Earl, Ceci, and Flynn Jones
in Italy, 1992. Photo courtesy of
Fabrizio Biamonte/Roller.

James Earl Jones with President and Mrs.
William Jefferson Clinton at the Lincoln
Memorial during Inaugural festivities,
January 1993. Copyright David Hume
Kennerly.

Three generations: Robert Earl Jones in
background; James Earl and Flynn Earl
Jones. Photograph courtesy of Michael
Tighe. Copyright Michael Tighe.

for the ultimate performance. But I did not want to pull any "star" pressure tactics. For the longest time, I hesitated to speak about the one scene without Troy that troubled me more than anything else.

It was actually the epilogue scene after Troy dies. It begins with the child coming out into the garden. It ends with Troy's brother Gabriel lifting his trumpet and trying to blow his dead brother into heaven. Gabriel was hit by shrapnel during the war. Most of his brain was blown away, but he came back from death. An actor must play Gabriel as mentally impaired, but not as dumb. He is a deceptively simple character, in that he is not simple at all.

August told Frankie Faison, the actor playing Gabriel on Broadway, that his job in the family was to judge Troy as to his fitness for heaven. "You almost came back from the brink of death solely to perform that mission," August said.

Lloyd added his advice as director. "You are here to shepherd your troubled brother into heaven."

Frankie and I had worked together before; I had directed him once in a student production at New York University. He was my understudy in *Of Mice and Men*. We could talk to each other, and perceiving the difficulty he was having with directions for the scene, I discussed it with him.

"These two concepts are not really in conflict," I said. "They are really the same thing—you can be both judge and shepherd or savior. You almost trusted it one day, and you've got to go back and try to trust it again until you feel comfortable with the concept that you have one single mission on that stage." Frankie grew into that scene; it was terribly moving.

At first Carole did not want the play to end as it did. August was determined that the scene with Gabriel and his trumpet should be left in the play, and Lloyd agreed with him. I tried to be objective. I suggested that Carole needed to see the play herself a few times without that coda scene. I watched it with them, and I realized that without that scene, the play was an even more depressing experience.

There still was no true catharsis written into the script, but the coda did move you beyond the depression. Carole was right that the coda was a "cop-out," but at least it was something. It enabled the audience to go away absorbing the best parts of the play.

Convinced that the resolution must come when father and son have their final confrontation, I began to focus on that scene. Troy is an "outcast" after his infidelity. Even though he is still the man of the house, he is uncoupled from everyone. His best friend does not see him anymore. His wife does not sleep with him anymore. The last person to break away from him is Cory. They stand on the brink of physical combat—then Rose intercedes. That is what is written in the script. One day I begged Lloyd to let us see what would happen, even with nothing written, if Rose does not come in. He agreed, and the scene became an improvisation—the symbolic and literal struggle between the father and son over a baseball bat. This was a symbolic sketch, not written by the playwright, and in that sense, not a legitimate part of the play.

But it worked. In that sketch, the father and son learn that they cannot kill each other. The bond between them is too strong. No one intervenes. They discover this for themselves, face-to-face. It was the first clear lesson in the whole play. They learn, and we learn, that no matter how bold or bad or desperate they are, they cannot kill each other.

From that point on, I noticed that I could leave the theatre each night absolved of carrying depression home with me. Once that sketch was accepted and woven into the performance, for the first time, I could go home and look at Flynn asleep in his bed, and feel a sense of peace.

That began to happen in the last week in San Francisco. Without any help from August, we began to refine that scene. He said he could not rewrite it, but he did agree to take the mother out of any intercession between father and son.

When the mother came on stage, I still went into the house with a burning hatred of the son, and knowing that he hated me just as fiercely. But somehow, as we wrestled over that bat and put it down, we rose above that hatred.

As a father in real life, I knew how uncomfortable it had to be to live with such animosity. Knowing my own relationship with my own father, I know how deadly wounding it is to live with. And I went home wounded every night, until we changed that scene.

I think many black people who came to see *Fences* came in search of a hero. Black women in particular, living through the deep frustrations of our time, watched me go up on that stage and play a man who could be a hero. But eventually Troy fails—his son, his wife, himself. There is a moment when the worm turns. They found that hard to accept. Here is a man with all the potential of the wonder of mankind. There is all that potential for Troy—and for his son. And Troy, quite simply, ruins it, destroys it—and some black members of our audiences smarted from it. This story is about a man in trouble, about a whole family in deep trouble. We do not give the audience the ascendant hero and the happy ending. Some people got very upset. Stuck with the story of a "failed garbageman," they felt betrayed.

I know I was a thorn in the flesh for August and Lloyd, but it was only because I cared so much about this play. Actor Oskar Werner observed that a good actor can bring only as much insight to a character as the playwright invests in him, while a great actor reveals more about the character than you could know if you were to encounter him in the flesh, in real life. That is the task we set for ourselves as actors. I felt I knew Troy Maxson in my bones, and I wanted to reveal him, in all his complicated humanity.

I was often troubled during the long run of *Fences* by the sounds of inappropriate laughter in the audience, when there was nothing really funny. When the death of Troy's mistress is revealed, some audiences would laugh or even applaud. When Troy walked on stage carrying his baby, the infant Alberta died giving birth to, some audiences would laugh derisively at the man's gall. The issue was the salvation of the child, yet the audience avoided that by laughing, hassling the scene. "Drown the baby." Or—"You should have thought of that when you stuck it in there!"

As with *Othello*, I am always unhappy when I feel an audience is dancing around and away from the pain. Jessica Tandy talked to me about her experience in *Streetcar Named Desire* years ago: whenever Stanley began his assault on Blanche, laughter would erupt in the Caucasian, middle-class, WASP audiences who came to see the play. They would twitter and sometimes lapse into uncontrollable laughter at Blanche's humiliation. Jessica observed that whenever a playwright probes deeply into a painful area, the audience will often laugh nervously, as self-protection. I am convinced that the American psyche has found it more comfortable to laugh off tragedy than to cry about it.

Unlike film, stagecraft must often rely on the imagination. Death can be authentically bloody and horrible on film. On the stage, death has to be suggested, evoked. In the face of tragedy in the theatre, some audiences elect to laugh so they will not have to weep.

Lloyd would always say, "Don't worry about the inappropriate laughter." He attributed some of it to black audiences who were not used to theatre, but were accustomed to the tradition of response behavior in church. I contested that. I thought laughter from the audience might also suggest to us that something was not working as it should on stage, and that we had to examine that, to be sure we were doing the best service to the play.

I have misbehaved in all kinds of ways when I have been distracted by someone in the audience. I have interrupted myself to shout at a stagehand. I have told people, impolitely, to shut up. I have been guilty of expressing my displeasure with obscene gestures or words. "Stop popping that fucking bubble gum!" I once shouted. I have also, in more controlled response, simply paused and waited until the audience settled back into quiet attention. When you are working as hard as we work on stage, you need the audience to work with you and with the grain of the emotions in the drama. Like Ed Sherin, Lloyd wisely recommended that in scenes of extreme emotion, the more committed, concentrated, and focused we actors are, the better the audience will connect with us and the play.

As I look back at the long run of *Fences*, I see that every actor in our company grew in the course of a good, hard, artistic struggle to achieve the play every night. On certain nights, I lost faith in certain scenes, but you have to overcome that lack of faith during a long-running production. You have to regenerate yourself. And the play worked more often than not. You have to give a play and an audience a powerful energy. After a time—usually, for me, about six months into the performance—that kind of energy inevitably diminishes to a point of no return. It depletes the well, the mysterious source of the power to act. You have to know when to leave a role, or you have to replenish the well.

Ceci saw before I did the signs of my fatigue. When a character, like Troy Maxson, goes too deep, you can lose the energy it takes to go there every night. I began to lose patience in certain places where the play still remained unresolved. I try not to become a character so totally that I cannot make certain adjustments in what he sees and does. I have to become him, yet stay detached enough to observe him, to see how he is connecting to the audience, to discern if the audience is responding to him, and to adjust if they are not. As an actor, I am totally responsible for calibrating that connection between character and audience.

After a year in *Fences*, I knew it was time to leave.

The Great White Hope came along before the trend of assertive black males—with the Black Rambos superseding the Black Sambos.

Fences arrived after the Black Rambo vogue had run its course. Troy Maxson in *Fences* is the male of the fifties, but not just the black male. He is the universal male weighed down by modern society, fenced in, if you will. I believe that both these plays transcend black experience and black theatre. I believe they are accepted as powerful, relevant, universal theatre, built on universal human themes. In some ways, then, Troy and Rose Maxson are Everyman and Everywoman. That is their ultimate reality and their ultimate validity.

After all the angst, quite wonderful things came out of *Fences*. August won the Pulitzer Prize, and swept the other awards given to writers in the theatre—the Drama Guild, the Tony. I treasure the Tony given me for my performance as Troy Maxson.

Most careers evolve in stages. First you are a student, a genuine apprentice. Then you are an amateur. Then you begin to do professional work. After my student days, I remained an amateur actor, the difference between the amateur and the professional actor being that the amateur cannot make a living by acting, and has not yet, and cannot or will not make the final professional commitment. At first I was not at all sure I could make my living in the theatre, even though I was being paid for my work. Gradually, I began to believe I could make my living by acting, without maintaining a second career. Eventually, I made the irrevocable decision to go forward with acting as my sole career. *The Great White Hope* brought me to that threshold.

With the success of *The Great White Hope*, I decided that I could afford to be a married man with responsibilities. I had lived very frugally for many years, but I had only myself to consider. Then I began to think that Julienne and I could be married, and we were.

Ironically, the second pivotal transition in my career happened with *Fences*, my second thunderbolt role twenty years later. Then, long divorced from Julienne and happily married to Ceci, I realized that I did not have the energy for long-running stage plays anymore.

My focus turned to films and television. I often chose to do films and television work so that I could afford to go back and do good theatre. Unfortunately, there is no parity between wages paid to stage actors and wages paid to actors on television and in the movies.

Now I have a different agenda from those early days. There is the deep responsibility to my family. Ceci and Flynn are two good reasons why I cannot go broke every two years. But when I think about returning to the stage, I have to admit to myself—as I march on past my sixty-second year—that I no longer have the physical energy or the psychic stamina to sustain a Broadway run of a year. Six months, maybe—and even that is immensely taxing. But I no longer have it in me to play a role on stage for a year, as much as I love the theatre, as much as it is my real home.

PART FIVE

VOICES AND SILENCES REMEMBERED

23.

HOMESTEADING

All my life I have wanted to make a haven, a home for my family.

JAMES EARL JONES

"Home House" my aunts in Mississippi call the place my great-grandparents built in Arkabutla Township, Mississippi, long before I was born. Wyatt and Sharlett Jeter Connolly's Home House sheltered their children and grandchildren, and stood staunch at the center of the little universe of acres and family and heritage they created in Tate County, Mississippi. The houses their children built radiated from that hub, tied to it by the spokes of land Wyatt parceled out to his sons and taught them to farm. Not all of them stayed there. One son, incurably infected with wanderlust, threatened to gamble his birthright acres away. Another son, Nimrod, steadfastly farmed his own land and his errant brother's land. Ed, the responsible eldest son, farmed his land and at the same time built a successful construction business in nearby Coldwater, moving his family into town to a fine house he built for them there.

My own grandfather, John Henry, finally sold his land to pay for the move to Michigan. I never used the words "Home House," but I understand what they meant to earlier generations of my family, and how they cherished the freedom to build their own place on their own land. Imagine coming up through slavery to hold in your hands the deed to your own land, and to read with your own eyes the words you had once been forbidden under pain of law to read and write.

I revere the toil and pride, the dignity and hope that empowered my great-grandfather, acre by acre, seed by seed, to plant his crops in soil by all theory too thin and poor to yield, and harvest money crops, and invest the money in more land and in wood and mortar for the house he built with his own hands. Then he built a church to serve as his family's spiritual home, and to use every other day for a school. The land made that possible, the land was sanctuary and security, the land was the pathway to the future. The land was home.

I was blessed to grow up in the country. Even during the Depression and the war, there were certain advantages in being a farm family. You had healthy food when others were rationed. You were self-sufficient. Growing up as a child on the farm with livestock and the fields, I was grounded in a work ethic determined by nature more than by man. The land gives you that sense of validation. It challenges in you a self-reliance.

In the early 1970s, then tied to the city, I hungered for my own home. I considered for a time a New York brownstone, but home to me meant the country. When Norman Landau, a friend of Julienne's and mine, asked me to ride up into Dutchess County, New York, to look at some country property with him, I went along to keep him company and get out of the city. He was the prospective customer, and I was just along for the ride. That Saturday we explored an incredible uphill property, eight acres of secluded woods, with a stream of clear, cold water running behind it, wildflowers everywhere, silence broken only by birds, insects, wind. I drank from the stream, tasted the pungent, edible wildflowers, imbibed the stillness and the air— and envied my friend the chance to buy this land. Norman decided the place was not big enough for him and his family, and later found a place in Connecticut.

"Are you sure you are not interested in the New York land?" I asked him. He assured me he was not. I could not forget the place, and I went back and bid on the property. I had no idea then what I might do with it, other than drive up and enjoy walking on my own land, leaving the city behind and retreating into the country where I had always felt most at home. A friend who once drove up with me said, "You know, trees like to be slapped." She would go over to one tree after another, hugging and slapping them. I laughed at the idea, but she insisted. "Trees respond to touch," she told me. I would go up and slap the trees once in a while. Over the years, I have had to take down some trees for one reason or another, but they got plenty of slapping while they stood.

* * *

The first time I had tried to build a house alone, it was for my mother Ruth on the land in Michigan. I never finished that house, and I have always carried my regrets about that. Eventually, my uncle H.B. decided it was best to demolish it, and he salvaged the masonry and used it on his own place. The hole I dug for the basement is still there, but it is barely a hole anymore. Ruth's house could have been a whole house, and I always carried a heavy, heavy misgiving about not finishing it. I had built other people's houses, but for a long time, that misgiving affected my ability to build my own house. My love for the new land in upstate New York freed me from that, and I began to look about for a design for my homestead.

I had my country land, but little money to improve it. Yet with the help of a local builder, I started building a simple kit house. No mortgage—just stop and go, stop and go. Go when I had money. Stop when I ran out. The house would stand vulnerable as Ruth's stood in Michigan; the construction was ongoing but there was no one to look after the site. When I got really desperate about the security of this house-in-progress, I found a way to enclose it enough so that I could live there from time to time and work on it by myself—an empty shell with a working fireplace in a little den where I could sleep.

The model of the house was displayed on the roof of Abercrombie and Fitch in New York. It was a chalet, all open, built of glass and redwood. Over time, I finished the house in the country. It was my refuge. In April of 1975 while I was playing Lennie in *Of Mice and Men* at the Eisenhower Theatre at the Kennedy Center in Washington, a telephone call brought me some terrible news. There had been a fire. My house was totally destroyed. The question—was it arson?

Providentially, no one was home. I was staying then in Washington. I kept three vehicles on the property, including an old Austin Healey sports car parked next to the house. Some of the neighbors who discovered the fire saw the car there and feared I might be inside. The tires of the car melted from the intensity of the blaze. The fire consumed trunks of irreplaceable memorabilia—photographs, scripts, letters. As Ceci says, out of that fire grew the scar tissue of my life.

When the fire was reported at 10:23 P.M., the local volunteer fire department brought five trucks and sixty men to the fire scene. By 12:25 A.M., it was extinguished. The house was gone, a complete loss—and with it, a temporary loss of trust in my community. "Total destruction," the official report said of the physical damage.

I could not consider rebuilding until I knew what had caused the fire. If it was racially motivated, there was "total destruction" far beyond glass, redwood, furniture, and memorabilia.

The arson investigation was led by Butch Anderson of the sheriff's department. He understood my anxiety and addressed it straightaway. "I want to assure you that this fire was not racial. Whatever happened to your house was not a KKK-type thing, as you as a black person might feel. It had to do with burglary, not with you."

"I need to know that," I said, "because I am inclined to want to rebuild."

"You should definitely go ahead and rebuild," Butch told me.

"No way," my accountant said when I told him. "If they don't want you there, why do you insist on rebuilding?"

I said I would investigate further. I pieced together from fact, rumor and several sources a classic story involving a vast network of stolen goods, and a witness protection program. Someone involved in this complicated scam decided to loot houses where he heard there were firearms. When I had a shotgun repaired locally, word got out that I might be a collector.

It was easy enough to break in. Then the burglar put a candle in the middle of the floor to see where he was going and simply neglected to put it out when he left. The house went up like kindling. Investigators were unable to find any metal that would qualify as melted firearms. I also collected silver, and there was no melted silver.

The house was looted before it was burned down—by "unintentional arson."

Convinced that the fire was not an act of hatred or terrorism, I called the builder who had helped me put up the house. "Get a bulldozer," I said. "Let's clear this land and start over again."

This time I designed my own house, and I designed into it all the paranoia that the fire awoke in me. From a magnificent old silo, I built a tower and a turret. My stone house has everything but a moat and a cannon position.

This new house has come to be a phoenix. Over the years, I have given it my own rough shape. I have brought my wife, Cecilia, to this homestead, and she has softened the stone and stubborn spaces and jagged angles with love, grace, and laughter. She has added soft light and gentle colors as counterpoint to the bold artifacts a man collects. Her family—her father Bill and her mother Fran, her brothers and sister and their spouses and children—have truly become my family. Their talk and laughter fill the rooms of our house at holidays. Flynn complains if they are not there, if, as he says, "there is not enough chaos." An only child, he thrives in the cheerful whirlwind of a large, loving family.

The drive up to my New York farm is nothing like the drive into the homestead in Mississippi or the farm in Michigan. The land wears a different face, the roads travel different contours, but the peace of the land and the woods enfolds me, gradually supplanting the stress of travel and work I bring with me out of the city. City people have a hard time handling the silences when they first come out to the country. After a certain period of solitude, I myself experience an aloneness that is sometimes disturbing, but the country eventually cleanses my spirit and purges my body of the sounds, fumes, and toxins of urban life. I think cities feed psychological stress and tension in many ways, including an overload of electrical forces and energy. When you go to a country cabin without electricity, you will be surprised at how tensions fall away.

Some practitioners advocate that urban dwellers removed from the country find a space in the yard or the garden and dig a hole deep enough to enfold the body. Lie down in the hole. Make sure your body can lie just below the surface of the ground. Stay in this hollow of earth. You will be surprised how rested you will feel simply because you have escaped for a moment the man-made influences. You have retreated for a moment to Mother Earth's very simple electrical systems. For the chemical and electrical balance of the body to be calibrated, you have to stay close to the earth itself, align yourself with its polarity so that your body can find harmony between the interior world and the exterior universe.

Once we become detached from nature, we begin to think we can do without it. The lights of the Great White Way overpower the stars. It is very hard to see the brightest constellation when you live in or near a city. The dark solitude of the country reunites you with the universe of the stars. The woods and hills restore in you something primal in yourself. The sea's pulse sets your own heartbeat.

When I found my own country landscape in New York, I was delighted to find in its center a winter pond. Henry David Thoreau wrote in *Walden* about his pond in winter, where "a perennial waveless serenity reigns as in the amber twilight sky. . . . Heaven is under our feet as well as over our heads." My own winter pond is very small but very important to my family and me, and when I was able to afford it, I brought in some equipment to clear away some of the growth and discover if there was a spring feeding the pond. If so, I wanted to stimulate it. The area is pear-shaped, and I wanted to keep it that way, but to make a dam of the muck and debris we cleared from it. Flynn and I populated the winter pond with fifty fish—all bottom-feeding fish—catfish, goldfish, carp, the huge

Chinese goldfish. We wanted living creatures to inhabit our water. We planted lilies around the edge and I devised a fountain to aerate it in the summer so the fish can thrive. It has been fascinating to see the pond grow a life of its own, and it is a laboratory of discovery for Flynn and me.

When the pond is full, I can stand in water up to my chin. I believed that if the pond was deep enough, the fish could survive the winter. At certain depths the water is a barrier to the extreme cold, and Flynn has seen fish swimming under the ice near the edges. Thoreau wrote of the quiet winter parlor of the fishes, "pervaded by a softened light as through a window of ground glass, with its bright sanded floor the same as in summer."

Modern civilization is so overwhelmingly dominated by technology that we lose our spirituality. To rupture the bond with nature is to risk destroying the spirit. It is dangerous to try to conquer nature—to kill rain forests or grizzly bears or even gentle winter ponds. We should not let our need to industrialize and modernize overcome our affinity for nature. We find a spiritual wisdom in the natural world that is hard to retrieve once it is lost. There are aspects of the universe far beyond our powers to observe or understand.

I have the illusion that I am timeless. The idea of the future, or retirement—none of it really makes any sense. I think of relinquishment, but not retirement. At some point I am going to give up a lot of commitments that, in the past, I have made almost reflexively. I am going to make a deeper connection to the country. I find more and more fulfillment there, in the house and the land and the family.

Flynn is the future. He measures time for Ceci and me, and it will be measured different ways at different times as he grows up because *he* will be different. Flynn is a graceful, wonderful person. He is already a gifted artist. Once when an adult friend of his told him she had trouble remembering jokes, he said to her, "Make a picture in your head. Remember by drawing a picture of it in your head." He instinctively understands visual memory. Our friends and neighbors in the country, Ernie and Kay Mott, are like family, and Flynn's drawings adorn their walls and refrigerator as much as ours. He gives them his pictures for presents.

Ernie Mott has been my friend, my neighbor, and my guide to the history and the woods of my chosen country land. When I was introduced to Ernie, he said to me, "So, Jim, what do you do?"

"Well, I'm an actor," I confessed.

Ernie replied, "I've never seen you in anything!" He had not a clue to who I was, and I loved that. We just connected person to person. We can talk hunting and fishing and Army life and barbwire fences. With Ernie, I can be completely myself.

Ernie has the kind of garden I would have if I could spend more time in the country. We used to go in together on livestock, and slaughter and freeze meat for the winter. Once, Ernie raised a pig that we slaughtered for the pork. Ernie and I use every bit of an animal we slaughter, from making candles from the tallow to thread from the guts. We grew up in the same way as farmers, and appreciate the economy and necessity of nature. Ernie shares his garden with us—the sweetest, whitest, most delicious corn. Kay has taught Ceci how to freeze it in its own juice so we can enjoy it all winter, along with beans and broccoli and other homegrown riches.

Ernie and I are very much alike. We are former Army Rangers, former farmers, woodsmen. We are loners. We adore the isolation of the woods. We can go for days without talking. It drives our wives mad. We have walked the woods and hills in all seasons. One of our favorite old paths runs past my property and leads down the hill to what used to be a mission school where he and other kids, in trouble or not, were sent.

Ernie is a fine hunter and woodsman, and one day early in my time in the country, we hiked along the creek, talking woodsman's lore. Ernie knelt by the creek and pulled a plant from the moist bank. He bit off part of it and gave me the rest.

"Try that," he said. Swamp marigold—crisp, succulent, delicious. The rest of the day we walked through the woods so Ernie could show me various wild plants you could eat. I avoided mushrooms, for they tend to change. A mushroom that has been gathered and eaten for generations in one place can suddenly be identified as poisonous elsewhere. The man from whom I bought my land took me through the woods showing me edible mushrooms—he was an expert.

"It's hopeless," I told him, "unless I photographed and recorded what you have told me. I would never trust my memory to come in here later and pick mushrooms to eat."

Ernie has shared with me a journal his grandmother kept of her life here in the late nineteenth century. She churned so much butter in a day, picked so many beans, gathered so many pounds of honey, walked so many miles down the mountain and back again to deliver her harvest to market. That was her life.

Ernie and I read her journals and say, "Boy, it is good to live here. It would have been good to live in those times." Ceci and Kay read her story and say, "God, what a woman. Oh, God, you worked so hard—you still do—to keep a home and raise children." She was weighed down by the need to churn the butter, pick the fruits and vegetables, sell them at the market, scrub clothes, and care for the family. But somehow there was enough energy left over for her to write a journal and preserve it all: "I was here. This is what I did."

She had to gather so much honey for sale, had to raise the children, tend the garden and the fields. If you have nothing beyond that in your life, that is what you write about. Survival was the overriding fact of her life, and reading her journals, I can see more clearly the personal history of this country land I love.

* * *

Ceci calls our home in the country my mistress, yet she understands what the place means to me, and she does not begrudge me my time there. She knows how my work can deplete my energy. Ceci is a wonderful actress. She loves to work, but she is not driven. She is all professionalism on the set, but once she leaves the set, she is all wife and mother, all family. She is my best adviser. She understands my work because it is her work, too. We share the vocabulary of theatre and film, and I trust her judgment. We can talk shop in the best ways, and she has been central in my career decisions. She and Flynn always are. They are my anchorage.

Ceci has said that she and I have everything in common but our backgrounds:

I look at him and think, "Lord have mercy, we two! Of all the people that you think you might be matched with in this lifetime would you have imagined a person of a different color, a person of a different generation?" But we understand each other. We know that we have found our life mates in each other. We are such different people. He is the introvert, I am the extrovert. We know that it is remarkable that our marriage can survive without question in this particular profession, especially in an industry swarming with barracuda and people who will do anything for an intro, will sell anything to the tabloids. Jimmy is a wonderful, endlessly interesting, complex, funny, sexy man. I know it is miraculous that we have Flynn. There was Robert Earl, then James Earl, now Flynn Earl. Our family is our grounding, as well as (and here comes the cliché) our bit of immortality.

Jimmy is defined by his work, but never to the exclusion of his family. I believe truly that Flynn and I are the rock for him, and I like to flatter myself by thinking that we are his springboard for the remarkable resurgence of his amazing career. I have to laugh when he talks about retirement. This guy will drop in his tracks. He will never retire. He cannot *not* work. Work has sustained him and fulfilled him. That twenty-five acres of land is his mistress. I never have any qualms about sending him back to his "mistress" when he has any time off. I say, "Go, putter around, and unplug the phone, just *be.*" He loved the country on first sight. I have to admit that I had to learn to love it. It is very isolated up there, and massive and scary at night when you are there alone in a thunderstorm on that mountain.

The first time I walked into the kitchen he had built, I saw this huge room surrounded by windows—and no cupboards. "Excuse me. Uh—where do you put the dishes?" I asked him. The man looked at me like I had grown a mushroom from my forehead.

"They go in the sink, of course," he said. Sure enough, every single dish was piled in the sink, and when he wanted to eat, he just took the top dish and washed it off. Needless to say, my "dowry" went to completely overhauling the kitchen.

Jimmy is very dear to credit me with "civilizing" him. Let's face it: the man is a farmer. I don't know if he would have been as fabulous and gifted a farmer as he is an actor, but I suspect so. Anything he puts his mind to he does brilliantly.

I now have come to regard the country as the place I would most like to be. Someday we will live there year-round, especially as Flynn is already so very rooted in the land, like his father. He can't wait to get back there. That is where we are making our home, year by year.

While Jimmy the artist is fulfilled and defined by the work, Jimmy the farmer has absolutely no use for the trappings of celebrity. God, how refreshing! It is the work itself that matters to him—the work, and the family and the land, not necessarily in that order, I think.

Ceci says that I have built the house with stones the color and texture of the sky just before a storm blows up. She says that for the sake of our souls, what we really miss most in California is weather and fragrance. In California, the weather so seldom changes. There is perennial sunshine. Pollution obliterates the fragrances of flowers and trees. Even a decade ago you could enjoy in springtime the waft of jasmine or orange blossoms. Now you rarely smell anything.

In the country, we have raised ducks, guinea hens, Nubian goats, rabbits, chickens, cats, cows, pigs, Great Danes. We have a horse. I try to be a citizen of my community. I can go into the village nearby and do errands and meet my neighbors at the garbage dump and still keep my privacy. I serve on the board of Harvest with Heart, a program which distributes fresh produce to people who need it. I am still close in memory to the boy who met the train bringing grapefruit and other food into Michigan during wartime.

For generations, as far back as I can see, my family has worked to build a haven, a safe home. My own homestead grows out of my love and reverence for the Mississippi farm born of my great-grandfather Wyatt's foresight and industry, and then for the farm in Michigan which my grandfather John Henry, my papa, bought on faith and worked with skill. I hand that legacy and the future on to my son Flynn with the hope that one day he too will find his own true home.

24.

JOURNAL

• My conviction grows that language is not natural to man. Because of my stuttering, I came at language standing on my head, turning language inside out, trying to discover the motivation, the truth of a character—not from his intellect but from the sounds he makes.

• I have never traveled to anyone else's drumbeat. Some people have called me a rebel. I qualify as one. A lot of it is inadvertent, unintentional, not a gesture at all, just me, just the nature of myself, finding my own drumbeat.

• Hamlet makes a curious little speech: "Words, words, words." Most of the actors who play Hamlet play him as a smartass, which he was not—or as a nut, which he was not—or as one who was thinking of being a nut, which he was not. Most actors handle that fragment of a speech—"Words, words, words"—as if it were a joke, and not anything meaningful. Hamlet was driven by rage, and some of that rage encompassed the futility, the duplicity of words.

Flynn will do that sometimes. He'll say something, and I'll say, "What did you say?"

"Nothing," he'll answer. "Never mind." He knows that if those words didn't convey his message the first time, they won't—even if he tries again.

• One of the hardest things in life is having words in your heart that you can't utter. Cyrano de Bergerac could do the words for everybody but himself. He had to help this "animal" evoke the words Cyrano himself wanted to speak to the woman he loved. Language is still a mess, still futile. Yet we stay hooked on the potential beauty of words.

• I have always thought it quite wonderful and necessary to keep connected to nature, to a place in the country landscape where one can rest and muse and listen. Flynn and I share a love of the woods. We collect stamps and baseball cards. We travel together whenever we can as a family, but we try not to disrupt Flynn's school schedule. We have been to Italy recently, and to Alaska, where Flynn and I drank glacier water and then pissed off the edge of the glacier.

I believe my son shares with me this visceral love for nature. Flynn and I can also escape into nature. Away from civilization and even from Ceci, whom we both adore beyond words, we can take sleeping bags out to the woods, eat what we want, pee outdoors, sleep under the stars.

• I have narrated Stravinsky's "opera-oratorio" *Oedipus Rex* with the Cleveland Symphony and the Baltimore Symphony, using the English narration written by e.e. cummings rather than the French libretto written by Cocteau. I played Oedipus in a production adapted by John Lewin and staged at the Cathedral of St. John the Divine in New York. It seems to me that most people overlook the central theme of this classic myth, a theme carrying special resonance for me. When the king heard that the new male child was going to be trouble for him, he said to the queen, "Get rid of him." And the queen said, "All right." That is the tragedy: not that Oedipus slept with his mother and killed his father, but that when he was a helpless infant, the father said, "Get rid of him," and the mother said, "Okay."

• There runs through my family a tendency toward religious zeal. Robert Earl's father was a self-ordained preacher of some exuberance. My grandmother Maggie Connolly demonstrated her religious fervor through shouting and other dramatic, exotic behavior at church, and through the hymns she sang all day everyday on the farm at home. Depressed the hell out of me.

• When I was in the Army, I would go to chapel. About a third of my unit was Catholic, either from Puerto Rico or the Philippines, or immigrant boys from the Northeast or Midwest. I couldn't understand the religious fervor which would inspire some of these soldiers to kiss the feet of the statues or wail in ecstasy. They reminded me of Maggie.

• My grandmother Elnora was a certified, official "saint," a member of the Sanctified Church, where the women members are "married" to Jesus, much as Catholic nuns are. She was called a saint, a classification, like "elder" or "sister," used by this particular church. St. Elnora. She wrote me frequent letters, and every other line was devoted to God and Jesus, so much so that the letters were more like prayers than communiqués. She was busy giving obeisance instead of trying to get her thoughts across. I found her letters very difficult to read. When I was overseas once, she sent me a Christmas card, which I didn't open. I put off reading it. Then, before I returned home, St. Elnora died.

I carried that card around with me a long time after her death before I opened it. I was afraid that finally she had said something lucid, and I had missed it before she died. But it was like all the other letters. To whomever she addressed them, Elnora was still writing letters to God.

• Despite her sanctified ways, there was a certain grace about Elnora. She always dressed in white flowing dresses that came down to her lower calf. She was a beautiful woman, in the mode of the Gibson Girl. I remember once when I was living in New York, Ruth came to visit, and Elnora was in the city, too. We were all going to see a play. We picked Elnora up in a cab. She was wearing her customary white dress, with a big oversized button over one breast. The button said, "Jesus Is the Answer." Elnora climbed into the cab wearing her button, and the cabdriver said, "Oh—and what is the question?"

She didn't take it in as being cynical. She was always a gentle person, a lady. With dignity and charm, she proceeded to tell him what the question was. I can still see her there in the front seat of that cab patiently explaining the question to the driver. She accepted his question as genuine, and gave him a reply.

• I used to sit with Irishmen in bars on the Lower East Side, and when we got around to talking about religion, they would say, "Nah—you're ain't no Catlick. You ain't no fucking Catlick." They were usually trying to pick a fight, but I am not a bar fighter—or a crusader. I would always pass.

• My voice is for hire. My endorsement is not for hire. I will do a voice-over, but I cannot endorse without making a different kind of commitment. My politics are very personal and subjective.

• Just before Robert Kennedy died, Ted Kennedy asked me to help in his brother's presidential campaign. "Will you be with us in New York?" Ted asked. I replied, "I'll be there. I'll read anything you want. I'll help in anyway I can." Then Bobby was killed. Even with that heartbreak and disillusionment, I considered giving the same support to Hubert Humphrey, but his message got so mealymouthed I declined. All I did that year was to stand up for Paul O'Dwyer, who was running for mayor of New York City. That was the extent of my active political involvement that year.

• When I was asked about Malcolm X on the "Dennis Miller Show" in 1992, I voiced the idea that at the beginning Malcolm expressed some crazy ideas, and that it was when he got more sane that they killed him.

• I was appointed by Richard Nixon to serve on the National Council of the Arts. I served in spite of the Nixon era. When his

V.P., Nelson Rockefeller was governor of New York, he found that it worked for him to be very good to the arts in New York. He believed the same thing could happen nationally while he was vice president. He made sure there was a lot of funding for diverse cultural elements of the country during that administration, encouraging funding for Native American arts and crafts, as well as work produced by blacks and Orientals. There was strong outreach into Appalachia to ensure that those artisans were stimulated and encouraged. All of us on the council looked at it as a "sugar tit." You get the baby growing, and then that baby has to prove himself commercially and stand on his own.

• I was playing in Ibsen's *Hedda Gabler* at the Yale Repertory Theatre in New Haven when the Connecticut Commission on the Arts fell into jeopardy. When I heard the state planned to cut funding for the commission, I offered to testify. Culture is as necessary for humanity as food, I said then, and I still believe that. Once a state eliminates its access to the arts, it sets up the machinery for the decay of civilization. I would rather sacrifice well-paved roads than good theatre. "Please give me a road that's passable," I argued then, "as long as there's a place to go on that road." Of course, the state should not attempt to censor or control the arts. Patronage should not ever confer that dangerous privilege.

• I was in the Army, digging Catholic chapel. I decided to take my instruction in Catholicism. I studied the material, took my training, and it came time for my baptism and confirmation. I went to talk to the priest. "Father," I said, "there are some things I can believe and some things I can't. For instance, there is the Virgin birth—"

"Now, son," the priest told me, "we don't want to lose you over a little thing like that! The Church is not a definition, it is a flowerpot out of which you grow."

The Army sermons were very clear. The Jesuit chaplains had fine

minds and spirits, and positive things to say. But when I got out of
the Army, it was different. The sermons I heard in New York were
angry or petty. They made me angry in turn. The ceremony was fine,
of course, but the sermons were crap, and I finally said, "I've had
enough of that." I occasionally went to confession to say that I had
nothing to confess. I'd stay away for a while and then go back and
confess some more.

• I think if I joined the Catholic Church for any reason beside those
early associations with the Polish farmers in Irons, Michigan, it was
because it was the one church in which the cathedrals had marvelous
aesthetics—stained glass, art works, statuary. Music from the
Gregorian chants was moving, beautiful, and soothing, in ways I did
not find true of the spirituals Maggie sang all the time at home. The
music did not depress me—partially because most of it was in Latin,
and the little Latin I know didn't get in the way.

• Once in the early days of my life in New York, I persuaded Robert
Earl to accompany me to a Catholic church in the Village. The
sermon was the most anti-Semitic diatribe I have ever heard. I said,
"On all the days I choose to bring my father to church, this priest is
dishing out this bullshit." But we sat it out.

When they started passing the collection plate around, Robert
Earl pulled his wallet out of his pocket as if he were in a holdup, and
put it on the plate, as if to say, "You are trying to rob my mind. You
might as well rob my pocket, too." I retrieved his wallet, and said,
"Let's go."

• Ever since I was allowed to leave the church in Michigan when I
was about fourteen because of the stuttering, I've tried to be as
independent about church and religion as I could be. Ceci and I were
married by a renegade Catholic priest at the United Nations chapel.
Flynn has not been baptized. His grandfather Bill Hart and I would

like him to be a Catholic. His grandmother Fran would not. The decision will be Flynn's. Only he can break the tie. I want to expose him to all the great religions of the world, and someday, for his own reasons, he will choose or not choose something that suits his spirit.

• I am a member of the National Rifle Association, but not a political member. I just throw the political mail from NRA into the trash. Charlton Heston campaigns on behalf of the NRA. He says, "Here I stand." When it comes to the right wing politics of the NRA, I don't get into that. I just believe in my right to have a gun in my house. Ceci, on the other hand, is a member of the antigun lobby, so we pretty much cancel each other out.

• When I came out of the Army, I brought every weapon I was trained to use—my .45, my M1, my carbine. I fully expected back in the repressive 1950s that someday I might be responsible for a cadre of people in an urban riot. I came out and heard Malcolm X warn the people to go out and get their shotguns. Hell, I thought people had their shotguns already. I came out of the Army fully expecting the worst. Thank God I have not had to face the worst. I am thankful that I have been able to serve my society in a creative way. I believe in the value of artistic endeavor in a society. Maybe art cannot always change minds, but art can change hearts.

• I think there is always the danger that actors will be caught in the ideology of a system. I think what my career stands for is the fight to retain the right of the artist's vision, and not the society's agenda. I have never thought of myself, professionally or personally, as a role model. I reject that as a mission. Therefore, I do not presume to give advice—about acting or politics or life in general.

• The artist's job is to convey an experience. Artists must reach as many people as possible. When some black writers began to write to very narrowly focused themes, I began to challenge the concept of "black theatre." There was a conference in Harlem when we talked about these issues. "There is no such thing as black theatre," I said. "Theatre is oriented around a language, and not a life-style or culture or subculture. Skin color cannot define theatre, or any art form, or any true culture."

Likewise, it has been a disappointment to me that playwrights usually depict black characters in conflict only with the white world. That oversimplifies. Human beings are caught up in far more gripping struggles than insane contests solely between racial or cultural groups. "Whitey" is often the least of the black man's problems or interests.

• I have probably gotten more roles crossing cultural boundaries than most actors of my time. The first summer that I joined Joe Papp as a spear carrier in productions for the New York Shakespeare Festival, he cast me as Michael Williams in *Henry V* because he thought in those days of the Vietnam War that the play would have a new and sharper impact with a black actor in that role. When King Henry is walking among his troops, he is walking among men who do not come from the upper echelons of society. If they had complaints, those complaints would be strong and clear.

Casting a black actor as Michael Williams intensified that role in those times, especially when Williams speaks forthrightly to the king, not knowing the man he is addressing *is* the king disguised as a common man. There is a debate about the justice of the war, and one soldier holds that soldiers must obey the king. Therefore, if the cause is wrong, the king is to blame, not his soldiers.

• When I played Claudius with a white Gertrude and a white Hamlet, I felt a certain initial discomfort because we made no attempt to explain. But I tried to forget as fast as I could—and hope the audience would forget as fast as they could—that I was a black Claudius. I wanted to be Claudius.

• I think with plays that are strong enough, it is much easier to transcend any superficial exterior definitions and focus on the personhood of the characters in the play. *Hamlet* is different from a play such as *Picnic,* for instance. I would never have played the role of Hal in *Picnic* because the play is fragile, and very much dependent on a certain place and time. If you inject an Oriental or black Hal, the play does not hold up.

• Over time, there has been a tradition of having Mediterranean Caucasians play Native Americans. It used to be that all the Indians were played by dark-skinned Caucasians—Jeff Chandler, for instance, and Burt Lancaster. That was Hollywood, and the critics and the public accepted that casting. Get it?

• I once wanted to play a woman—the ghetto mother Sister Sadie in Clifford Mason's *Sister Sadie and the Sons of Sam.* That's all I want to say about that!

• I love to play renegades, rogues, and ramblers. They are not really bound by social trappings anyway. Race does not matter.

• There is a difference between nontraditional casting and integrated casting. If I were to play Big Daddy, for instance, I don't want to go on stage and play him as a black man. That would be called integrated casting. I think that would be an erroneous view of what Tennessee Williams wrote. In the context of Williams's dramatic world, on that Southern plantation, the man has to be white. To really achieve the playwright's purpose, I would have to go on stage and convince the audience, by makeup, acting, or both, that I was a white man. That would be my job as an actor. I want very much to play Big Daddy in *Cat on a Hot Tin Roof.* I had done the role in workshop productions, but I would like to do it full stage sometime. I would first play it in whiteface makeup, as Olivier played Othello in blackface. Then, after I had conquered the role, I would wash off the whiteface. I would endeavor to create the illusion of being Caucasian, of portraying the essence of that character with such depth that you would forget such surface issues as skin.

But that is where my conservatism comes in. If the play falls apart because of a certain type of casting, I think the casting is wrong. If the play is strong enough, then any casting is right.

• I do not know if it is true that all actors want to direct and all directors want to act, but in 1972 I tried directing and decided I had better stick to acting.

Joe Papp gave me the chance to direct Chekhov's *The Cherry Orchard*. My vision of Chekhov's play was to create a cultural overlay, taking the Russian text word for word, and casting it with African-Americans of all different cultural and genetic variations. I liked the idea of looking at a serf coming into his own, making a place for himself against all of the guidelines prescribed by his culture.

My papa, John Henry, was a kind of Lopakhin, even down to clearing the plum grove in Mississippi and the land in Michigan. Like Lopakhin, he was a practical pioneer, loving the land but willing to subordinate it to the good of his family, his people, and working *with* instead of *against* the grain of change. He lurked somewhere in my consciousness as I began to conceive my production of *The Cherry Orchard*.

I wanted to use all Afro-American actors in the production, but I wanted to keep the play set in Russia. I didn't want to set it in Africa or in New Orleans.

For many painful reasons, I couldn't make the production work. Another director took over, and I played the role of Lopakhin.

• *The Cherry Orchard* was in many ways artistically traumatic for me. Do I want to direct again? Oh, surely. I tried again, in fact, in a production at New York University. I directed *The Road to Rome*, a Robert Sherwood comedy with a large double cast.

Now, if I were directing, I would choose a play with two characters, or a movie, or a television film. I think I had a geniune talent for directing that got lost in the machinery.

• I think of directors as parents, who have to love each member of the cast as children, and care for, nurture, and assist them, as if they were the parents of these children. A director can love his cast of actors, but he must not bed one of them. Actors who become lovers during a production are asking for problems, I think, but that is a more private matter. For the director, it is very different. The director bears the burden of reponsibility for the whole production. He must love his actors for the sake of the project, not for any individual gratification.

A director is like a shepherd. He has to be a dictator, too. When you are producing a story there is no democracy—in the theatre or in the movies.

• I have loved working in the plays of Athol Fugard over the years, and his plays in particular dramatize vivid experiences which reverberate with relevant issues and themes—*Master Harold . . . and the Boys, Boesman and Lena, A Lesson from Aloes, The Blood Knot.*

What is wonderful about Fugard's characters for me is that they are elemental men—such as Steinbeck has written in Lennie in *Of Mice and Men,* August Wilson has written in *Fences,* and Shakespeare has written in many of his plays—kings as well as rogues. I think Athol has reached the point where the young blacks of South Africa have said, with a certain amount of hostility, "Thank you, it's our turn now, we will speak for ourselves." In the light of that change Athol has had to turn his focus more to the tragedy of the white people—which has numbered my days of working with him. Yet he has written a new play of confrontation between a black man and a white man, an inmate and a guard, both of whom have killed members of the opposite race. Surprisingly, the guard is there to ask forgiveness of the black man. It is a shock to everybody, but that is

Athol's point—the white man has to do that, he must do that—he must apologize. The black man must accept the apology. We all gain grace by it. We have to move on.

• By his definition, Athol is not a director, although he has directed many of his plays. He was still under state arrest in South Africa when *The Blood Knot* was produced in this country, and so could not direct it. He does not direct, he says. He simply gathers his cast of actors together, and when they need help, he tells them wonderful stories, real stories about his life in the kind of situation which is the focus of the play. He is a constant poet with a strong sense of music. Athol conducts more than directs.

• I have always wanted to make a record album on which I would sing songs such as "Red River Valley"—and "Shenandoah" and "Danny Boy." I would name my album *Songs James Earl Jones Likes to Sing Whether You Want to Hear Them or Not!*

• From the outset of my career, I have worked better with women than with men. I joined my first professional association with Toby Cole at the Lucy Kroll Agency when she happened to see me step in for Ivan Dixon in *Wedding in Japan* in 1957. When Toby left to become a writer, Lucy assigned me to Dorothy Petrie, a wonderful agent, tall and pretty. I used to visit the Petries' house, and got to know Dan and their children. Dorothy got pregnant and had twins. Then *The Great White Hope* phenomenon happened to me, and Lucy gave me more and more of her attention and counsel.

• My key assistants have been women—Sharyn Bamber, Sally Seamon, Jane Aire, Regan McLemore, Coddy Granum, Risa Shepherd, Bobbie Edrick. Another of "Earl's Girls" is Jan Eckman, my commercial agent, the most effective I've ever had. Lucy has been in my life since the fifties, of course. Over the past few years, as she has reduced her work load, her associate Barbara Hogenson has become more and more involved in my professional life.

• Starting with the aunts I loved as a boy, I have always idealized women. I have always held a faith and trust in the women I have worked with. Seldom have they disappointed me. From agents to directors to co-stars to assistants to co-authors, I have cherished these women who have been my colleagues, and my friends.

• When Flynn was younger, he invented an invisible dog named Caesar. Caesar was superhuman and all-knowing, and only Flynn could see him. Caesar was all the things Flynn would like to be. If we were flying on a jet, Caesar ran along on foot on the ground, keeping up despite the speed—and most likely ensuring the safety of our flight. Caesar knew the answers to questions I can't answer with a bachelor of arts degree. If Flynn asked me a question and I gave him ten answers, he was not satisfied. "Caesar will find out, Papa," Flynn would tell me. Caesar was Flynn. Your own need to be shines out of any dream or creation you imagine.

• Flynn has an uncanny ability, perhaps because he is an artist, to find his way in new territory. I can be lost in a new city on a tour. We have never been there before. The driver will take us from the hotel to a store, and back to the hotel again. The next day, I will say to Flynn, "Let's go back to that store. Which way do we go?"

Flynn will say, "Papa, you turn here, and then there, etcetera, etcetera." He has been able to guide me this way since he could talk. Because a child's mind is not clouded with other tasks, the little tasks he takes on are total. And Flynn has a powerful visual-spatial grasp of his world. Already, he possesses a reliable inner compass.

• Once, that I know of, my mother Ruth got very angry with me, angry enough to express herself. Her third husband was creating problems for the family. My aunts Ozella and Helen, her sisters, asked me to talk to Ruth. Her husband would constantly tease her and belittle her. The less sexually attractive she became, the more he belittled her. He was a photographer, and he began to take head shots of members of our family and superimpose the heads on magazine photographs of nude bodies. He was sick, it was sick behavior, and the aunts asked me to intervene.

After I challenged Ruth about tolerating his behavior, she skipped over all the facts and got straight to the point with me: "James Earl, your father didn't do me any good. You haven't done me any good. This man at least lets me breathe free in his house. He lets me make a home with him."

• Ruth was born August 24, 1910. She was seventy-five years old when she died. In that final year, she tried to write about her life. Here is some of what she said about herself then:

> Here I am almost to my 75 birthday . . . I have been around. [I was the] second to oldest of 10 kids. I have been trying to dabble in poetry as far back as that . . . I feel all used up. What got the old gal agoing was I have just moved into a new apartment. The place is named Phoenix Place. . . . It sounds poetic so I will try. The emblem is the phoenix bird. I don't know the connection. . . .

The first funeral I remember was my grandfather John Henry's mother's. I was barely four years old then, and we still lived in Mississippi. Into the soil covering my great-grandmother's grave, someone drove a pointed stake to mark where the headstone would eventually go. I was terrified, thinking that the stake was being driven into my great-grandmother. I avoided funerals for a long, long time after that.

The next funeral I attended came years later, when Sidney Bernstein died. He had produced Genet's *The Blacks* and Fugard's

The Blood Knot. Pete Seeger sang "Red River Valley" and I read a piece from *The Blood Knot.* The last funeral was my mother's.

• John Henry and Maggie—Mama and Papa—died in separation, but they were buried together. In her last years, Maggie had gone to live alternately with their daughters Helen and Thelma in Grand Rapids. Often she would make reference to her grandson as "that James Earl!" Eventually, when she could no longer be cared for at home, she was committed to a caretaking hospital, where she died.

John Henry never wanted to sever his ties with the land. He had gone down the road from the farm to live with daughter Bessie. He was later committed to a caretaking hospital in Manistee. There, he would save his daily aspirin all week so he could get a real "buzz" during the weekend. He stayed in the hospital until his death.

I passed on going to my grandparents' funerals. I did not visit their graves until I was in the midst of my psychotherapy. I decided to go to Dublin to the cemetery. There, I stood at their gravesites and talked to them.

• Ruth died in 1985. My mother's funeral was a very silly event because nobody dies on that side of the family. Of ten children, she was then the third to die, only the first since her sister Ruby died at the age of nine or ten.

We didn't know how to behave at Ruth's funeral. Consequently, we all were very silly, and that was good, because it made it more of a homecoming than a wake or a funeral. We buried Ruth in Michigan in the fall. Harvest time.

• Geraldine Page's memorial service, held in a theatre, was a joyous occasion. Her husband Rip Torn conducted it like a good country preacher. If any of us got up there and talked too long, he'd say, "Okay, get off. Get off. Let's move it along."

He had opened the service by standing and saying hello to the standing-room-only audience. We applauded for about five minutes running. We applauded Geraldine into heaven, very much as Troy Maxson's brother Gabe picked up his bugle and blew his brother into heaven. As people talked, we tried to define Geraldine. Everybody had a different story to tell about her, a different Geraldine.

• When Lucy started urging me to write down my memories, I resisted. "I'm not ready yet. They're not done yet." Lucy told me that no matter what the artist feels about his work, it is his obligation to put his story on paper and let history decide if it is relevant. It is difficult to define one's self. But I see now that some aspects of my life do have their own individual rounding out, their own individual conclusions. And as Lucy, Penny, and Robert keep reminding me, mine is very much a life and career in progress.

• Most people are surprised to learn that I am a stutterer. Of course, I have learned to compensate for the problem, and, most of the time, to transcend it. Often we stutterers are thought of as calculated or calculating, careful-thinking people. We are only trying to find the word we can use to move on with a conversation.

• Moving to Michigan influenced the accent, inflections, and enunciation of the sounds of my voice. But no matter how long I lived in Michigan, or how many courses I took in speech and English, or how much experience I have had as an actor, whenever I go home to Mississippi, I can always revert to the Mississippi language we shared as a family, our very Southern black dialect. There are members of the family there who still doubt that they really see me on television or in movies.

"That ain't you, is it?" they say hopefully. "You ain't no actor, is you?"

• While it is natural for the voice to utter sounds, language is not natural to man. When we move into the speech mode, the brain's electrical energy changes. For the stutterer some "switch" goes awry, some electrical current runs askew. The motor of language is ignited by a crisis state in the brain. I quickly discovered when I first started doing voice-overs that certain irritations set in. You get so nervous during certain passages of script that you can't get through them. You can't make them work. They lack something. I read somewhere that the EKG reading goes up when a human being stands in front of a microphone and lifts a page to read. Some crisis state exists.

Yet when I read great literature, great drama, speeches, or sermons, I feel that the human mind has not achieved anything greater than the ability to share feelings and thoughts through language.

• I was sufficiently warned by all my teachers in college and since then not to become obsessed with my voice. Once you start listening to your own voice, you risk becoming trapped into affectation. The speaker's last concern should be how he sounds. The listener, not the speaker, should be aware of how the voice sounds. The speaker should be concerned with what he seeks to communicate by the sound of his voice.

• I do a lot of commercials. That has become an important facet of my career. More and more often, however, I find myself being invited to functions and awards ceremonies to deliver speeches. I am still not good at speeches. The stage is what I do best. I have a problem with anything that is not well scripted. I don't plan to shun all public life. I just want to choose events which are personally important to me—to put my voice where it really counts.

• When I was a student at the American Theatre Wing, my acting teacher played an old Edison recording of Sarah Bernhardt during

World War I. She went onto the battlefield among French soldiers after a massacre by the Germans, and began to curse the war. Her voice lifted into a primal sound, transcending screaming or yelling or oration. This was pure language—exploding beyond the words and their articulation into pure emotion embodied in pure sound. I don't even speak French, but I understood her voice without understanding her language.

• A modern writer may be content to evoke a character's *emotion*. Shakespeare was never content until he found a character's *passion*. There is nothing more moving or powerful than the power of the Word when beautiful language is married to deep passion. The voice is the instrument for the expression of that power. Emotion is resultant, responsive. Passion is active, aggressive.

• "You have about forty different ways of sliding," people used to say to Ty Cobb. "How do you decide which way to slide?"

"I don't think about it, I just slide," he answered.

So it is with an actor's voice. You hope you have worked so hard for so long that you don't have to become self-conscious and think about it. You just use it organically, as the instrument of your art.

• During my boyhood years of silence, I never actually thought, "Gee, I would love to know how to talk. I would love to know how to deliver one of Shakespeare's soliloquies effectively." But there was a yearning, an indefinable yearning. Whenever I would meet a stranger, someone in the family would say, "This is James Earl. James Earl, say hello to Mrs. So-and-So." I couldn't and wouldn't. In my silence, I was robbing myself of any presence. I am who I am. I was denying myself that—or something that had been set loose in me denied it.

Poetry and my professor helped me to discover once and for all that I could communicate verbally. I reclaimed my voice from that long silence. I rediscovered the joy of communication. I wanted to make up for the lost years when I did not speak. Eventually, inevitably, you yearn to lift your voice out of the silences and say, "This is who I am. For what it's worth, this is how I feel—and this is who I am."

* At this point, I am very tired of saying *I*. I think I shall stop saying *I* for awhile.

Hamlet spoke of "Words, words, words." As he says in the end, "The rest is silence."

CHRONOLOGY OF THE CAREER OF JAMES EARL JONES

(A Selective List of Theatre, Movie, and
Television Performances)

THEATRE PERFORMANCES

[Note: year given is year of opening; some runs extended into the
following year]

1950–53   At the university and community theatres in Ann Arbor,
Michigan, appeared in the following plays, among
others: *The Birds, Much Ado About Nothing, A Sleep of
Prisoners, Once in a Lifetime*

1953   At Manistee Summer Theatre, Manistee, Michigan,
appeared in the following plays, among others: *The Dark
Tower, Father of the Bride, Philadelphia Story*

1955   At Manistee Summer Theatre, appeared in the following
plays, among others: *Green Grow the Lilacs, I Remember
Mama, Dial "M" for Murder, The Caine Mutiny Court
Martial, Twelfth Night*

1956   At Manistee Summer Theatre, appeared in the following
            plays, among others: *Dark of the Moon, The Tender Trap,
            The Desperate Hours, Othello,* playing Othello for the first
            time
1957   At Manistee Summer Theatre, appeared in *Teahouse of the
            August Moon, Romeo and Juliet,* among others. In New
            York, appeared in workshop productions of *Taffy, The Big
            Knife, Heaven Can Wait, among others.*

PLAY	ROLE
1957 *The Egghead*	Understudy (Broadway debut)
Wedding in Japan	Sergeant Blunt
1958 *Sunrise at Campobello*	Edward
1960 *The Pretender*	Jessie Prince
The Cool World	Harrison Thurston
Henry V	Williams
Measure for Measure	Abhorson
1961 *The Blacks*	Deodatus Village
Clandestine on the Morning Line	Roger Clark
The Apple	Actors used their own names
Romeo and Juliet	Gregory and Apothecary
A Midsummer Night's Dream	Oberon
King Richard II	Lord Marshal
1962 *Moon on a Rainbow Shawl*	Ephraim
P.S. 193	Mario Saccone
The Merchant of Venice	Prince of Morocco
The Tempest	Caliban
Toys in the Attic	Henry Simpson
Macbeth	Macduff

	PLAY	ROLE
	Infidel Caesar	Cinna
1963	*The Love Nest*	George Gulp
	Othello	Othello
	The Last Minstrel	Mr. Ash
	Mister Johnson	Mister Johnson
	Next Time I'll Sing to You	Rudge
	The Winter's Tale	Camillo
1964	*The Blood Knot*	Zachariah Pieterson
	Othello	Othello
	Emperor Jones	Brutus Jones
1965	*Danton's Death*	Georg Buechner
	Baal	Ekhart
	Coriolanus	Tribune
	Troillus and Cressida	Ajax
1966	*A Hand Is On the Gate*	Black poetry readings
	Bohickee Creek	Arnie and Bo
	Happy Ending	Arthur
	Day of Absence	Mayor
	Macbeth	Macduff and then Macbeth
	The Peace Creeps	Roscoe
	Othello (New Mexico State)	Othello
1967	*Emperor Jones*	Brutus Jones
	Of Mice and Men	Lennie
	The Great White Hope	Jack Jefferson
1968	*The Great White Hope* (Broadway opening)	Jack Jefferson
	Othello	Othello
	The Blood Knot	Zachariah Pieterson
1970	*Les Blancs*	Tschembe Matoseh
	Boesman and Lena	Boesman
1971	*Othello*	Othello
1972	*Hamlet*	Claudius
1973	*The Iceman Cometh*	Hickey

PLAY	ROLE
The Cherry Orchard	Lopakhin
King Lear	King Lear
1974 *Of Mice and Men*	Lennie
1977 *Paul Robeson*	Paul Robeson
1978 *Paul Robeson*	Paul Robeson
(Broadway opening)	
1980 *A Lesson from Aloes*	Steve Daniels
Hedda Gabler	Judge Brack
1981 *Othello*	Othello
1982 *Othello*	Othello
Master Harold . . .	Sam
And the Boys	
1983 *Master Harold . . .*	Sam
And the Boys (U.S. tour)	
1984 *The Day of the Picnic*	Ulius Vkumbi
1985 *Fences* (Yale Repertory	Troy Maxson
Theatre)	
1987 *Fences* (Broadway opening)	Troy Maxson
1988 *Fences* (Los Angeles)	Troy Maxson

MOVIES

1963 *Dr. Strangelove or: How I Learned to Stop Worrying and Love the Bomb*

1967 *The Comedians*

1970 *The Great White Hope*
      The End of the Road
      King: A Filmed Record . . .
      Montgomery to Memphis (Narrator)

1972 *Malcolm X* (Narrator)
      The Man

1974 *Claudine*

1975   *The River Niger*
1976   *The Bingo Long Traveling All-Stars and Motor Kings*
       Deadly Hero
       The Swashbuckler
1977   *A Piece of the Action*
       Exorcist II: The Heretic
       The Last Remake of Beau Geste
       The Greatest
       Star Wars (Voice of Darth Vader)
1980   *The Empire Strikes Back*
1981   *The Bushido Blade* (also called *The Bloody Bushido*)
1982   *Conan the Barbarian*
       Blood Tide (also called *The Red Tide*)
1983   *Return of the Jedi*
1985   *City Limits*
1986   *Soul Man*
1987   *Allan Quartermain and the Lost City of Gold*
       Matewan
       Gardens of Stone
       Pinocchio and the Emperor of the Night (Voice only)
       My Little Girl
1988   *Coming to America*
1989   *Best of the Best*
       Field of Dreams
       Three Fugitives
1990   *Grim Prairie Tales*
       The Grand Tour
       Into Thin Air
       The Ambulance
       The Hunt for Red October
1991   *I Can't Lose*
       True Identity
       Convicts
       Terrorgram
       Scorchers

1992   *Patriot Games*
        Sneakers
1993   *Sommersby*
        Meteor Man
        Excessive Force
        The Sandlot

TELEVISION

James Earl Jones appeared on single or limited episodes of programs noted below, unless they are identified as movies made especially for television, as television series in which he had a starring role, or as programs for which he was host or narrator.

1961   "The Catholic Hour"
1962   "Look Up and Live"
1963   "Look Up and Live"
        "East Side, West Side"
        "Camera Three"
1964   "Stage 2"
        "Channing"
        "The Defenders"
        "Camera Three"
1965   "As the World Turns" (Series)
1966   "Look Up and Live"
        "Dr. Kildare"
        "Camera Three"
        "Neighbors"
1967   "Tarzan"
1968   "WNET Playhouse"
        "Tarzan"
1969   "Ed Sullivan Show"
        "N.Y.P.D"

1973	"Theater in America" *King Lear*
	"Black Omnibus" (Host and narrator for series)
1974	"Bell System Family Theatre" *The Cay*
1975	"Happy Endings"
	The UFO Incident (Movie) (Also known as *Interrupted Journey)*
1976	"A Day Without Sunshine" (Narrator)
1977	*The Greatest Thing that Almost Happened* (Movie)
	Jesus of Nazareth (Movie)
1979	*The Mad Messiah* (Movie)
	Roots II: The Next Generations (Role of Alex Haley)
1979–80	"Paris" (Starring role in series)
	The Golden Moment: An Olympic Love Story (Movie)
	"The Guyana Tragedy: The Story of Jim Jones" (Movie)
1980	"Mobil Summer Show" (Host)
1982	"ABC Afterschool Special"
	Amy and the Angel (Movie)
1984	*Atlanta Child Murders* (Movie)
	The Big Vegas Hotel Wars (Movie)
1985	*Me and Mom* (Movie)
1986	"Faerie Tale Theatre"
	"Highway to Heaven"
	"Wonderworks"
	"Mathnet"
1987	"CBS Schoolbreak Special"
1988	"American Playhouse"
	"Garfield and Friends"
	"L.A. Law"
1989	"American Playwrights Theatre"
	"Saturday Night with Connie Chung"
	"Long Ago and Far Away" (Series host)
1990	"Reflections on the Silver Screen with Professor Richard Brown"

"Gabriel's Fire" (Starring role in series)
Heat Wave (Movie)
The Last Elephant (Movie) (Also known as *The Ivory Hunters* and *White Gold)*
The Last Flight Out (Movie)
By Dawn's Early Light (Movie) (Also known as *The Grand Tour)*
"Hard Ride to Glory: The Black Athlete in America" (Host and narrator)

1991   "Biography" *Muhammad Ali*
"Pros and Cons" (Co-starring role in series)
"Portrait of Cuba and the Caribbean" (Narrator)

1992   "The Creative Spirit"
"JFK Conspiracy"
"Earthworks" (Narrator)
"The Day the Nation Cried" (Narrator)
"Percy and Thunder"

1993   "Great Brown Bears"
"Lincoln" (Narrator)
"Race for Life: Africa's Great Migration" (Narrator)

HONORS AND AWARDS (A SELECTIVE LIST)

1962   Village Voice Off-Broadway Award (Obie) for best actor in the Off-Broadway theatre
Theatre World Award as most promising personality
Presidential appointment to the Advisory Board, National Council on the Arts

1964   Drama Desk Award for best performance by an actor, *Othello*

1965   Vernon Rice Award for *Othello*
Obie Award for best actor in the off-Broadway theatre

1969   Tony Award for best performance by an actor, *The Great White Hope*

	Drama Desk Award for outstanding performance, *The Great White Hope*
1970	Academy Award nomination for best performance by an actor, *The Great White Hope*
	Drama Desk Award, *Les Blancs*
	Honorary Doctor of Humane Letters, University of Michigan
1971	Golden Globe Award, Most Promising New Actor
1973	Drama Desk Award for outstanding performance, *Hamlet* and *The Cherry Orchard*
1974	NAACP Image Award, Best Actor
1975	The Golden Hugo Award
	The Gabriel Award
	Golden Gate Award, San Francisco International Film Festival
1976	Grammy Award
1980	Honorary Doctor of Fine Arts, Princeton University
1981	Medal for Spoken Language, American Academy of Arts and Letters
1982	Office of Black Ministries' Toussaint Medallion
	Honorary Doctor of Humane Letters, Columbia College, Los Angeles, California
	Honorary Doctor of Fine Arts, Yale University
1985	Theatre Hall of Fame
	Emmy Award, outstanding children's programming
1987	Tony Award for Best Actor, *Fences*
	Drama Desk Award for Best Actor, *Fences*
	Outer Critics Circle Award for Best Actor, *Fences*
	Distinguished Performance Award, Drama League of New York
1990	ACE Award for Best Actor
1991	Emmy Award, Outstanding Actor in a Television Drama series
	Emmy Award as Outstanding Supporting Actor in a Miniseries or Special

Los Angeles Film Teachers Jean Renoir Award
Commonwealth Award for Distinguished Service in
the Dramatic Arts
1992 National Medal of the Arts
NAACP Best Actor Award
NAACP Hall of Fame Image Award

INDEX

387